ALABAMA F

IN THE TWENTY-FIR

ALABAMA POLITICS
IN THE TWENTY-FIRST CENTURY

WILLIAM H. STEWART

THE UNIVERSITY OF ALABAMA PRESS
Tuscaloosa

The University of Alabama Press
Tuscaloosa, Alabama 35487-0380
uapress.ua.edu

Hardcover edition published 2016.
Paperback edition published 2021.
eBook edition published 2016.

Typeface: Meridien

Cover image: Alabama State Capitol Building, April 13, 2007; photograph by Donnie Shackleford
Cover design: Gary Gore

Paperback ISBN: 978-0-8173-6027-6

A previous edition of this book has been cataloged by the Library of Congress.
ISBN: 978-0-8173-1927-4 (cloth)
E-ISBN: 978-0-8173-9024-2

To Connie and Trey

Contents

Illustrations

Figures

Tables

Acknowledgments

The origins of *Alabama Politics in the Twenty-First Century* date back to the fall of 2008 when I met with Daniel Waterman, editor in chief at the University of Alabama Press, to discuss a book I had always wanted to write. While it would identify the major structural characteristics of Alabama state government, it would stress the *politics* inherent in all aspects of government. Mr. Waterman believed that there would be a substantial audience for such a book both within Alabama and beyond its borders. It would be scholarly in terms of using the latest research findings, but it would be written in non-technical language that would be understandable to the interested citizen and suitable for classroom use—classes in state government generally as well as classes focusing mostly on the Alabama scene. Mr. Waterman and the assistant to the director of the press, Ms. Blanche Sarratt, have been of indispensable help in the work necessary to publish this book. In the editing phase Ms. Dawn Hall has saved me from several mistakes had her keen observations not been made prior to the book's being put in print. She has also made the manuscript much more user-friendly to all who will read and use it.

The anonymous referees who read the manuscript of *Alabama Politics* made helpful suggestions related to literature that would strengthen it from the perspective of comparative state politics and also assist the author in making his points come across to the reader more effectively.

Even as a professor emeritus I continue to meet regularly with highly informed and motivated students for discussions of contemporary state politics, particularly over breakfast and lunch. I am especially indebted to brothers John and Mark Hammontree with whom I have had a standing Friday morning breakfast engagement at Northport's City Café. (Mark took over where John had left off.) I am indebted as well to Jared Culver, a recent UA law graduate, who now works in the office of US Senator Jeff Sessions. Also working in Washington is a skilled writer-alumnus, Barry Phelps, now with the US Bureau of the Mint but formerly on the staff of then Vice President Al Gore.

I am also very appreciative to Mr. Norris Green, legislative fiscal officer, and Mr. Timothy A. Lewis, state law librarian, who furnished me with much of the information presented in the chapter dealing with the expenditures of state government. In addition, Andy Benefield, another UA grad, was helpful in assembling the data needed for nonfiscal charts, graphs, and tables, which appear in the pages to follow. Steven Noles, a very skilled attorney and Harvard grad, provided invaluable assistance in connection with discussions of the legal cases discussed in the book.

Professor Michael DeBow, professor of law at Cumberland School of Law of Samford University, deserves special thanks—for his continuing friendship and support during the time the manuscript was in preparation and for answers to questions about court cases I frequently posed to him both in e-mails and during lunchtime discussions.

Secretary of State John Merrill has also been of continuing assistance. Secretary Merrill was formerly a distinguished member of the Alabama House of Representatives and was extremely helpful in my understanding of the nuances of legislative behavior.

Finally, I am indebted to my wife, Connie, and my son, Dr. William H. "Trey" Stewart III, for their encouragement and patience during the time it took to produce this book. Especially was this true during the period in which I was seriously ill—not long after work on the projected book started.

Inevitably in a book of this scope, errors either of fact or of judgment will occur despite multiple readings by several highly observant readers. For these I take full and complete responsibility.

1
Portrait of Alabama

Before launching a study of Alabama politics, it is essential for us to understand the environment in which political processes and institutions operate. An appreciation for the political milieu is essential in explaining how and why political actors behave as they do in contemporary Alabama. This environment has changed considerably in recent years (although there are relatively stable aspects), and a picture that might have been clear a relatively short time ago could be out of focus now.

Where Is Alabama and What's It Like?

You will find Alabama on the map in the east south central region of the United States. An Alabamian lives in the "real South." When one person was asked to identify the heart of the "real South," he said it was definitely "somewhere around Alabama."[1] It has also been said that Alabama represents "the quintessential South."[2]

A Snapshot of Alabama Politics

An Alabamian's vote is not continually solicited by national politicians. Its severest critics have identified the state's political reputation as that of a "political backwater."[3] The state has never produced a president. Only one vice president (William R. King) came from Alabama, and he died a month after taking his oath of office. John Sparkman, at the time the junior senator from Alabama, was the unsuccessful Democratic nominee for vice president in 1952. At present, the state is not typically one of the leading players in national politics, although it has produced some powerful politicians in the relatively recent past (most notably George Wallace, who is the subject of chapter 2).

What has been true of Alabama in most recent presidential elections, as on November 6, 2012, has also been true in a majority of the other southern states. Political scientist Harold Stanley notes that in the 1990s, even though there was an all-southern Democratic slate twice (1992 and 1996), its victories (those of Clinton-Gore) did not depend on southern support.[4] In this century, Republican southern support was crucial in George W. Bush's successful White House bids. Each time, however, the fact that Alabama would be a red state come November could be taken for granted. Since Alabama is usually off the beaten path in terms of national general election campaigning, even the most gifted Alabama politician of today can realistically aspire to no higher national office than that of US senator.

Alabama's Image

Although as we will see later in this book (especially in chapters 5 and 8), black and white Alabamians have become increasingly polarized politically, it is nonetheless true that progress in overcoming racial prejudice has been made—even if actual behaviors do not always jibe with that of the Finches of *To Kill a Mockingbird*.[5] Harper Lee's novel, set in a small southern Alabama town in the 1930s, is one of the most admired literary works in the world. The prolific Alabama writer Wayne Greenhaw called *Mockingbird* "Alabama's and perhaps the world's best novel."[6] Its leading character, attorney Atticus Finch, is pointed to as "the most enduring fictional image of racial heroism." An Alabama teacher, Heather Langford of Notasulga, said she wanted her children to read *Mockingbird* and "know that if there were more people like Atticus Finch, the world would be a much better place."[7]

Alabama's image, especially from the early 1960s to the early 1970s, was best represented by Wallace—a mostly negative symbol. Indeed, Wallace has been given as one of the reasons "why Americans hate politics." National columnist E. J. Dionne makes reference to Wallace's opportunism in changing from a racial liberal following a defeat at the polls to a man who "pledged never again to be caught on the tolerant side of racial politics."[8]

A substantial number of Alabama's current generation of "most influential" people occupy no elective office.[9] A list compiled in 2009 named twelve. Only two, then-governor Bob Riley and US senator Richard Shelby, had been chosen at the polls. All of the group were male and there was only one African American among them, Dr. Joe Reed, the head of the Alabama Democratic Conference since the 1970s (and formerly associate executive secretary of the Alabama Education Association). The average age of these dozen "power brokers" was calculated to be sixty-five.

Alabama Attitudes

Approximately one-fourth of the Alabama population is African American. An examination of political behavior with this formerly subjugated segment of society will be an important component of a political portrait of Alabama. Politicians of today no longer have to carry what historian Virginia Van der Veer Hamilton referred to as "the albatross of race."[10] Still, Alabamians are subject to continuing allegations of intolerance, most recently in the case of Hispanics and the controversial immigrant law (proclaimed to be the "nation's toughest") of 2011 (discussed in chapter 3).

The Alabama population does not consist simply of blacks and whites. This fact was confirmed by the results of the 2010 census and was responsible for the immigration law mentioned in the previous paragraph. Most Alabamians have lived in the state all of their lives and aren't apt to accept the notion that newcomers (wherever they are from) should immediately have the welcome mat set out for them.

The 2010 Census

Between 2000 and 2010 Alabama's Hispanic population rose 145 percent—from a total of 75,830 Hispanics to 185,602 (+109,772). Hispanics now made up 3.9 percent of the state's population. Even newcomers to Alabama from other states do not quickly become key players in the state's politics, however, so it is not surprising that it presently has no prominent Hispanic politician.

Alabama's total population rose at a modest 7.5 percent between the 2000 and 2010 censuses. (The 2000 population was tabulated at 4,447,100; 2010, at 4,779,736.) The southern growth rate average was 14.3 percent. In- and out-migration have been virtually the same. The 2010 census showed approximately 100,000 entering the state from elsewhere, but another 100,000 leaving.

The state's largest metropolitan area is Birmingham-Hoover, with 1.1 million residents located in seven counties.

Huntsville is the second largest (510,088). Its population grew at the rate of 22 percent during the past decade. Forty-nine percent of the state's population lives in four metro areas, including these two—what is referred to as the I-65 corridor. (The other two metro areas located near I-65 are Mobile and Montgomery.) Prevailing political values are more likely to be those of residents of smaller towns within these metro areas than either the central cities or the more affluent suburbs.

Many residents of the less opulent suburbs are relatively recent migrants

Table 1.1. Population changes in Alabama counties

County	2010 Population	% Change from 2000
Autauga	54,571	+25.0%
Baldwin	182,265	+29.8%
Barbour	27,457	−5.4%
Bibb	22,915	+10.0%
Blount	57,322	+12.3%
Bullock	10,914	−6.8%
Butler	20,947	−2.1%
Calhoun	118,572	+5.6%
Chambers	34,215	−6.5%
Cherokee	25,989	+8.3%
Chilton	43,643	+10.2%
Choctaw	13,859	−13.0%
Clarke	25,833	−7.3%
Clay	13,932	−2.3%
Cleburne	14,972	+6.0%
Coffee	49,948	+14.5%
Colbert	54,428	−1.0%
Conecuh	13,228	−6.1%
Coosa	11,539	−5.4%
Covington	37,765	+0.4%
Crenshaw	13,906	+1.8%
Cullman	80,406	+3.8%
Dale	50,251	+2.3%
Dallas	43,820	−5.5%
DeKalb	71,109	+10.3%
Elmore	79,303	+20.4%
Escambia	38,319	−0.3%
Etowah	104,430	+0.9%
Fayette	17,241	−6.8%
Franklin	31,704	+1.5%
Geneva	26,790	+4.0%
Greene	9,045	−9.3%
Hale	15,760	−8.3%
Henry	17,302	+6.1%
Houston	101,547	+14.4%
Jackson	53,227	−1.3%
Jefferson	658,466	−0.5%
Lamar	14,564	−8.4%
Lauderdale	92,709	+5.4%
Lawrence	34,339	−1.3%
Lee	140,247	+29.9%
Limestone	82,782	+26.0%
Lowndes	11,299	−16.1%
Macon	21,452	−11.0%
Madison	334,811	+21.0%
Marengo	21,027	−6.7%
Marion	30,776	−1.4%
Marshall	93,019	+13.1%
Mobile	412,992	+3.3%
Monroe	23,068	−5.2%
Montgomery	229,363	+2.6%
Morgan	119,490	+7.6%
Perry	10,591	−10.7%
Pickens	19,746	−5.7%
Pike	32,899	+11.1%
Randolph	22.913	+2.4%
Russell	52,947	+6.4%
Shelby	195,085	+36.1%
St. Clair	83,593	+29.1%
Sumter	13,763	−7.0%
Talladega	82,291	+2.5%
Tallapoosa	41,616	+0.3%
Tuscaloosa	194,656	+18.1%
Walker	67,023	−5.2%
Washington	17,581	−2.9%
Wilcox	11,670	−11.5%
Winston	24,484	−1.4%

from rural counties. The Alabama economy of today is definitely more industrial than agricultural, and it has been many years since the typical state residence was a family farm.

Alabama has been classified as mostly "urban" for a long time, and population losses within the state have been most glaring in rural counties, including both African American and white majority population counties. In the Black

1.1. Population changes in Alabama by county.
Source: US Census Bureau

Belt, the Lowndes County population declined 16 percent between 2000 and 2010 (from 13,473 down to 11,299). Neighboring counties sustained double-digit losses as well. In the northern part of Alabama, white majority counties, including Colbert (54,984 / 54,428) and Jackson (53,926 / 53,227), had small losses when 2010 census figures were released.

The Quality of Life

Alabamians are known for their passion for big-time college football. While it is true that this diverts attention from political matters, this is the case in other parts of the country as well. Alabama has no major sports team franchises so fan interest centers on Alabama and Auburn collegiate football. Fans may have a degree of loyalty toward their teams that resembles religious zealotry.

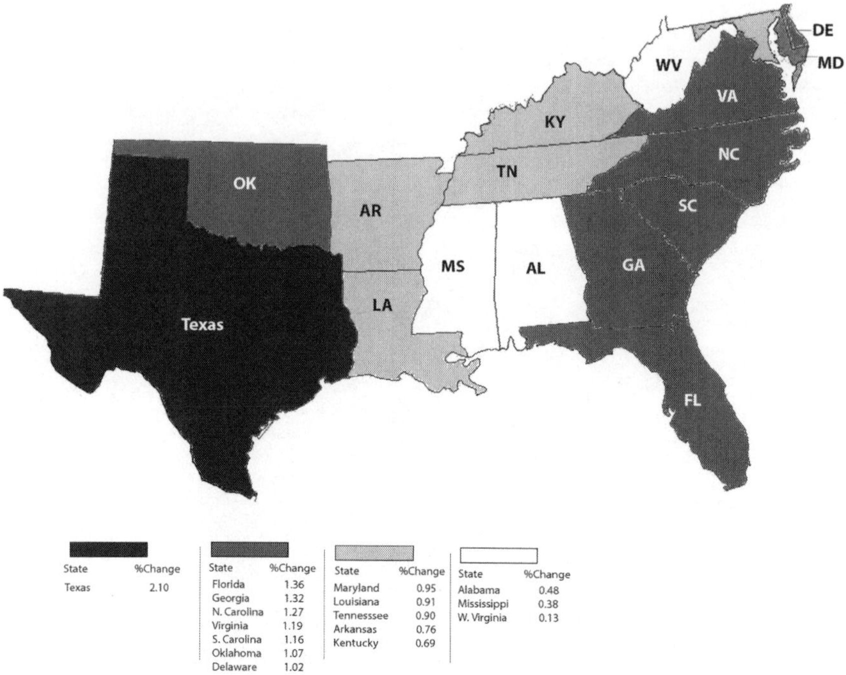

1.2. Population growth of the South. Source: US Census Bureau

Poverty and Education

The average Alabamian, even if not officially classified as impoverished, is by no means affluent either. Thus many don't have the luxury of being able to follow politics closely even if they were so inclined. In 2010 the percentage of Alabamians identified as impoverished was 17.3. The Alabama rate was a little higher than the 2010 national poverty rate of 15.1 percent.

For the most part, not being highly educated, the typical lower-income Alabamian is unlikely to want to sacrifice on Alabama's behalf. Surveys regularly indicate (as pointed out in chapter 14) broad support for more public revenue for public schools—while referenda returns show just as regularly defeat at the polls for proposals that would provide it. Higher taxes aren't popular anywhere, but in Alabama the antitax mentality has been especially virulent.

Even though there is ample statistical evidence to prove that it helps to increase earning power throughout life, Alabamians are continuing to be underappreciative of the value of education and, partly for this reason, un-

Table 1.2. Top ten poorest states (2011)

State	Median Income	Poverty Rate (%)
Mississippi	$36,950	21.3
Arkansas	38,600	16.5
Tennessee	40,026	16.1
West Virginia	40,824	15.7
Louisiana	41,896	18.0
Montana	42,005	13.4
South Carolina	42,059	14.9
Kentucky	42,091	15.5
Alabama	42,218	16.1
North Carolina	43,275	16.1

Source: 24/7 Wall St. http://247wallst.com.

willing to support it generously, especially with locally raised revenues. Alabamians on the average have a lower level of education than the residents of most other states. About 78 percent have finished high school. Just three states—Louisiana, Texas, and Virginia—have smaller percentages. Alabama ranks forty-third among the states in terms of receipt by residents of two-year college degrees and forty-fifth from the perspective of diplomas from four-year colleges.

And, demonstrating why the state so often serves as the higher educational training ground for other states to which graduates move, Alabama ranked fiftieth in terms of the earning power of people who have received college degrees in 2012.[11]

The "Status Quo Society"

Alabama citizens historically have had a preference for keeping things pretty much like they always have been. The typical Alabamian is "conservative," not just in politics but in other aspects of life as well. People living in areas of the country that seem more receptive to change may view typical Alabamians as uninformed or even ignorant. Based on this traditional predisposition, an orientation that is associated with lower levels of education, historian Glenn Feldman referred in the title of an article published several years ago to Alabama as "the status quo society" (specifically, the Alabama of the 1940s).[12]

Rural Alabama residents are still sometimes referred to as rednecks—a form of demeaning stereotyping that has not been consigned to the scrapheap to join equally offensive racial epithets. When a polling firm took a survey early in 2012 it asked questions of Alabamians and Mississippians that it had not asked of respondents elsewhere. These questions included whether or not they believed in evolution, that interracial marriage was acceptable, and that President Barack Obama was a Muslim.[13] In chapter 3, "Social Values and Politics," we will present findings from surveys related to attitudes on these subjects and political behavior. But the complete "portrait of Alabama" cannot be confined to simplistic stereotypes. In many respects, Alabama will be found to be just as advanced as more affluent, more educated states.

Modern Alabama

In 2009, when Alabama was competing with Washington State for an aircraft manufacturing plant, US senator Patty Murray of that state "challenge[d] anybody to tell [her] that they've stood on a[n assembly] line in Alabama and seen anybody building anything."[14] This statement was rightly contradicted. Toward the close of the twenty-first century's first decade, Alabama counted among its employers well over 5,000 manufacturing firms, approximately 200 of which had their headquarters in foreign countries. The most spectacular addition to the Alabama industrial pantheon came in 1993 with the announcement that a Mercedes plant would be built at Vance. Production began at the plant in 1997, and it is estimated that, since then, the auto manufacturer has contributed approximately $1.5 billion each year to the state economy. In some respects, economic changes have not been positive. For example, toward the close of the 1990s there were forty-eight publicly traded companies that had their headquarters in Alabama. However, at the start of 2010 this number had decreased to only nineteen.

Corruption and Church

Cynicism toward politics and politicians has been encouraged by highly publicized scandals at all levels of government. Chapter 4 will deal with public corruption mainly at the state level, and comparative data related to the American states generally will be presented. At the outset, it is obvious that Alabama has no monopoly on corruption. A recent book on New Jersey had the subtitle, "New Jersey's Culture of Corruption."[15] Even before its most recent governor headed to prison, Illinois's lieutenant governor (who would have to fill the vacancy) lamented that his state "ha[d] become an 'international laughingstock.'"[16] Late in 2010 the capital city of Alabama, Montgomery, was said to be "in a state of upheaval"—but this time due to something positive. At Governor Bob Riley's urging, the legislature had just passed a package of ethics reform bills that leaders hoped would permit Alabama "to shed a reputation for corruption."[17] We will discuss the politics of passage in chapter 4.

Surveys (the results of which are presented in chapter 3) indicate that

Alabamians are considerably more religiously oriented, and, as we will see in chapter 4 as well, this has important implications for Alabama politics. One veteran capital journalist, Dana Beyerle, referred to Alabama politics as "a hotbed of religion."[18] State politicians, he said, had almost invariably used religion in their campaigns. The Christian Right, discussed in chapter 3, has been a critical component of the Republican Party. While one negative aspect of Alabama's overwhelmingly conservative religious mindset once prominently included anti-Catholic bigotry, today like-minded Catholics and Christians of other persuasions are apt to coalesce politically (as on the issue of abortion, for example).

Alabama is becoming more diverse religiously, and this is having some political effects. The state was once almost monolithically Protestant, but this is no longer the case. The Eternal Word Television Network, a large Roman Catholic organization, is among the world's biggest religious operations and is headquartered in Alabama. Alabama's abandonment of old anti-Catholic prejudice was evidenced by the election of a Catholic US senator (Jeremiah Denton, a Republican) and governor (Don Siegelman, a Democrat) and by the win of Republican presidential aspirant Rick Santorum in its 2012 presidential primary. As in other states, there has also been observed both the increasing secularization of society and the growth in the number of people who profess to have no religious orientation.

Alabama is definitely not insulated from other national trends either, and the state suffered along with other states in the severe recession endured in the early years of the twenty-first century. Its recent unemployment rate has roughly paralleled the national level. Alabama's current governor, Robert Bentley, has pledged not take a salary until the jobless rate goes down to 5.2 percent. (It is presently about 8 percent.)

Policy and Politics

Governmental institutions in Alabama, and the officials voters elect to make policy through them, are similar in many respects to those in other states. This book has the goal of shedding light on the environment in which institutions function and how the processes and structures actually operate. We will make comparisons to and contrasts with other jurisdictions frequently (especially other southern states).

The fact that Alabamians like low taxes and apparently aren't concerned if public services don't get adequate funds has even been taken note of internationally. When a low tax consensus seemed to be building in Australia in recent years, this was said to represent "[a] little bit of Alabama" or "the politics of fiscal starvation."[19] We will discuss the politics of funding and administering public services in chapter 14.

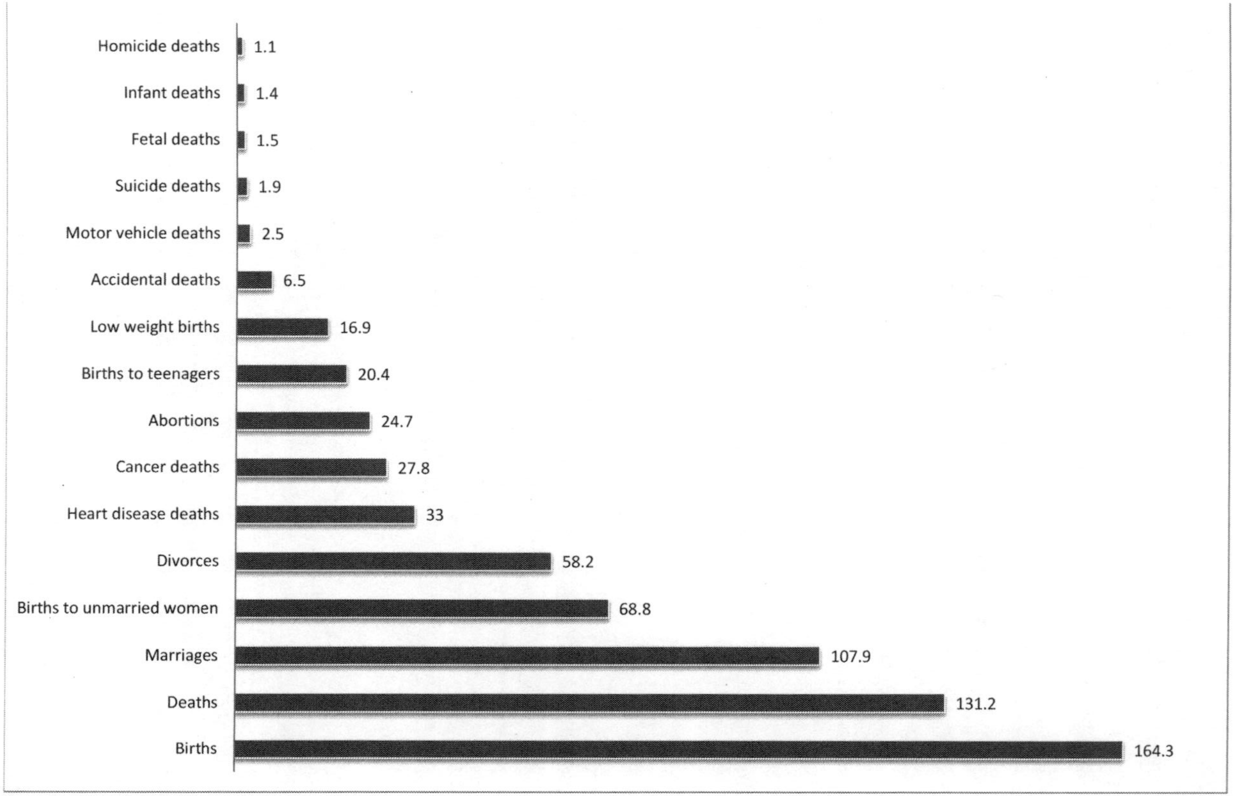

1.3. Alabama vital statistics, 2010. Source: Alabama Center for Health Statistics

How Government Functions

At times in its political past Alabama state government has been identified as dysfunctional. This was especially true when the Democrats controlled the legislature while the voters usually elected Republican governors. Since late 2010 Alabama has had party government under unified party control. One may be dissatisfied with the outputs of a conservative state government and its failure to act on a liberal agenda that the Republican governor and legislature would never agree to. But it is not now stalemated government due to partisan deadlock. Republicans have a "supermajority"—and *if* they are united and *if* they have the will to act (both uncertain political variables)—they can do so. V. O. Key had argued that a two-party system was healthy for American democracy because it provided better ways of resolving conflicts between competing groups, bridged the separation of powers, and helped voters make more rational choices at election time. As Richard Scher observes, "The efficacy of the [two-party] model [for Key] was not based on policy outcomes or outputs."[20] A two-party system did not exist in any southern state when Key advocated it.

Alabama and Southern Politics

A century ago, Alabama was an integral part of what was known as the Solid (Democratic) South. Even after Alabama ceased to be a predominantly rural state, the flavor of its politics shared much in common with other Deep South states.

Today the Alabamian who holds allegiance to a political party is most likely to identify as a Republican. Nevertheless, as in other parts of the country, professed independence of party tie has been on the rise.

To cite Scher again, he points out that, "For many people," including most of our readers, "traditional southern ways, including politics, are an increasingly dim memory."[21] One of the most recent studies of contemporary southern politics, written by former Alabama US representative (and professor) Glen Browder reminds its readers that in the early 1950s southern politics was very different than it is today. Before the rise to prominence of George Wallace and Martin Luther King Jr., it was an activity from which African Americans were systematically barred—an exclusion which they, for the most part, passively accepted.[22] This is no longer true in Alabama or anywhere else in the South. African Americans' movement into an active political role is the subject of chapter 5. They are a vital component of state politics today, and legal barriers no longer deny them opportunities for full participation. This does not mean that there are not continuing controversies over perceived barriers, however—such as the new requirement that a voter present a photo identification when they go to the polls.

The Civil War Legacy

Civil War nostalgia is confined to a continually decreasing segment of the population. Thus while mention of war reminiscences is warranted in this study, we will not need to linger for a long time on this subject. The Civil War (or War between the States) is not a matter of high salience for the average Alabamian of whatever ethnicity. Alabama observes three Confederate hero holidays, although mention in the media is generally rare except to note that state employees don't have to go to work then. General Lee's birthday (January 19) sometimes coincides with the day honoring Dr. Martin Luther King Jr., on which much more emphasis is placed.

Alabama and Washington

Even though most Alabamians have no desire to refight the Civil War, it would still be inaccurate to say that actions in Alabama (or, frequently, the lack of action) meet with uniform approval in Washington. Numerous instances will be cited where the US courts or the US Congress or president required the state of Alabama to do (or not do) certain things. At the same time many illustrations can be located to show close cooperation, especially after natural disasters.

US district judge Frank Johnson issued so many orders pertaining to Alabama in the 1950s and 1960s that he was sometimes referred to as the "real governor." Johnson served as a judge of the district court for the Middle District of Alabama (1955–79), and many of the cases ultimately decided by the Supreme Court started in his courtroom. Jack Bass and Walter De Vries note that, "Despite its relative political stagnation [they wrote before Republican dominance was achieved], Alabama ha[d] undergone fundamental social and political change." The stimulus for change had not been state officialdom, but the federal judiciary, especially Judge Johnson. These scholars credit Johnson with a "bold application of the law to correct long-standing practices of social injustices."[23] In an interview with Bass and De Vries, Judge Johnson was candid enough to say that there was no "political thicket" into which federal courts could not enter in order to correct legal wrongs.[24] In addition to many positive legacies of the federal court decisions relating to Alabama, they also resulted, as historian Wayne Flynt points out, in "a state deeply polarized along racial lines."[25]

There is a consensus among Alabama's political elite today that federal or-

1.4. Lister Hill. From the William H. Stewart collection

ders will always be complied with, even if sometimes only grudgingly. When state lawyers were defending the new immigration law in summer 2011, they referred to previous instances of defiance as "thankfully part of the past."[26] Whether this is completely true or not, the reader will have to determine in the course of reading this book. That the federal government is supreme and that it has the final say when there are conflicts is an established fact, however.

Overview

There are numerous indexes that attempt to show which states have the "worst" politics, and Alabama typically ranks fairly high on these unfavorable lists. Readers come to a book like this with different attitudes, beliefs, and orientations regarding government and politics, and I fully respect these. "Worst" and "best" represent value judgments that may be made differently by different people.

Alabama's Top Twenty-Five Most-Accessed Articles from September 2008 through December 2013

1. Scottsboro Trials
2. Harper Lee
3. Segregation (Jim Crow)

4. Birmingham Campaign of 1963
5. Agriculture in Alabama
6. Letter from Birmingham Jail
7. Montgomery Bus Boycott
8. Eugene "Bull" Connor
9. Modern Civil Rights Movement in Alabama
10. Climate
11. Plantation Architecture in Alabama
12. Minerals of Alabama
13. Alabama (an overview)
14. Cherokees in Alabama
15. Birds of Alabama
16. Martin Luther King Jr.
17. Creeks in Alabama
18. Insects of Alabama
19. Civil War in Alabama
20. Geology of Alabama
21. Selma to Montgomery March
22. *To Kill a Mockingbird*
23. Paul William "Bear" Bryant
24. Slavery
25. Coal Mining

Author's Viewpoint

One area where the author does not claim to be detached is in support of equal rights. No other change in Alabama politics has been as important as the part the state has played in the civil rights struggle since the 1950s. The roles of African Americans in Alabama politics will be presented frequently and the obstacles to their elevation to loftier positions than they have thus far been able to attain identified. Racism remains a problem with which Alabama (as well as other states) will have to deal for an indefinite future.

What's Ahead?

Not a lot of political news comes out of Alabama at the present time. When George Wallace was in his prime, however, Alabama became synonymous with its governor, and the nation paid very close attention to developments in the heart of Dixie. Wallace reflected an Alabama that is, in many respects, quite different from the state and people described both in the preceding pages and those that follow. And even though the literature on Wallace is voluminous and continues to grow, it is essential that a book on Alabama politics—including one from a contemporary perspective—devote a separate chapter to Wallace.

So the next chapter focuses on the legacy left by George Wallace, the most important single practitioner of Alabama politics in its history. Even though he died in 1998 one cannot deal with Alabama politics (almost two decades after his passing) without understanding the role Wallace once played and the influence his legacy continues to have today.

The subjects to be discussed subsequent to chapter 2 were chosen because, in my judgment, they are most critical to understanding Alabama as it functions politically at present—whether one is a student reader, an interested citizen who wishes to be better informed about his or her state, or a scholar curious to see how someone with the same vocation has attempted to synthesize a growing number of possible sources related to his chosen subject into a single book of only a few hundred pages.

2
The Wallace Legacy

George Wallace served far longer than any other Alabama governor (four terms in his own right and one cut short by the death of his wife, surrogate Governor Lurleen) before or since. The fact that Alabama is now one of the most Republican states in the nation was delayed until he was out of office.[1] The contemporary role African Americans played in state politics was, in contrast, accelerated by Wallace's obstructionism. Civil rights legislation passed during the Wallace era (and renewed thereafter) is aimed at assuring that no actions will be taken by governments in Alabama (and other covered jurisdictions) that infringe on black political rights. Wallace's apologies, although no doubt sincere, were not sufficient to remove the need for continuing federal surveillance.

George Wallace's Influence

Even though he has now been deceased for more than fifteen years, Wallace's name continues to be brought up in discussions of state politics more than any other. He both aspired to and attained a level of national prominence that no other governor had the audacity to even seriously contemplate.

Overview

During a federal bench trial relating to Alabama's property tax system (the modern origins of which date to the Wallace era) in the spring of 2011, reporter Brian Lawson observed that, "Wallace was the name most often used during the trial. His shadow loomed throughout."[2]

A new book about Alabama, past and present, takes the view that the Wallace era is not over and done with: "The 'Guv'ner' is gone but he dominated the scene for so long that he left an 'indelible after-image.' The state is still 'haunted' by him and his legacy."[3]

2.1. Lurleen and George Wallace, 1965–1966. Courtesy of the Alabama Department of Archives and History

Allen Tullos (on whose book reviewer Don Nobles was commenting) believes that, "The Guv'ner [Wallace] will haunt Alabama so long as the state fails to reconcile the quandaries he only stoked."[4]

Tullos's choice of the verb *haunt* to characterize the continuing Wallace influence is stronger than the assessment that will be made in this chapter.

Alabama's modern image has most often reflected the persona of George Wallace—a mostly negative symbol. The time Wallace dominated Alabama politics has been characterized in multiple ways, typically disapproving. Jack Bass and Walter De Vries, southern politics scholars quoted in the previous chapter and several times in this one as well, coined the expression "Wallace Freeze" to characterize the long period during which they believe Alabama was kept on hold by an absent or infirm governor.[5]

The Wallace Tenure

When he was inaugurated in 1963 Wallace was Alabama's youngest governor. When he left office four terms later (two were consecutive), he was the oldest. Between 1958 (the year of his first and only unsuccessful run for the governorship) and 1982 Wallace's name had been listed on voter ballots (mostly those of the "tantamount-to-election" Democratic primary) a total of nine times. When he initially won election in 1962, Alabama politics was, as his most successful biographer Dan Carter notes, "still the business of white folks."[6] By the time he left the governorship for the fourth time in 1987, however, this was definitely not true, and Wallace had good reason to thank black people for allowing him to continue to serve for such a long period of time. He retired from politics in 1987 (at the end of the fourth term) and died on September 13, 1998, in Montgomery.

Explaining Wallace's Success—and Lack of It

Wallace did not come close to achieving his major national objectives. Nevertheless, he would have to be regarded as the most influential Alabama politician in its history. Wallace was able to be as powerful as he was because of multiple factors, both personal and systemic. From a personal perspective, Wallace possessed much more political skill than most of his gubernatorial predecessors. His personality was an inherently dominating one. Richard Scher writes that it was not until the ascent of Wallace in the 1960s that Alabama began to exhibit the "cult of personality" that had previously characterized the politics especially of Louisiana and Georgia.[7]

Other native-born Alabamians (such as Helen Keller, Hugo Black, and Lister Hill) have had a more positive impact on the quality of people's lives, but Wallace was a powerful *politician*. The biographer whose book he liked best (Stephan Lesher) called him "the most influential loser in modern American politics."[8] The author of an obituary in 1998 took note of the fact that Wallace, at his height, was frequently regarded as "the most powerful politician in America."[9] In sharp contrast, in the post-Wallace years it has sometimes been open to question whether the incumbent governor was even the most influential politician in Alabama.

No Alabama politician today occupying any office gets anywhere near the attention that Wallace received. No governor since Wallace has had his picture on the cover of *Time*, *Newsweek*, or any other mass-circulation magazine. Wallace was even immortalized in the rock standard—"Sweet Home Alabama" ("In Birmingham they love the governor"). No other Alabama leader is credited with—or blamed for—changes that have occurred in national politics on his watch. No governor since Wallace (or before, for that matter) ever imagined that if he played his cards right, he could be the American political "king maker."

Wallace and the Civil Rights Movement

When he made his first successful gubernatorial race in the spring of 1962 George Wallace supposedly said he was "going to make race the basis of politics in this state." Today, race is no longer an open issue in Alabama political campaigns. Appeals for votes based on racial identity are not made anymore. It is a fact, however, that in the typical election an overwhelming number of whites vote one way (Republican) while African Americans in even greater percentages vote another (Democratic).

As previously noted, Wallace is frequently credited with giving a huge, although unintentional, boost to the movement for African Americans to secure equal rights not only in Alabama but everywhere. Bass and De Vries suggest that, "Perhaps the South and the nation required a George Wallace somewhere to serve as a catharsis by giving vivid expression to racism and bringing it to national consciousness, to vent the pent-up emotions of the mass of southern whites, who within a decade would be accepting the beginnings of a desegregated society."[10]

Wallace's cathartic function was demonstrated most clearly in the brutal response to the first attempted Edmund Pettus Bridge crossing in Selma on "Bloody Sunday" (March 7, 1965). The cruel images seen by people all over, along with the dramatic trek to the Alabama capitol two weeks later, furnished the needed impetus for the passage of the Voting Rights Act in just a few months. The initially unsuccessful bridge crossing, followed by the victorious march to Montgomery on March 21, 1965, was perhaps the defining moment of the civil rights movement.[11]

Wallace apologized on March 11, 1995, for his previous segregationist beliefs and actions. One sign of his change of heart, more than two decades before the formal apology, was when he crowned the University of Alabama's first black homecoming queen on November 17, 1963—not far from the spot where he had "stood in the schoolhouse door" to keep blacks out. One of Wallace's daughters, Peggy Sue, is the wife of the former chair of the state Democratic Party. On March 8, 2009, she was with the group of civil rights heroes who walked over the Edmund Pettus Bridge in Selma in another observance of "Bloody Sunday."

Wallace and Political Change

There was no blood shed in the Alabama Democratic Party as a result of Wallace's efforts to drive further wedges between the party nationally and its Alabama adherents. Within Alabama, however, Wallace fractured (to use a medical analogy) the Democratic Party, which today is only a shadow of its former vibrant self. The wounds he inflicted with his schismatic state and national campaigns were grievous indeed. At his demise the party that had enabled his rise to power no longer had the majority of white voters, and, because they constitute approximately three-fourths of the state's population, this meant consignment of the Democratic Party to a seemingly perpetual minority position in state politics. In presidential voting, the last time someone who wasn't a Republican (Democrat Jimmy Carter of neighboring Georgia) carried the state was in 1976, six years before Wallace was elected to his fourth and final gubernatorial term.

Political Recruitment Patterns

In the Wallace era candidates usually either recruited themselves based on an inbred or acquired passion for politics or were selected by the occasional local political boss. Even with Wallace, Alabama had no even loosely disciplined statewide political organization that routinely recruited candidates for various offices. (The schismatic state Democratic Executive Committee did not qualify as such.)

Wallace came from a political family, and the environment in which he grew up was one in which his male role models had few diversions besides politics. Humanist Maggie Riechers says that politics "seemed to run in the water" in the southeastern part of the state from which Wallace hailed.[12] In contrast, most recent Alabama governors have come from families that were not heavily involved in politics.

No contemporary Alabama politician has openly confessed to the ambition that Wallace did not even try to disguise. Historian Timothy Huebner, reviewing the Dan Carter Wallace biography, notes that: "During his years at the University of Alabama and in the Air Force during World War II, the Alabamian constantly made known his political aspirations; after the war, he leapt into politics at age 26."[13]

No contemporary Alabama politician has been as calculating as Wallace, reshaping himself to fit shifting political currents (although some have approached Wallace's level of pragmatism). Wallace as a young member of the Alabama House of Representatives had as his mentor and role model the left-leaning Big Jim Folsom. However, when race was beginning to dominate state politics, he abandoned the Folsom brand of populism and switched to a strongly segregationist approach. Scher notes that even before Wallace had made the change from a nonracially oriented populism, he had "projected some of the insolence and danger he later used to great advantage."[14] This behavioral style was typical of populists.

Political Style

As we will see, especially in chapter 9, the campaign style of both Folsom and Wallace was distinctly of the traditional southern variety and bears little resemblance to the much more staid, businesslike approach of today. Numan

Bartley and Hugh Graham observe that, "Wallace talked the language of the common white folks in Alabama" and had "an impressive ability to voice the hopes, fears, of average white people" in the state.[15] Before Wallace arrived on the scene, V. O. Key had noted in some of the Alabama politicians he had observed "a wholesale contempt for authority and a spirit of rebellion akin to that of the Populist days."[16] Wallace perfected this political style. Scher says that his "dark angry intensity" was "designed to have . . . listeners react emotionally, and to focus on form rather than substance."[17] No recent Alabama politician has been so strong that another ambitious man or woman would greatly fear going contrary to his wishes. When Wallace was in his prime, however, it was risky, sometimes even reckless, to go against his expressed desires. He had "powers of intimidation" and "the ability to crush those who oppose[d] him."[18] Until his debilitated physical condition prevented him from doing so, Wallace was able to coordinate the activities of the executive and legislative branches to a degree that has eluded more recent governors even when, as in Wallace's day, the same party (now the Republican Party) decisively dominates both.

Change in the Governorship

Albert Brewer had sought unsuccessfully to defeat Wallace, now with one full term under his belt plus his late wife Lurleen's fifteen months in office, in the 1970 gubernatorial race with the promise to be a full-time governor. Brewer told Alabama voters that this was what the state most needed—someone who would devote all of the time available to performing gubernatorial duties. (It was generally accepted that Wallace would use a second term to launch another race for the presidency.) Even before the assassination attempt in 1972, Scher says that "there were numerous complaints from legislators, other state executives, and even his own staff that George Wallace was unable, or unwilling, to attend to the administrative tasks of his job."[19]

The voters rejected Brewer's argument, however, and returned Wallace to Room 100 at the state capitol. A majority of the white electorate did not see a problem with Wallace's part-time approach to governing.

Wallace had never been a full-time governor. One aide recalled a time when, "We were talking about spending $110 million of the taxpayers' money and the governor of this state was gone . . . he was standing over by the window eating a Baby Ruth."[20] This sort of gubernatorial inattention would be unheard of today.

Even as a part-time governor Wallace was more powerful than many full-timers have been, however. For example, he was able right away to determine who would be the House speaker, the president pro tem of the Sen-

2.2. Albert Brewer taking the Oath of Office after the death of Governor Lurleen Wallace. Courtesy of the Alabama Department of Archives and History

ate, and the chairs of House and Senate committees. While he was at full strength, the Alabama governorship was ideally suited to the ruthless personality Wallace brought to it.

After the assassination attempt on Wallace in 1972, the old system of gubernatorial influence over the legislature broke down, and collapsed completely with the election of the first modern Republican governor (Guy Hunt) to succeed Wallace in 1986. Even in the new era of Republican governors and Republican legislatures, no chief executive has succeeded in exercising the amount of legislative influence Wallace had when he took office initially in 1967.

Relations with Washington

Relations with Washington were already strained when Wallace succeeded John Patterson in January 1963, particularly due to Patterson's botched handling of the Freedom Rider desegregation efforts early in May 1961. Under Wallace, however, conflict between Alabama's approach to race relations and that of the national Democratic administrations escalated much further. The

2.3. Cover of George Wallace inaugural program from January 1971. From the William H. Stewart collection

pattern of federal involvement in Alabama administrative activities embraced but was not confined to racial discrimination in education. It was also notable in the areas of prisons and mental health. With respect to prisons, legal scholar Larry Yackle says that Wallace "sought political gain from the [Alabama prison] crisis." Wallace claimed that "thugs and federal judges" had "just about taken over society." "A vote for George C. Wallace" held out the promise of changing this situation, however (according to Wallace).[21]

At present, Alabama's administration of federal grant programs is generally fairly routine. This was not the case in Wallace's day. The "Alabama Syndrome" had federal architects of new programs in Washington always taking into consideration how any discretion that might be granted to states in spending federally allocated money would probably (in their view) be abused by Wallace.[22]

With the exception of the Roy Moore Ten Commandments and same-sex marriage controversies, relations of Alabama with the federal courts have also been more tranquil in the post-Wallace era. No recent Alabama politician, including Moore, has used comparable terms to those of Wallace in his attacks on Judge Frank Johnson (Wallace called Johnson an "integrating, carpetbagging, scalawagging, race-mixing, bald-faced liar").[23] All recent governors have upheld federal law as interpreted by the courts, even if they personally disagreed with the rulings.

State Programs

Wallace's name, like Richard Shelby's, appears on many buildings throughout Alabama, especially on the campuses of the public two-year community colleges that Wallace founded. These institutions have enabled many young people to go to college who otherwise would have been unable to. Education scholar Stephen Katsinas says the community college system "reflect[ed] George Wallace's pragmatic, populist politics."[24] But Bass and De Vries contend that the Wallace colleges were "developed with little planning or provisions for staffing" and thus "compare[d] unfavorably with similar postsecondary programs in Florida and the Carolinas, which were established in an orderly manner and based on population trends rather than political influence."[25]

Wallace never signed any "no new taxes" pledge. During his time in office, when he proposed new programs, as he frequently did, new revenue sources were recommended to pay for them. For example, Wallace secured the adoption of a two-cents additional beer tax to finance his new junior college system during the first year of his first term in 1963. The lieutenant governor at the time, James Allen (who later served as a US senator), helped secure passage of the tax by breaking a filibuster against it. At this time, lieutenant governors, although not elected as part of a gubernatorial ticket, frequently acted as the governor wished—as Allen did here.

Wallace's biographer in the *Encyclopedia of Alabama* gives him credit for attempting to reform Alabama's tax structure, although he failed to do so.[26] Actually, in the middle years of his era, as the anti-property-tax mood was gathering steam around the country (most notably in California), Wallace resorted to modern demagoguery and led in the effort to install new barriers to increasing Alabama's already lowest-in-the-nation property taxes.

When Judge Lynwood Smith declined, in October 2011, to order constitutional reform of Alabama's property tax laws, he specifically mentioned Wallace along with a powerful interest group whose influence has been pervasive for a long time. Judge Smith wrote that, "The [Alabama] Farm Bureau [which is now known as the Alabama Farmers Federation] with assistance from an extraordinarily popular governor [George Wallace] was able to ensure the enactment of legislation that protected the interests of the large, rural landholders, guaranteeing that some of Alabama's wealthiest citizens paid some of its lowest taxes."[27]

Wallace did try to reduce tax earmarking by shifting funds from the Education Trust Fund to the General Fund. However, the Alabama Education Association (AEA) first demonstrated its new political muscle by successfully resisting this proposed reform. Having more positive results were the efforts of Governors Fob James and Wallace to establish a trust fund into which money from state offshore oil and gas well leases would be deposited.[28]

Voters approved constitutional amendments creating and then strengthening the trust fund in 1982 and 1985 as advocated by Governors James and Wallace. It was subsequent governors (not Wallace) who approved the raiding of these funds, most recently in September 2012, to help meet current needs and avoid further tax increases.

Even though critics allege that the Wallace administration was corrupt (and some of these allegations aren't difficult to prove), Alabama's original ethics legislation was actually passed in 1973 (during his second term). He had vowed that he would sign the most stringent bill that the House and Senate were willing to pass. Each chamber thought the other would reject a tough bill, but neither did—and Wallace promptly signed it into law.[29] While frequently critical of Wallace, as we have seen here, Bass and De Vries write that Wallace was "a man whose reputation even among political enemies in Alabama [was] one of personal honesty."[30] Holding public office for a long time did not enrich him.

Conclusion

Ever-increasing numbers of Alabamians remember nothing about Wallace personally, and his name is only something they see attached to buildings and institutions or read about online or elsewhere. Just as it would be a serious omission to exclude Wallace from consideration, it would also be a mistake to overestimate the current influence of a man, even one so important as he was, who has been dead for more than fifteen years. The political problems Alabama has today are not mostly attributable to George Wallace—although he did contribute to making the tax system more regressive and the education bureaucracy much more expensive to maintain.

Wallace was not evangelical and did not try to exert political influence through appeals based primarily on religious values. Nevertheless, Bass and De Vries argue that he "fully understood the fundamentalist Protestant outlook that dominates much of the South and serves as a force for right-wing politics."[31] In the post-Wallace era many politicians have used religious beliefs to advance their own political fortunes much more explicitly than he ever did, and it is to an examination of the influence of religious and social norms on Alabama politics that we will now turn.

3

Social Values and Politics

In the fall of 2010, 68 percent of Alabamians surveyed said that they attended church on a weekly basis.[1] Only 12 percent said they never attended. Alabama church attendance is much higher than that found in more secularized states. Among the states, Mississippi ranked number one in terms of the percentage of its people who believed in God and prayed regularly. Like Mississippians, Alabamians also ranked highly on the importance of religion in their daily lives (more than 70 percent affirming its high importance). A polar opposite, only 7 percent of Alaskans said that religion was "very important" in their lives.[2]

We will begin our discussion in this chapter with an explanation of that aspect of Alabama conservatism that is doctrinally grounded—specifically in concepts derived from the Old and New Testaments.

The Christian Right

Alabama, along with Mississippi, frequently is cited as one of the states in which the political might of religiously oriented citizens has been most pronounced. A term very frequently used is in this context is the "Christian right" or the "religious right."[3] Political scientist Alexander Lamis has defined the Christian right as consisting of "those who are interested in an array of conservative social and cultural issues."[4] The Christian right has helped keep Alabama in the Republican presidential column in the last nine elections. Since self-identified "born again Christian" Jimmy Carter carried the state in 1976 (see the Wallace role in chapter 2) no other Democrat has been able to. Political scientist John Green notes that when Bush won in 2000 his southern triumphs "depended heavily on religious constituencies, especially observant evangelical Protestants, the prime constituency of the Christian Right and the core of traditional southern Protestantism."[5]

As we will see when we discuss political parties in greater depth in chapter 8, a division exists in the Republican Party between members who are primarily business oriented and those who are motivated mostly by their religious beliefs. The upset gubernatorial victory of Republican Fob James in 1994 (after an earlier term as a Democrat) was undoubtedly aided by his (and especially his wife's) appeal to conservative Christian voters. Jim Folsom Jr., the Democratic nominee, had assumed the governorship when Guy Hunt was removed from office (see chapter 4), and he typically had good relations with business interests.

The Christian Right and Political Preferences

The largest potential component of the Christian right in Alabama would be Southern Baptists. They number approximately 1.1 million believers in about 3,300 churches.[6] Well over a half-million additional Alabamians belong to Baptist churches that are not allied with the Southern Baptist Convention. (Many African American Alabamians are members of these Baptist congregations as well as other theologically conservative denominations and vote heavily Democratic.) Approximately 70 percent of Alabamians of all ethnicities self-label themselves as born again Christians.[7]

An exit poll conducted during the March 2012 presidential primary found that of the three remaining serious contenders for the Republican nomination at this time, former Pennsylvania Senator Rick Santorum was most favored by self-identified born again Christians, ranking ahead of former US House Speaker Newt Gingrich and former Massachusetts Governor Mitt Romney (the party's ultimate nominee).[8]

In the following sections we will discuss some of the most important disagreements involving values and politics in Alabama. The discussion is definitely not comprehensive, however, because there are some significant omissions. Those selected are among those where there has been the sharpest division of opinion. The values controversy originating in Alabama in recent years that received the greatest national and even international news coverage involved a prominent public display of the Ten Commandments.

The Ten Commandments

The origins of the dispute relating to the Ten Commandments were in the Etowah County circuit courtroom presided over by Judge Roy Moore. Judge Moore posted a small placard containing the Commandments that he had personally made shortly after his appointment to fill a vacancy by Governor Guy Hunt in 1992. He also regularly asked Christian ministers to offer prayers during the opening of court.

For what opponents of the posting and the prayers regarded as a consti-

3.1. Ten Commandments monument and Alabama Supreme Court Justice Roy Moore. Source: *Birmingham News*

tutionally impermissible merging of church and state, Moore was ordered by Montgomery County Circuit Judge Charles Price to remove the plaque and stop the prayers. When he refused, the governor at the time, Fob James, said that, if necessary, he would use the National Guard to prevent the plaque from being removed.[9] Before the matter regarding the Etowah court could be finally settled, Moore ran for and was elected to serve as the chief justice of the Alabama Supreme Court. (In the March 2012 Republican primary he was renominated for the position from which he had been removed in 2003. In the November general election he defeated his Democratic opponent and resumed his leadership of the Supreme Court and state judicial system in January 2013.)

After Moore was sworn in as chief justice in 2001, he installed a 5,280-pound monument containing the Commandments in the rotunda of the judicial building on Dexter Avenue. Just as he had been locally, Moore was now sued at the state level in federal district court. Judge Myron Thompson ruled on November 18, 2002, that the monument amounted to an unconstitutional abridgement of the needed division between church and state and ordered that it be removed.

The monument would have been acceptable had it been part of a display featuring other historic sources of law, Thompson held.[10]

Moore's own reaction to Thompson's decision was that, "It's a sad day in Alabama when a federal judge enters into the state and tries to disestablish a justice system by saying you can't acknowledge the foundation of that system."[11]

When Moore defied Judge Thompson's order by refusing to remove the monument, his eight colleagues voted to suspend him from his chief justice position and put the monument in storage. The Court of the Judiciary, consisting of retired judges and presided over by former governor and former Criminal Appeals Court Judge John Patterson, upheld the suspension. The fall 2003 "trial" of Moore was accompanied by large demonstrations around the judicial building and was extensively covered by national and international media.

That Moore would mix his religious views with a state function was not unusual behavior in Alabama. Historically, representatives of state authority, from public school teachers on up, freely injected their personal religious beliefs into their official activities. Controversies have been most numerous in public education.

Same-Sex Marriage

In early 2015, Chief Justice Moore once again found himself in conflict with the federal judiciary, this time on the question of same-sex marriage. After a federal district court ruled that the Alabama Sanctity of Marriage constitutional amendment was invalid,[12] Chief Justice Moore sent a message to all sixty-seven county probate judges telling them to disregard the federal court ruling disallowing Alabama's ban on same-sex marriages. Approximately one-third of the judges issued the federally approved licenses while the remainder would not, citing the Moore letter. Then, on March 3, 2015, the Alabama Supreme Court ordered probate judges to stop issuing same-sex marriage licenses. This ruling came as a result of a request from two religiously conservative groups.[13] Normally, the Alabama Supreme Court does not make rulings except in real cases, although it does issue advisory opinions in response to legislative requests. In this instance it did, however, due to their perception of the public interest in this matter and their inevitable concerns with possible voter reactions at the time of the next elections.

Religion and Schools

Until US Supreme Court decisions, especially in the 1960s, outlawed it, Christian education was always an integral part of public education in Alabama. Even after the Court ruled against Bible reading, Alabama (along with five other states) still specified in law that religious services be conducted in public schools. Governor George Wallace said that if the Supreme Court attempted to put a halt to Bible reading in an Alabama classroom, he would go himself to that class and read the Scriptures to the students.[14]

In a survey by the *Press-Register* of Mobile prior to the 2010 gubernatorial primaries (in which only Republican aspirants returned survey forms), all candidates said they supported school prayer.[15]

A series of lower federal court decisions has stirred up the most political controversy related to religion in the schools in recent times. In *Wallace v. Jaffree* (1985), the US Supreme Court upheld lower federal court rulings that found the state to have acted improperly. The Alabama legislature, it was decided, had passed an unconstitutional law when it empowered public school teachers to lead students in prayer or moments of silence.[16] In the late 1990s a federal district judge ordered a halt to school-sponsored prayers in DeKalb County. He also voided a state law permitting prayer at school events and prohibited schoolteachers from leading their students in religious activities.[17]

This decision was referred to as the Alabama Secular Humanism Decision and was widely circulated. The 11th US Court of Appeals ruled afterward that Judge Ira Dement had gone too far when he barred voluntary student-led prayers. In these and other controversies, the Republican Party in Alabama positioned itself on the side of religious faith and portrayed the Democratic Party as an agent of secularism (which has few open adherents in the state). Alabama Democrats sought to show that Republicans did not "own" this issue, however, and frequently introduced bills in the legislature to increase the use of the Bible as a work of literature (as would be constitutionally permissible). Republicans generally opposed these initiatives, mostly because of the unstated reason that they didn't want Democrats to lure away the religious conservatives who were increasingly moving toward their party.

The teaching of the Bible related to the origins of human life on Earth has also been politically controversial, competing in Alabama, as in other conservative states such as Tennessee, with scientific explanations. Science textbooks for many years have featured a disclaimer to the effect that evolution is only a "theory." The National Center for Science Education assigned Alabama an F grade based on its tentative endorsement of teaching evolution.[18] Putting matters in a broader comparative perspective, American studies scholar Christopher Clausen is not surprised that "believers [such as those in Alabama] find it hard to go along with secular or scientific claims that contradict what they regard as revelation. This familiar state of affairs," he continues, "has often been described as a revolt against modernity, whether it occurs in Alabama or Saudi Arabia."[19] He also points out that, "Religious conflicts in multi-faith America are mild compared to countries that have only one faith or virtually no faith at all."[20]

As we saw in chapter 1, Alabama has been an entity with an overwhelm-

3.2. Congresswoman Terri Sewell. From the William H. Stewart collection

ingly male leadership, and some religious groups help perpetuate this pattern in the state at large by denying women in church the top leadership positions, such as filling pulpits.

Gender Roles

Even though Alabama has always been a male-dominated society, there are some fairly progressive milestones related to women's rights in Alabama's past. For example, it was the third state in the Union to authorize married women to make wills (in 1843), following Connecticut (1809) and Texas (1840).[21] With regard to the ballot, however, Alabama never ratified the Nineteenth Amendment granting woman suffrage. Despite this, the necessary three-fourths of the states did so by 1920. Alabama also declined to ratify the unsuccessful Equal Rights Amendment to the US Constitution as proposed by Congress in 1972 (one of fifteen nonratifying states). The election of women to public office in Alabama has been inconsistent as far as different branches and positions are concerned. In the appellate judiciary, three of the nine Supreme Court justices were female in 2012 as were three of the ten judges of the courts of appeals. The chief justice was a woman until she resigned in mid-2011. A Republican woman, Twinkle Andress Cavanaugh, was the first of her gender to chair one of the state's two main political parties. (She is now a member of the Public Service Commission.) In April 2012, of thirty-one statewide offices, women occupied ten.

Political progress of women has been slowest on the legislative front. In fact, in the early years of the twenty-first century, Alabama was in last place as regards gender and legislative composition.[22] There are now nineteen women in a 140-member legislature (five senators and fourteen representatives). This figure represents 13.5 percent of the total membership.

Speaking of federal offices, it was only in 2010 that the first women were elected to Congress from Alabama in contested races. Terri Sewell, a Democrat, had the distinction also of being the first African American woman to represent Alabama in Congress. (Martha Roby was elected at the same time as a Republican congresswoman in southeast Alabama.)

In terms of appointive boards, white men constitute the overwhelming majority of members, even though the population of Alabama is about 52 percent female. To reiterate what was noted in chapter 1, a survey in 2009 to identify Alabama's dozen most influential people included no women and only one African American.

Women's rights is another area in which Alabama has needed federal goading to act in ways favorable toward a group being discriminated against. It took action by the federal judiciary to secure for Alabama women the right to serve on juries in 1966.[23] The 2009 Lilly Ledbetter Fair Pay Act, named for an Alabama woman, was a federal not a state law. This law is designed to ensure that there is no pay discrimination between men and women—specifically, to guarantee that women doing the same work as men get the same pay for it. Alabama Republicans in Congress voted against this legislation. Conservative opposition to the Ledbetter Act was traceable not to any religious belief but to values of laissez-faire capitalism favoring minimal governmental intrusion in private business. In order to be in a favorable competitive position for the "best and brightest," potential large employers, both public and private, have, however, frequently been more advanced than the state government in making progress to remove recently recognized forms of discrimination.

Sexual Orientation

In 2006 a Birmingham district elected Alabama's first openly gay state representative, Democrat Patricia Todd. Previous to this, in the 1990s, Alabama had added the amendment (774) to the constitution declaring that Alabama courts did not have to recognize the validity of same-sex marriages performed elsewhere. When Alabama passed its "marriage amendment," it was the twentieth state to do so. Despite such actions as these taken presumably to promote the sanctity of traditional marriage, in 2011 Alabama was fourth among the states in terms of divorcing couples.[24] Alabama legislators have not been willing to pass a hate crimes law or a law specifically targeting bullying motivated by hostility toward someone's sexual orientation.

Reflecting back on the traditional Alabama (and southern) tendency to be unwelcoming toward the new and different, it should not be surprising that it would be among the first of the states to attempt to discourage people who have not entered the United States legally from settling in Alabama. As we saw in chapter 1, however, thousands have done so. Restrictive immigration regulation would not be supported by any major set of religious values, and some religious groups have been very vocal in their opposition to Alabama policies in this area.

Immigrants

The move to deal with "outsiders" began with the English as the official language movement that had an impact in Alabama as well as other states. In 1990 Alabama adopted a constitutional amendment (509) to this effect by a 9–1 margin.

The anti-immigrant backlash also manifested itself in the controversy over driver's license testing in multiple languages. In the 2010 Republican gubernatorial primary campaign, unsuccessful candidate Tim James made as one of his principal issues the demand that the state return to single-language testing. His TV ad on this subject "went viral" and was seen by millions throughout the United States.

In 2007 Alabama was estimated to have a minimum of 85,000 immigrants. In a ranking of the states, Alabama was twenty-eighth.[25]

Comparatively, the "politics of immigration" had become more salient in southern states generally following the terrorist attacks of September 11, 2001. States like California and New Mexico, in which immigration had been a major political issue for a long time, were now joined by states such as Alabama and Georgia where it had not previously been on the agenda.[26]

California and New Mexico did not respond as restrictively as Alabama and Georgia, however.

The Alabama House passed an immigration bill, HB 56, in April 2011. At that time Mickey Hammon said he believed that the measure he and his Senate cosponsor (Scott Beason) had sponsored was "stronger than Arizona's controversial law and would attack every aspect of an illegal immigrant's life."[27] Most of the opposition in the House came from Democrats, especially the African American majority within the party. The law went so far as to criminalize knowingly offering a ride to an illegal immigrant. The Senate sponsor of the immigrant bill was quoted as saying in a talk to a Republican Party group that, with respect to illegal immigrants, government officials should "empty the clip, and do what has to be done."[28] He later explained that he was speaking metaphorically and meant only that multiple tactics as contained in the new immigrants' bill should be used.

Scott Beason said further that, "Democrats do not want to solve the immigration problem because they know this is a fact that when more illegal immigrants move into an area, when their children grow up and get the chance to vote, they vote for Democrats."[29] Governor Bentley signed House Bill 56 into law on June 9, 2011. The Georgia governor had signed his state's new immigration bill a few weeks earlier, on May 13. Bentley had capitalized on anti-illegal immigrant sentiment in his winning 2010 gubernatorial campaign.

The immigration act was the last plank in the Republican "Handshake with Alabama" platform to be approved. With the passage of this law, Alabama was said to have "vaulted past Arizona with what is being called the most restrictive law in the nation."[30] Alabama now became, in the words of veteran AP political reporter Phillip Rawls, the "epicenter of the fight over the nation's patchwork of immigration laws."[31] This was despite the fact that, unlike Arizona, Alabama shared no border with Mexico and had a comparatively small nonnative population. Critics of the law feared that it had "resurrected ugly images from Alabama's days as the nation's battleground for civil rights a half-century ago."[32] President Barack Obama himself criticized the new law: "It's a bad law. The idea that we have children afraid to go to school, because they feel afraid that their immigration status will lead to being detained—it's wrong."[33]

The most serious challenges to the Hammon-Beason law were filed in federal district court by the US Justice Department, which asserted that it "conflict[ed] with federal law and undermine[d] federal immigration priorities."[34] The most stringent aspects of HB 56 have not survived legal challenges, and it is generally regarded as a dead letter.

Group activity during the litigation phase of the immigration act mostly involved mainstream religious organizations such as Episcopal, United Methodist, and Roman Catholic church leaders in addition to traditional rights groups like the ACLU and the Southern Poverty Law Center. Evangelicals did not play prominent roles in demonstrations related to the immigration law. This is in sharp contrast to the role they have historically played with respect to the sale and consumption of alcoholic beverages.

Alcoholic Beverages

For many years after 1901 the most important sociopolitical issue in Alabama was alcohol beverage sales. Prohibition sentiment traditionally has been strongest in the more evangelical north. South Alabama, containing more Catholics and Episcopalians, has had more wet sentiment than north Alabama.

One political observer, Steve Flowers, has noted that, "Unlike their neighbors to the south, north Alabamians were Bible-toting teetotalers. Most of the counties north of Montgomery were dry. Most of the Black Belt counties settled by the Scotch Irish were wet and enjoyed their bourbon."[35] There was a parallel to this pattern in Mississippi. V. O. Key noted that in the Magnolia State prohibition received less support in the delta whereas, "The preachers of the hills fight demon rum and their followers vote for prohibition, while the sinful delta votes for liquor."[36] Some Black Belt counties were legally dry, however, and part of the explanation was the desire of white elites to keep liquor out of the hands of African Americans who might be emboldened by it.[37]

When the Alabama legislature came under prohibitionist control in 1914, the new majority passed the "bone dry" law banning the manufacture and sale of alcoholic beverages in the state. This was five years before national prohibition was made part of the US Constitution in 1920 through the Eighteenth Amendment. The Anti-Saloon League was one of Alabama's strongest interest groups during the period dating from approximately 1900 to the end of national prohibition in 1933.[38] Prominent aspiring politicians such as Hugo Black widely publicized the fact that they were nondrinkers.[39]

Just as Alabama went dry before the nation, it also remained legally dry after the nation had repealed prohibition. Under the leadership of Governor Bibb Graves, Alabama adopted a county option system for selling alcohol in 1935. Distilled spirits originally could be sold only in state stores while beer was available in "package" stores.

Beginning in the 1970s the political power of wets was sufficient to get a change to where communities within dry counties could vote to allow the sale of alcohol within their jurisdictions. Initially, the minimum population required for a separate municipal vote was 10,000. Due to a change made in 2009, the minimum is now only 1,000 (down from 7,000). At present, twenty-seven of the state's sixty-seven counties are dry. Due to the subcounty option, however, after November 2012 votes there was only one county, Clay, in which no alcohol sales are allowed.[40] In neighboring Mississippi, thirty-four of eighty-two counties prohibit the sale of hard liquor. The political reason for the move to divide urban (city) and county (rural) voting on alcohol sales is because country folk typically voted dry while city dwellers cast wet ballots.

The state generally allows alcoholic beverages to be sold Monday through Saturday. However, public opinion, led by business interests, has moderated to allow Sunday afternoon and evening sales where local representatives and senators agree that local residents should be given the right to vote on it. Alabama is not the only state where Sunday liquor sales have been politically controversial. Thirteen states still prohibit them.

Governor Robert Bentley formerly was a member of the state House of Representatives from a Tuscaloosa district and regularly kept Sunday alcohol sales from reaching the referendum stage. Things were different as governor:

"When I represented my local community, I voted against Sunday alcohol sales and things of that nature. As governor . . . I don't feel I should impose my views on everybody in the State."[41]

While Catholics have no problem with the liberalization of alcoholic beverage laws, they frequently work cooperatively with conservative (and prohibitionist) Protestants when policies related to abortion are considered.

Abortion

Political scientist Richard Scher identifies abortion as an area in which modern demagoguery (having abandoned race) is now practiced with "simpleminded, emotional, irresponsible approaches" that are probably counterproductive in dealing with a serious problem.[42] Until the 2010 elections African American state legislators, along with some of their white Democratic colleagues, generally were able to block the passage of legislation designed to undercut *Roe v. Wade*.[43] Even so, in 2002 Alabama became the first state in the country to mandate that physicians performing abortions do ultrasounds and give patients the opportunity to see the results. The voluntary ultrasound law did not appear to affect the abortion count, which was approximately 11,300 in 2010. The legislature also approved "choose life" license plates, which several other states have as well. NARAL Pro-Choice America (formerly the National Abortion and Reproductive Rights Action League) pays attention to state actions likely to affect the conditions under which abortions may be obtained (thirty-nine Alabama items have recently been listed at its website). NARAL has been critical of many of them, such as required waiting periods.[44]

Antiabortion actions such as Alabama has taken thus far represent "symbolic politics." Even if the legislative action doesn't bring about any substantive change, supporting legislators believe that they are, by passing largely ineffectual laws, still putting themselves on the side of responsible sexual behavior and undiminished parental authority.[45]

In his successful gubernatorial general election campaign in 2010, as would be expected, the Republican, Robert Bentley, took an antiabortion position, while his Democratic opponent, Ron Sparks, did not. Sparks was quoted as saying: "I'm not going to punish women for making a decision on their bodies."[46] In contrast, physician Bentley said: "I will never stop believing we must protect innocent lives in this country." After taking office, Bentley's wife, Diane, addressed an antiabortion rally. The House of Representatives approved a bill banning abortions after twenty weeks, and it cleared the Senate shortly before the legislature adjourned its 2011 regular session. With Governor Bentley's signature Alabama became the sixth state to outlaw abortions at the twenty-week point in a pregnancy. According to a capital reporter, the newly empowered Republicans had been "eager to prove their pro-life credentials."[47]

In the judicial arena, a Supreme Court, now totally Republican, authorized a woman whose unborn baby was fatally injured in a vehicle accident to sue on account of her loss.[48]

Previously, a fetus incapable of life outside the womb could not have been the object of such a suit.

Just as Catholic clerics and conservative Protestant ministers have different views on alcoholic beverages, they also part company when it comes to the life and death issue of capital punishment. While Catholic leaders have come increasingly to oppose the taking of life (whether at its inception or hastening its end), conservative Protestants are generally supportive of capital punishment. For the most part, however, considerations of race rather than those of religion have been more important in this area.

Capital Punishment

Political scientist Alexander Lamis identifies capital punishment as one of the issues on which the Democratic Party nationally was "weak" and which could thus be used to stigmatize it, driving larger numbers of southern (white) conservatives into the GOP ranks.[49]

There were twenty-five executions during the time Republican Bob Riley was in office (2003–11). His total was the most since the two terms of Governor Bibb Graves (1927–31, 1935–39) when there was more than double that number. Until federally prohibited in 1977, people could be executed, and frequently were, for such noncapital crimes as rape.[50] Governor Riley said, "I believe in the death penalty. I believe it's a deterrent. If we can save one life by having it, I think we should keep it."[51]

Due in part to federal restrictions on potential subjects of capital punishment the number of executions also has declined in other jurisdictions besides Alabama. Further, it should be remembered that there was a lapse in all state executions between 1967 and 1976. The moratorium was formally imposed in 1972 through a US Supreme Court decision that state capital punishment laws generally were in conflict with the federal Bill of Rights guarantee against cruel and unusual punishment.[52] Since execution in the electric chair (nicknamed Yellow Mama and in service since 1927) was believed to be in jeopardy constitutionally, Alabama switched to lethal injection in 2002.

In the 2005, 2006, and 2009 legislative sessions the Senate Judiciary Committee approved a death penalty moratorium. During the last full year of a Democratic Senate (2009), the measure passed the full Senate after getting a 6–1 favorable committee vote, but it did not pass the House. Its chief proponent, African American Democratic Senator Hank Sanders, expressed his frustration when he said: "The death penalty, the death penalty, just like no new taxes, so people react viscerally on it."[53]

Weaker Democratic support for capital punishment in Alabama is mainly due to the fact that historically a disproportionate number of African Americans have been executed in the state. Alabama ranked twenty-seventh in population, but ranked second in executions in 2010.[54] Alabama had more executions per capita than any other state. There was an eight-month informal moratorium during 2007–8 as states deliberated different combinations of lethal injection drugs in hopes that the one they opted to use would withstand federal judicial scrutiny. A majority of the US Supreme Court voted in 2008 that executions could begin again.[55]

In almost a decade and a half there has been only one instance of a gubernatorial commutation of a death sentence. This occurred in 1999, when outgoing Republican Governor Fob James commuted the sentence of a woman who had been convicted of participating in the brutal murder of a teenage girl. The most commonly presented reason for the governor's commutation at the end of his time in office was that he didn't believe in the execution of women.

Partisan judicial elections may make the exercise of the death penalty more likely since aspiring jurists (or incumbents) don't wish to be perceived by Alabama voters as being "soft" on crime. The interest group most vocal in its support of capital punishment in Alabama with no moratorium is Victims of Crime and Leniency.

Politicians occupying the position of state attorney general have been especially strident in their support of the death penalty. Charlie Graddick, in the early 1980s (then a Democrat but who later switched back to his original Republican identification), was said to have advocated electrocuting people "until their eyes popped out."[56] Even before Republicans assumed a position of strong dominance of statewide offices in Alabama, members of the party were more likely to occupy the attorney general position because they were perceived as tougher on criminals, including unwavering support for the death penalty.

One of the aspects of the Alabama capital punishment system that arouses the most controversy is the freedom that trial court judges have to override a jury's sentence of life without parole for someone whom they have convicted of aggravated murder and substitute the death penalty. Although critics oppose this judicial discretion because there are no fixed standards, it was held to be constitutional in *Harris v. Alabama*.[57] Approximately 20 percent of convicts on Alabama's death row are there because the trial judges in their cases overrode a jury's recommendation of life without parole and substituted death. In Delaware, another state with judicial overrides, appointed judges have more often used their discretion to overturn jury verdicts for death.

Alabama's continued use of the death penalty tends to reinforce a negative image of the state, not only in other states that don't allow it but also sometimes abroad. Before Australia would agree to extradite a man in connection with the death of his wife on their honeymoon, Alabama officials had to agree that he would not be subject to capital punishment were he to be convicted.[58] (He was acquitted.)

Conclusion

As noted at the outset of this chapter, there are numerous other areas of public policy where social values strongly influence the kind of politics that is found. This is the case most notably with respect to drugs and, to a lesser extent, smoking and other forms of tobacco use. At this point, however, we will turn to a discussion of allegations of corruption in Alabama state government. Corruption by individuals in or out of office is condemned by all religious value systems just as it is in those with a secular foundation. Yet values of moral codes, whatever their basis, are frequently inconsistent with actual behavior.

4
Corruption in Alabama Politics

The subject of bad behavior by public officials is one of the oldest in books on politics. Some writers, taking a more beneficent view of human nature, have argued that the best way to prevent public corruption is to start out with morally upright people in positions of responsibility. Others have taken a more critical stance and have said that the tendency of humans to behave corruptly is so strong that a multitude of laws is needed. These laws mandate what officials must and, more importantly, must not do. They also provide stiff punishment for those who disobey the laws. As a practical matter, this is not an either/or situation. Voters do try to choose those who they believe will behave themselves once in office, but their representatives have also enacted punishments for those who don't. Public corruption is obviously not confined to one level of government or one political system. However, our emphasis here will be on Alabama state government.

Research on Corruption

Scholars have sought to identify variables associated with the incidence of corruption in different jurisdictions both within the United States and internationally.[1] We will be identifying important variables throughout this chapter. It is not unique to Alabama—that much is obvious right away. Political scientist Peter Rodriguez and his colleagues have pointed out that, "All governments are beset in their pursuit of legitimate objectives by the presence of corruption."[2] As a simple experiment, do an Internet search using the keywords "Alabama" and "corruption" and see how many items you generate—no doubt, a lot! However, little would be gained by simply enumerating instances of wrongdoing. The approach to be used here will be that of identifying some of the most significant allegations of corruption in recent years, but, more consequentially, showing the relevance of misconduct for the way Alabama state government operates.

We examine corruption from different perspectives in this chapter. The most obvious way is to identify different types of corrupt activities, such as graft. Corruption also may be considered in the institutions in which it is said to occur, the traditional legislative, executive, and judicial branches, for example, as well as from the perspective of public policy. A major policy area impacted by corruption in Alabama in recent years has been postsecondary education. Corrupt behaviors can be classified into minor and major. Actions may be taken that go against a minor, obscure law unintentionally. Or they may offend the most important laws that are on the books to protect the public interest. We will be looking here at major allegations of corruption, especially in the vicinity of the capitol, and at the same time making comparisons and contrasts with other states.

A Culture of Corruption?

We will present evidence later in this chapter suggesting that corruption in Alabama government is considerably above the American state average. Observations based on reports in the news media tend to confirm this finding.

Corruption and Politics

Former representative Benjamin Lewis (R-Houston County) commented: "I think we have a culture of corruption in Montgomery."[3] An individual who was involved in the gambling prosecutions to be discussed further on said he was told that the Montgomery political environment was "a sea of sharks," and that the formula for success was to "show people the color of my money."[4]

Some politicians have joked about corruption. Perennial (and always unsuccessful) candidate Ralph "Shorty" Price mused: "If you can't steal enough to last you the rest of your life in two years [the length of the gubernatorial term he recommended instead of the constitutional four], you ain't got enough sense to have the office in the first place."[5] A much more successful politician, the late governor James "Big Jim" Folsom said, "Sure I stole, but I stole for you."[6]

The proclivity toward corruption appears to be unrelated to party affiliation. Of the two Alabama governors (one incumbent and one former) convicted in recent years, the first was a Republican, the second a Democrat. Among less prestigious officials at both the state and local levels of Alabama politics, those implicated in alleged corrupt activities also have included Republicans, Democrats, and those who were elected on nonpartisan ballots. Since most prosecutions have been of Democrats during the period stressed in this book, Democrats have been more likely to allege partisan vendettas than Republicans.

Historical Perspectives

Alabamians have a long history of distrust of government, and allegations of corruption, even if unproven, only intensify their negative attitudes. Historian Harvey Jackson says that as early as the end of Reconstruction, "run-of-the-mill Alabamians had become convinced that trust put in government was trust misplaced."[7]

Southern Democratic apologists frequently pointed to Reconstruction as "an orgy of corruption, spoils politics, high taxation, profligate public spending, and massive debt, all spearheaded by the Republican Party."[8] Such allegations contributed for many years toward the maintenance of the solidly Democratic South and impeded Republican growth.

Stereotypically, politics have been viewed as more corrupt in the South than in other parts of the country. Of the white supremacist Democratic South, the noted Alabama civil rights activist Virginia Foster Durr wrote to a friend: "Underneath southern life there is a sort of swamp—such deep corruption that it seeps through all the crevices and crannies of life. . . . It is like living in a closed room all the time and simply struggling for air."[9]

Other critics have lamented the prevalence of corruption in the places where they lived as well.

National Rankings

In the South of today, political scientists have looked for correlations between political corruption and other indicators of the quality of life. Corruption appears to be positively associated with higher levels of income inequality. Among regions, inequality is somewhat higher in the South. (Incomes are definitely lower in the region.) At the state level, of the top eight states ranked by the extent of income inequality, three (New York, Connecticut, and Illinois) are outside the South. Each of the others, including Alabama, is a southern state.[10]

The Public Integrity Section of the US Justice Department lists Alabama at number four when ranking the states from most corrupt to least corrupt.[11] Using per capita as the basis for rankings, Illinois (where a sitting Democratic governor was impeached in 2009) is eighteenth based on the number of guilty-of-corruption verdicts the federal government obtained in the period 1998–2007. Alabama had 252 convictions during the survey period. Since its population at the time of the 2000 census was 4,627,851, this meant that its convictions per 100,000 residents equaled 5.4.[12] In another ranking from worst to best, Alabama was sixth based on the observations of journalists covering state capitals.[13] Louisiana also typically ranks high (in this survey, second) or low, depending on the survey format. Its corrupt tendencies are said to be attributable in part "to the prevailing French attitude that a political office was a piece of property that the officeholder should use for profit."[14]

Cases of Corruption

The next sections present a series of case studies that highlight allegations of corruption and the outcomes of proceedings against those accused of misfeasance in office. Each illustrates the impact of corruption on the kind of government Alabama has had in its recent past.

Governors Hunt and Siegelman

Governor Guy Hunt's felony conviction on April 22, 1993, of using money from an inaugural fund for private purposes, resulted in his automatic removal from his position and the immediate ascension of Lieutenant Governor Jim Folsom Jr., to the governorship. He served until Fob James thwarted his bid for a full term in 1994. Hunt was given no jail time, although then-attorney general Jimmy Evans had recommended it. Instead, he had to pay substantial fines and perform community service. On March 31, 1998, Hunt received a pardon from the State Board of Pardons and Paroles "on grounds of innocence."

Proceedings were initially brought against former governor Don Siegelman in federal district court in Tuscaloosa in October 2004. However, after a jury was selected, Judge U. W. Clemon ruled that there was insufficient evidence to try Siegelman and dismissed conspiracy charges related to health care contracts.

The second Siegelman proceedings were in federal district court in Montgomery beginning on June 6, 2006. Other individuals, most notably former HealthSouth CEO Richard Scrushy, were also tried along with Siegelman before Judge Mark Fuller. The primary charge against Siegelman was that he had appointed Scrushy to the Certificate of Need (CON) Board, which rules on the justification for proposed new health care facilities, in return for a contribution to liquidate the debt of the governor's failed lottery campaign. Following the lengthy trial, Siegelman and Scrushy were convicted on June 29, 2006. Each was sentenced to seven years in prison.

Extensive appeals followed on multiple grounds. One of the most important arguments that defense lawyers made was that in Alabama politics, as in politics as practiced elsewhere, officials with the power to appoint frequently choose those who make contributions to their campaigns or favored causes.

The contention of Siegelman that got the most national attention was that his prosecution was politically motivated. Leura Garrett Canary was the US attorney for the middle district of Alabama at the time the Siegelman case arose. She was married to Bill Canary, president of the Business Council of Alabama, one of the premier Republican-oriented interest groups in the state. Ms. Canary said, however, that she had recused herself from any involvement in the case.

Mobile *Press-Register* investigative reporter Eddie Curran had written a long series of stories prior to the Siegelman trial. His investigations convinced Curran that the Scrushy contribution to the unsuccessful Siegelman lottery foundation campaign was not of the usual "pay to play variety." Witnesses in the Montgomery trial testified that Scrushy had been coerced into making a $500,000 contribution to pay off expenses incurred in promoting the lottery because he had previously raised $350,000 for the campaign of Republican Fob James, whom Siegelman had defeated in 1998. The $500,000 Scrushy donated to Siegelman represented the $350,000 given to James "plus interest."[15]

After he had served nine months in prison in Louisiana, Siegelman was released on bond in 2008 and was able to continue with his ultimately unsuccessful appeals as a free man. The US solicitor general, Elena Kagan, later a Barack Obama appointee to the Supreme Court, urged the justices not to accept Siegelman's request that they consider his appeal. They didn't, and he returned to the federal prison in Louisiana on September 11, 2012.

In conclusion, it can probably be said that the prosecution of former Governor Siegelman *was* political in the sense that it illustrates the workings of the two-party system and the incentive that one party has to "get something" on the other.

The same thing was true in the early 1990s when Democratic attorney general Jimmy Evans had the incentive to "catch" the newly reelected Republican governor, Guy Hunt. He pressed felony charges in connection with actions that, if both had been of the same political party, might have been viewed as relatively inconsequential.

According to *Birmingham News* columnist Robin Demonia, "pursuing corrupt politicians in Alabama falls mostly to federal prosecutors" because "few county district attorneys have the stomach for it." Demonia claimed that local "prosecutors [took] a pass when they [saw] public corruption [because it was] a lot easier to go after criminals who have no political power, no big-money lawyers and no opportunity to hit back hard."[16] The two-year college corruption scandal is examined next in this chapter. When prosecutions relating to the postsecondary institutions were drawing to a close, Demonia likened it to "a long-running opera brought to you by the federal government."[17]

The Two-Year College Scandal

Outside the realm of the top executive position in Alabama, the governorship, the most drawn-out litigation relating to public corruption in recent years dealt with the Alabama Community College System.[18] Over a period of three years dating from 2004, when a raid was conducted on the Alabama Fire College, seven people were the objects of guilty verdicts rendered by juries. One was acquitted, and ten pled guilty. The most prominent of those who confessed was Chancellor Roy Johnson, who made a deal with federal prosecutors to provide needed incriminating testimony in return for lighter financial and jail treatment (six and a half years) for himself.

Administrative reform, as with the establishment of the Alabama Community College System to provide a chancellor and unifying mechanisms for the large network of two-year schools, has been widely applauded because it was in accord with expert opinion on educational administration. With the passage of time, however, the bureaucratic mechanisms, as well as the institutions subject to coordination, became what political scientist James Simmons labeled "a source of self-serving corruption and inefficiency."[19] At the time the community college scandal arose, the institutions had financial ties with approximately forty state legislators by way of their or their relatives' salaries or business dealings. These were the people to whom the term "double-dipper" was applied. They drew not one but two incomes from Alabama state government. Furthermore, their college employers benefited from having lobbyists-in-place in the legislature.

Gambling

Gambling has been associated historically, not only in Alabama but elsewhere as well, with a higher incidence of corruption. This activity tends to have lower levels of social acceptance and is more susceptible to corruption than something that is routinely regarded as legitimate. Generally, activities that are less widely sanctioned are subject to more regulation, as we saw in chapter 3 with respect to alcoholic beverages. Perhaps surprisingly, gambling has not been subject to any systematic state regulation in Alabama.

The Alabama Constitution has contained a general proscription against gambling since it went into effect in 1901 (Article 4, Sec. 65). It is defined as games of chance with prizes awarded to winners. Even card-and-paper bingo falls into this category since winning is based on luck, not skill. Despite the constitution, charitable organizations frequently hosted bingo games to raise money to support their programs as well as to give older people something fun to do. Betting on racing animals (dogs or horses) was made legal in the 1970s.

Two case studies illustrate the intimate connection between gambling and politics. The Siegelman situation previously examined raised serious allegations of corruption only after the fact, while the second controversy involved alleged corruption in the legislature as gambling interests were seeking to pass favorable legislation.

The Lottery

The first vote on a statewide gambling plan came in 1999 when Governor Siegelman's lottery proposal went before the voters. Siegelman had based his winning 1998 gubernatorial campaign largely on a lottery to fund college scholarships, on the model of Georgia's Hope Scholarship program. Siegelman's victory over incumbent Republican Fob James and subsequent polling data indicated that the lottery was likely to pass muster with the voters.

Despite the pessimistic forecasts (from their point of view), conservative Protestant churches strongly campaigned against it. One religious message against the lottery was that, "Gambling brings ABC—addiction, bankruptcy, crime and corruption—as surely as night follows day."[20] The leaders of the antilottery campaign had sufficient political wisdom to realize that even in a religiously oriented state such as Alabama, a campaign arguing that gambling is morally wrong would not have as good a chance at succeeding as one based on historic public cynicism and distrust of government. Ultimately, the Siegelman lottery plan was voted down 54 percent to 46 percent. For several years after this referendum, gambling receded as a major statewide issue. Republican Bob Riley succeeded Democrat Siegelman in 2003, and he did not support it. Within the still Democrat-dominated legislature, however, several leaders, especially in the Senate, saw expanding and taxing gambling as a win-win proposition. During the first decade of the new century, numerous bills to expand gambling were introduced in the legislature.

Casinos and Electronic Bingo

The legislature spent most of its last two regular sessions under Democratic control (2009 and 2010) debating bills that would increase gambling beyond

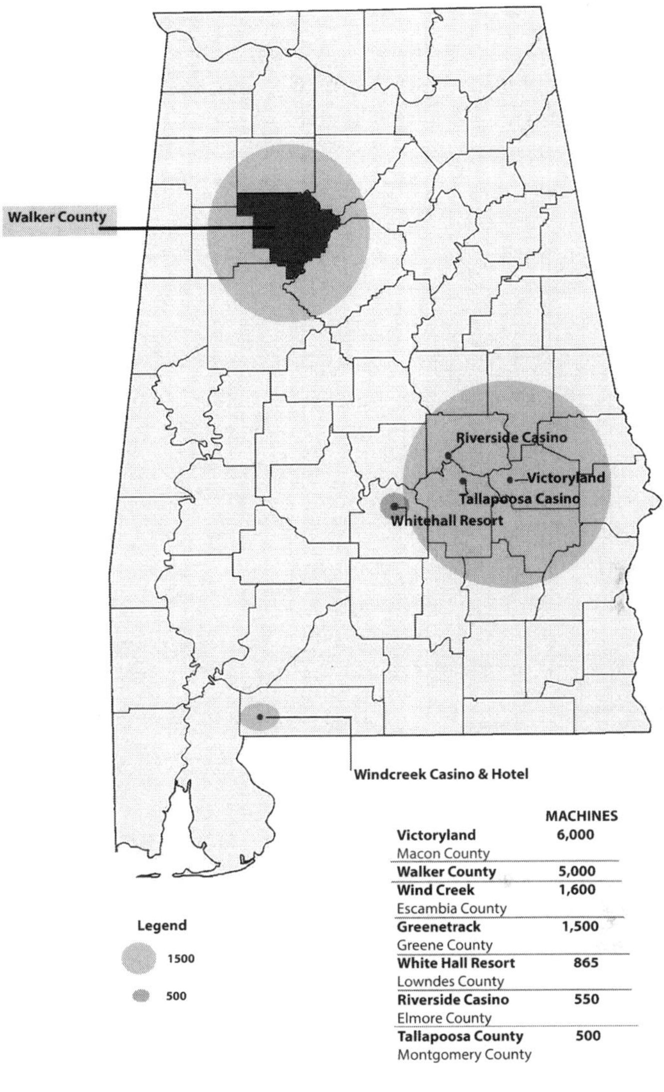

4.1. Major bingo operations in Alabama. Source: Gambling operations, government records

dog-horse racing and not-for-profit bingo. Over the years, Republicans had been creeping up in numbers in the legislature, and it seemed possible that they might actually gain a Senate majority in the November 2010 elections. (In fact, they won both houses.) If Republicans assumed a legislative majority, there would be little chance of gambling expansion passing because one of the key components of the Republican base, conservative evangelicals, strongly opposes it.

In some localities, law enforcement officials started to strictly interpret what the Alabama Constitution had to say about gambling and to shut down bingo games. In response, legislators from the areas affected started to introduce constitutional amendments to assure that churches and lodges would not have their bingo games raided. Seven amendments, beginning with Jefferson's in 1980, had been added to the state constitution by the end of 2010. Generally, it was specified that all net revenue had to be spent on charitable activities. (Because of their lack of home rule authority, localities could not handle this ostensibly trivial matter themselves.) The situation was made confusing in part because the definition of "bingo" was not uniform across the amendments. One editorial writer observed that, "bingo has three different definitions depending not so much on the game as where it is played."[21]

In one case, the Alabama Supreme Court, in November 2009, gave its opinion on what constituted bingo. According to the high court, there were six standards that bingo had to meet in Alabama to be legal:[22]

1. Each player uses one or more cards with spaces arranged in five columns and five rows, with an alphanumeric or similar designation assigned to each space.
2. Alphanumeric or similar designations are randomly drawn and announced one by one.
3. In order to play, each player must pay attention to the values announced; if one of the values matches a value on one or more of the player's cards, the player must physically act by marking his or her card accordingly.
4. A player can fail to pay proper attention or to properly mark his or her card, and thereby miss an opportunity to be declared a winner.
5. A player must recognize that his or her card has a "bingo," i.e. a predetermined pattern of matching values, and in turn, announce to the other players and the announcer that this is the case before any other player does so.
6. The game of bingo contemplates a group activity in which multiple players compete against each other to be the first to properly mark a card with the predetermined winning pattern and announce that fact.

The state's largest newspaper, the *Birmingham News*, found that the Supreme Court's ruling had "define[d] legal bingo in a way that bears little resemblance to the games being played" at casinos involved in court litigation.[23] The disputes over what was legal and what was illegal continued unabated.

Even without any new laws being passed, electronic, or video, bingo was becoming much more popular than the traditional type, and new clienteles were developing. Also, it seemed promising as a way for both the state and local governments to raise badly needed revenues in a political climate in which there was strong opposition to any new taxes. One survey taken at the time the gambling controversy was raging in 2010 found that 72 percent of the respondents favored taxing gambling as a means of generating new income. About 25 percent favored outlawing gambling throughout the state.[24]

A survey in 2009 had found that 36 percent of the respondents favored funding education with gambling revenue, while 19 percent supported gambling no matter what the state proceeds were used for. Forty-four percent were against it to fund any program. These results show a lack of a solid consensus on gambling and help explain why nothing passed the legislature.[25] An AP poll of legislators the same year indicated that many of them did not favor taxing and regulating gambling as a way to deal with the state's financial crises. Only about a third said they supported expanding gambling.[26] (A constitutional amendment requires a three-fifths majority in each chamber to pass.)

Even within the ranks of legislative gambling supporters there was division as individual senators and representatives sought the most favorable terms for their own localities (or themselves as possible entrepreneurs). A bingo bill came before the Alabama Senate on March 3, 2010, but the 18–16 vote by which it was approved was three votes shy of the 21 required to bring it up for debate (since the budgets had not yet passed). On March 30, however, a much-amended electronic bingo bill sponsored by Senator Roger Bedford (D-Russellville) did get the requisite number of Senate votes. The bill would give special protections from new competition for gambling businesses already in operation.

Not only were small storefront gambling operations flourishing in places like Walker County (Jasper), but elsewhere much larger gambling enterprises were either being planned or were already in operation. The projected new establishments, sometimes referred to as "upscale resorts" or, in legislative language, "points of destination," would include hotels with hundreds of rooms, restaurants, live shows, and other Las Vegas–style amenities. Jobs were being provided or were in prospect for thousands of employees, probably a majority of which would be African American. One establishment (VictoryLand) was identified as "the largest bingo facility in the world." It had six thousand bingo machines, "more machines than in any Vegas casino."[27]

On a heavy business day patrons would spend about $21 million. Those who were involved in either constructing or operating such huge facilities believed that they would be "too big to fail" because of the loss of jobs and revenue that would occur if they did. The largest proposed gambling site was Country Crossing in southeast Alabama, estimated to cost $87 million.

As we have just seen, even without legislative action, there was already large-scale electronic gambling in Alabama. Also, according to federal law Native Americans are allowed to have gambling games of their choosing if the state in which their lands are located allows any form of gambling. Based on this doctrine, the Poarch Creek Band of American Indians had casinos in Atmore, Wetumpka, and Montgomery County.

The Riley Raids

Governor Riley could do nothing about Native American gambling. However, to combat what he regarded as illegal electronic bingo casinos elsewhere, he established a task force in December 2008 to raid them. A Riley appointee directed the raids, and the intervening group consisted mostly of state troopers. (A fuller discussion of the political controversy the raids created is presented in chapter 12.)

In the 2010 Republican gubernatorial campaign, all but one aspirant gave at least mild support to the Riley raids. On the Democratic side, both candidates denounced them. In the general election campaign, the Democratic nominee, Ron Sparks, was strongly opposed to them, and his main platform plank ("the cornerstone of his campaign"[28]) called for expanding and taxing gambling. The Republican nominee, Dr. Robert Bentley, said he favored a referendum in which voters would have the option of legitimizing casinos or banning all gambling, including card-and-paper bingo. However, since he became governor there has been no serious effort to have a referendum on any aspect of gambling.

The Native American casinos are increasingly profitable for their operators. In the case of Alabama, specifically, revenues received by Poarch Creek Indian Gaming increased by 61 percent in 2010 (from 2009) and this was the fastest rate of growth among Indian casinos in all of the twenty-eight states that have them.

Given the huge stakes involved in the proposed expansion of electronic gambling in Alabama, it is not surprising that the entrepreneurs and their lobbyists would go all out, especially in 2010, to win legislative approval of the needed constitutional amendment. With African Americans very much in need of the jobs the expansion of gambling would provide, the outlook for victory at the polls was good—even if Republicans should pick up some previously Democrat-held seats in white-majority counties. (We have previously noted that, ultimately, they won both legislative houses.) Republicans were, of course, aware of what Democrats were thinking. They apparently communicated to federal law enforcement officials that violations of the law might be occurring as the language of a gambling expansion constitutional amendment was being worked out behind the scenes.

The Bingo 11

Shortly after the favorable Senate vote for expanded gambling in March 2010, federal officials announced that they were investigating the circumstances under which the bill was passed in the upper chamber. One gambling entrepreneur, Mickey Gilley, confessed to investigators that he had, in effect, sought to buy legislative "yes" votes for the gambling referendum bill that had cleared the Senate.[29] Eleven people were indicted by a federal grand jury and accused of being involved in a scheme of bribing legislators in order to get their votes in favor of this gambling referendum measure.

Gambling interests had contributed to the campaigns of most of the senators who had voted for the gambling bill that passed on March 30. Only a few of these were accused of any wrongdoing, however. The money was sometimes laundered many times and numerous new groups were formed to hide who was contributing to whom.

During their first trial (June 10–August 29, 2011) the defendants collectively were referred to as the "Bingo 11." The most prominent among them was gambling magnate Milton McGregor. Records showed that during recent campaigns he had contributed $1.9 million to more than fifty PACs that, in turn, gave to favored candidates, or to other PACs. One of the defendants was an employee of the Legislative Reference Service to whom McGregor had been making payments. He was accused of writing gambling bills that were especially profitable for McGregor. (He died before the second trial.)

The main evidence presented at the first bingo trial consisted of recordings made by Republican legislators who had reported what they felt were attempted bribes to the FBI and were asked by the federal authorities to record subsequent conversations. During the lengthy trial in the summer of 2011, no testimony was offered in which "bribe" was specifically mentioned, and prosecutors had told jurors in advance not to expect such testimony. Defense attorneys argued, ultimately successfully, that their clients had been involved in no more than politics as it usually works in Alabama and elsewhere. In addition, the legislators who wore recording devices would be adversely affected by a large turnout at the polls in the planned November referendum. If gambling were to be voted on at the same time as legislative candidates, it could hinder the Republican drive to get control of the legislature. The prosecution was further damaged when one cooperating legislator recorded his own racial slurs. This helped to keep the focus off of corruption. For about a week, jurors deliberated the defendants' fate. On August 11, 2011, they delivered a verdict that found none of the accused guilty of any of the charges against them. On the others they reported themselves to be deadlocked. Two of the

"Bingo 11" were acquitted in the initial trial. On March 7, 2012, following a more abbreviated second trial before federal judge Myron Thompson, the remaining defendants were acquitted of all the charges that had been leveled against them.

Ethics Reform

Until 2010, the most important law on the books aimed at preventing and/or punishing public corruption was the Ethics Act of 1973. The existence of what was then regarded as a strong ethics law in Alabama was not what would have been expected. (See chapter 2 for a discussion of the circumstances surrounding the passage of this law.)

Over time it was discovered that the independent anticorruption agency created by the 1973 law, the Alabama Ethics Commission, was not strong enough. The main power that it lacked was that of subpoena. In contrast with Alabama, thirty-seven state ethics agencies were empowered to compel witnesses to cooperate with them.

When Alabama reformed its ethics legislation in 2010, after close to forty years' experience with the previous act, it was not acting in a vacuum. It was among a group of southern states responding to instances of allegedly corrupt behavior by public officials.[30]

Governor Bob Riley called the new Republican-dominated Alabama legislature into a lame-duck special session in December 2010.[31] Shortly after they assembled, both House and Senate passed seven bills, which the governor quickly signed into law. City and county officials and employees, as well as their counterparts at the state level, were bound by the provisions of the new laws.

One of the major elements of the new legislation was setting limits on the amount of money a lobbyist could spend on a public official he or she was trying to influence. At the time the session was called, no report was required until a lobbyist had spent $91,000 on a particular legislator. This was changed to prohibit public employees from being given anything of greater than "minimal" value. In 2012, after complaints that students were being prevented from giving their teachers Christmas presents, the law was amended to allow gifts worth no more than $25.

Also, lobbyists must now receive orientation training on what Alabama ethics laws both permit and prohibit. In September 2011, former Governor Riley, who registered as a lobbyist when he became a private citizen again, was among a group that received this instruction.

Another restriction was placed on "double-dipping," most often involving legislators who were also teachers. The new ethics legislation prevented teachers from serving as legislators. As will be noted in chapter 7, the law also provides that dues for organizations such as the AEA and the Alabama State Employees Association, some of which would go to PACs, could no longer be automatically deducted from employee paychecks. To prevent hostile legislators from retaliating against the Ethics Commission by cutting its funding, the agency is guaranteed no less than one-tenth of one percent of the General Fund budget. The package of new ethics laws passed by the Republican legislature was the subject of mostly positive assessments. In the most optimistic interpretation, the new laws "open[ed] a new era in state politics."[32] The current director of the Ethics Commission, James Sumner, said the laws would "change the culture of Montgomery."[33] They signaled Alabama's "new day in ethics."[34] However, a reformist spirit is difficult to sustain in any political arena.[35] After the enthusiasm that leads to the passage of the reform legislation subsides, there is a tendency for political behavior patterns to revert to the old ways of doing things. Embedded political cultures are not easily changed. As national columnist David Brooks pointed out, "It is really hard to turn around complex systems. Government can't solve everything."[36]

Ethnicity has not been a significant variable in the case studies of alleged corruption presented in this chapter. As already noted in chapter 1, whites occupy most important positions of leadership, so they would likely be the ones guilty of corrupt behavior at the state level—if it occurs. Had our analysis extended to the local level there would have been numerous examples of misconduct in both black-majority and white-majority jurisdictions, although most black officials and white officials conform to the law most of the time.

At this point we will turn to an examination of the roles of African Americans in Alabama politics. Undoubtedly the biggest change that has occurred in Alabama politics in the last half century is the important part that African Americans have come to play in it. The difference between today and the pre–Voting Rights Act period is hard to overemphasize.

5

African Americans and Alabama Politics

When the 1901 constitution was being drafted, one convention delegate was candid enough to say that it "shows too plainly that our purpose [is] to keep the [Negro] out of Alabama politics."[1] The constitution, along with extralegal forms of subjugation, enshrined white supremacy and consigned blacks to a totally subordinated political and social position until the mid-1960s.

The Age of Segregation

The African American disfranchising effort was not confined to Alabama. Historians J. Morgan Kousser and James McPherson point out that the condition of African Americans deteriorated throughout the South at this time.[2] Conventions to effectively abrogate the Fifteenth Amendment as well as to subjugate blacks in many other ways were taking place in many other southern states. The age of segregation, which historian Robert Dean Pope dates from 1877 to the 1950s, having the aim of first establishing and then perpetuating the Jim Crow system, was at its fiercest.[3]

From the time of the 1901 constitution until the passage of the Voting Rights Act of 1965 blacks were virtually shut out of the Alabama political process. Beginning with the Montgomery bus boycott in the previous decade, however, blacks were able to exercise influence if they were committed so strongly that they were willing to suffer physical and verbal abuse for the cause of equal rights—as well as go to jail (instead of those who committed the outrages against them). Tragically, some blacks, as well as white allies, lost their lives in the struggle for justice.

It was not until the Voting Rights Act and its vigorous enforcement by federal authorities that African Americans could vote freely. In time this would include being able to vote for candidates of their own color who had a good chance of being elected. They would also be able to speak out in the same forums as whites and have their voices heard.

In this chapter we focus mostly on the roles African Americans played in recent years in Alabama politics. It would probably be helpful, however, to first look back nearly a century and a half to when the polls were initially opened to newly emancipated slaves.

Historical Perspective

Blacks went to the polls in Alabama for the very first time early in October 1867, when they voted in a referendum that led ultimately to the constitution of 1868.[4] After federal troops had been withdrawn from the South by the mid-1870s, however, they were no longer allowed to participate in this way with their white fellow Alabamians. Historian Wayne Flynt writes, "Race increasingly defined all political discourse, reducing both class and section to secondary importance."[5] This schism worked to the disadvantage not only of blacks but of whites as well.

At the beginning of the Civil War, Alabama had been one of the more affluent of the American states. But cotton production, the source of most of Alabama's wealth, was almost totally supported by the institution of slavery, and, in 1865, slavery had ended. Before the devastations of war, the Alabama population had been about 960,000, and close to half were slaves. The population was badly decimated during the years 1861–65 with the loss of at least 25,000 wartime casualties. In the postwar period blacks were no longer chattel available to passively do their former masters' bidding. In time many would go back to the fields, but the human and economic losses sustained during the war would never be recouped. While an abundance of cotton was planted by large and small growers alike, when harvested it was worth only about half as much as it had been before the war.

Beginning of the End

The exercise of power by federal authorities on behalf of unfairly treated blacks in Alabama and elsewhere in the South began most seriously about a century after the Civil War was being fought. The federal initiatives that began during the 1960s are referred to as the Second Reconstruction. Unlike the first, it did not end after only a few years. Even though new laws aimed primarily to protect the rights of blacks are no longer being passed, federal vigilance to ensure that previously enacted policies are fully enforced continues. In late summer 2012 in Birmingham the US Justice Department established a new civil rights unit to improve enforcement efforts.

5.1. Voters in Peachtree, Alabama, 1966. Courtesy of the National Archives and Record Administration

The Second Reconstruction

The Civil Rights Act of 1964 and the 1965 Voting Rights Act were passed as essential elements of the Second Reconstruction.[6]

These laws have been of huge significance in bringing about a new era of black participation in Alabama politics. Black empowerment today is mostly attributable to these two laws.

Federal Preclearance

Section 5 of the original Voting Rights Act required federal review of state and local actions affecting minority political rights in the covered jurisdictions. In the 1970s and 1980s the act was extended and strengthened to effectively require that blacks be represented in legislative assemblies basically to match their numbers in the total population. (We will see how this has worked with respect to the Alabama Legislature in chapter 11.) The most recent readoption of the Voting Rights Act came in 2006 when President George W. Bush signed a twenty-five-year extension into law. This extension was designed to further strengthen black voter influence and roll back US Supreme Court decisions viewed as weakening it.[7]

5.2. Civil rights attorney Fred Gray. Courtesy of the Alabama Department of Archives and History

Current Federal Oversight

One strongly Republican Alabama county (Shelby) has recently asked to be exempted from the Section 5 Voting Rights Act requirement that it preclear all voting-related changes with the Department of Justice or the Washington federal district court. Its attorneys argued that the preclearance mandate of the Voting Rights Act took it for granted that Shelby, if left alone by Washington, would purposely deprive African Americans of their right to vote. (All of Alabama is covered by Section 5 of the Voting Rights Act based on discrimination against blacks at the time the law was passed.)

Shelby County officials said that the situation there related to black voting was a completely different matter after more than four decades. If more recent voter turnout data had been considered when Congress renewed the Voting Rights Act in 2006, they would have shown that black turnout is roughly equal to that of whites throughout the state. In Shelby County specifically, more than 50 percent of the black voting age population was participating in presidential elections, putting the county on a par with other places around the nation. Continued congressional "interference" with Shelby County's "electoral autonomy," local attorneys argued, was "both arbitrary and without constitutional justification."[8]

The Shelby County chapter of the NAACP said preclearance for their locality was still needed, however. Based as it was on such old data, the US Supreme Court struck down the preclearance provision of the Voting Rights Act in *Shelby County v. Holder*.[9]

Another Birmingham metropolitan area jurisdiction, the small municipality of Pinson, had been exempted from Voting Rights Act preclearance requirements in March 2012. Federal court approval of the bailout was just a formality given a signed agreement between Pinson and the US Justice Department.[10]

Opportunities for Black Participation

With the increased Republican dominance in Alabama, further gains by blacks are particularly difficult, given that African American Democrats are generally on the losing side of the current political equation in the state. A white Republican candidate will probably beat a black Democrat in most cases. Currently, all thirty-five black members of the Alabama state legislature were sent to Montgomery by predominantly black districts. Due to racially polarized voting, blacks' chances of being picked in majority-white counties when legislators are elected from whole counties are not good. As a result, there are no longer any single-county at-large legislative elections in Alabama.

Just as Alabama did not remain one-party Democratic "forever," so, given inevitable population shifts and movements, it will not always be a deeply red state. For the near term, however, there is virtually no likelihood of a generous mix of black and white officials at the statewide level.

Population Shifts

Black dispersal from central cities to suburbs could make the construction of majority-minority districts (as districts to facilitate the elections of blacks are called) more difficult if normally accepted criteria of proper districting have to be followed.

Another factor is that with the opening up of more opportunities for African Americans in Alabama, the mass exodus of blacks from the state that occurred, especially up to the middle years of the twentieth century, has stopped. The 2010 census actually showed a modest increase in the numbers of blacks in the total state population (1,170,202 to 1,252,291).

Based on her own research and that of the other scholars on whom she relies, Susan MacManus sees problems ahead for the GOP. It is good for Republicans that they have been able to win over many rural residents who formerly were firm Democrats. However, the rural population is declining and the metropolitan areas that are gaining the most new residents are increasingly Democratic, not only made so by new blacks but by younger whites who are turned off by the social conservatism exhibited in recent years by the Republican Party. Also, Hispanics, who mostly identify as Democrats, are, as we saw in chapters 1 and 3, increasing their numbers as well. MacManus notes that, "When compared with their older counterparts, younger voters in today's South are more racially/ethnically diverse, more concentrated in urban areas, [and] more mobile." Regardless of their own ethnicity, "they are more likely to be racially tolerant." Finally, "the influx of more highly educated, moderate-to-liberal, mostly white retirees from the Northeast and Midwest, has somewhat diminished the political clout of older, native-born voters in some states."[11]

States that have recently been in receipt of most "snowbirds," as they are called, do not include Alabama. Alabama remains so solidly "red" that its firm place in the November Republican presidential column is unlikely to change anytime soon. (Note: Political demographers are already observing signs of a black-brown coalition in the neighboring state of Mississippi that could make it more two-party competitive fairly soon.[12]) According to the 2010 census results, Hispanics were more responsible for population gains than blacks in sixteen of the states classified as southern. The historic black-white dichotomy will therefore be altered in the South, including Alabama, if these population trends continue.

Blacks and Statewide Politics

The first African American to run for statewide office in Alabama was James T. Rapier, an unsuccessful Republican candidate for secretary of state in 1872. A serious black Republican candidate in modern times has still not run for statewide office, so evidence of the willingness of white Republicans to vote for an African American has not been tested. Anecdotally, the feeling is that such a candidate would stand a good chance of election.

The Elusive Governorship

In a survey conducted prior to the 2010 gubernatorial election, 53 percent of the respondents said that Alabama was ready for a black governor.[13] The black candidate for the Democratic nomination (Artur Davis) did not win, however, and, no matter who the Democratic nominee turned out to be (in this case Ron Sparks), he (there was no female candidate) would have been an instant underdog. (The Republican nominee [Robert Bentley] won by an overwhelming margin.) One African American state legislator had told a reporter: "I don't think we're ready yet to elect a black man governor."[14] A national legislator, DC representative Eleanor Holmes Norton, told journalist-commentator Gwen Ifill: "Artur can't make himself into a white old boy. I think it would be much more difficult given the state, not for Artur, but the state. Of all states, that's the worst state I could [think of] to run in. A terrible state."[15]

Barack Obama had done very poorly in the 2008 presidential election in Alabama (he fared about the same in 2012), and this did not (and does not) portend well for potential African American candidates in upcoming statewide races. However, blacks in Alabama enthusiastically received Obama's initial national win. His appearance on the ballot encouraged a strong African American turnout in the state, as it did elsewhere. Showing continuing racial polarization, however, was the fact that a *New York Times* reporter, Adam Nossiter, visiting northwest Alabama shortly after the 2008 presidential election, found strong "negative feelings about the race of President-elect Barack Obama."[16]

In the typical Democratic primary, black voters are estimated to constitute about half of the participants. In general elections, it is speculated that black voters represent about 30 percent. If these projections are correct, the successful Democratic candidate would need to get approximately 30 percent of the votes of whites plus nearly all of the votes provided by loyally Democratic African Americans. This is calculated using the following formula: $70X = 50.1 - 30(0.98)$, where $X = 0.2957$

Legend:
70 = white percentage of general election voters
30 = black percentage of general election voters
0.98 = percentage of black voters expected to cast Democratic votes
X = percentage of whites needed to vote Democratic for the Democratic candidate to win
50.1 = vote needed for a candidate to win the election[17]

With the mass shift to Republicanism by white Alabama voters in recent years, the estimated one-fifth of the white vote that Democrats need to win statewide has become increasingly difficult to secure. Both parties obviously would like to have the votes of blacks, but the Democrats presently have a lock on them (and have done the most by far to earn black support). For the most part, the very conservative tenets of the Republican Party have not appealed to African Americans. Blacks now constitute a majority of the members of the State Democratic Executive Committee. The Alabama Democratic Conference, identified more fully below, is an integral part of the official organization.

African American candidates are caught in a dilemma (but white Democrats are as well). If they appeal too much to their own ethnic group, they will alienate potential white supporters (the opposite being true for white candidates). On the other hand, if blacks appear to neglect black interests, as Davis was viewed as doing when he voted against the Obama health care plan in March 2010, they are seen as insensitive and overly opportunistic. Davis was attempting to run a race-neutral political campaign requiring him to appeal to white voters without alienating blacks. He was unable to do this successfully.

The Davis Debacle

Artur Davis had begun the 2010 election year with a big poll lead—30 percentage points. However, his campaign themes—which stressed a more progressive tax system, higher standards of public ethics, and reform of the bloated state constitution—never resonated with the Democratic primary electorate, alienating (or worse, boring) white and black voters alike. The loss of the black counties was what was most surprising, however. Senator Hank Sanders, a founder of the Alabama New South Coalition, criticized Davis's alleged neglect of black interests as reflected in the health care vote: "You can't seek to become Alabama's first black governor despite the black vote. That was a mistake of stunning proportions."[18] After his primary defeat Davis acknowledged that his successful opponent, Agriculture Commissioner Sparks, had run a campaign with more Democratic voter appeal—emphasizing a lottery and the expansion and taxation of additional forms of gambling. He then left the state for Virginia and moved rightward politically, speaking at the 2012 Republican National Convention.

Just as Obama's initial election to the presidency in 2008 was said to have "broke[n] the biggest glass ceiling in American politics," for an African American to be elected to the Alabama governorship or to a US Senate seat at some future time would amount to the same thing at the state level.[19] Something on this order actually happening, however, is very doubtful given the present "supermajority" status of the Republican Party in Alabama. Blacks have been able to celebrate numerous electoral victories below the statewide level, however.

Black Political Successes

Since the modern era of Alabama politics began for African American Alabamians with the passage of the Voting Rights Act in the mid-1960s, close to a thousand blacks have been elected to public office. In 2002, Alabama was reported to have 757 black officials. (This total included thirty-six US and state legislators, 569 city and county officials, fifty-six in law enforcement, and ninety-six in education.) Alabama's neighboring state to the west, Mississippi, had 950 black officials at the time this US census of black elected officials was made.[20]

Federal and Judicial Officials

Three African Americans have served in the US House of Representatives since the federal courts began requiring the drawing of minority-majority districts. Republican Jeremiah Haralson (1875–77) had been Alabama's last black member of Congress until Earl Hilliard was elected in 1992. The legislature had gerrymandered Haralson's district out of existence prior to the 1876 congressional elections. In 2010 Terri Sewell was elected as Alabama's first black congresswoman.

When Oscar Adams won a full term on the Alabama Supreme Court in 1982, following his appointment by Governor James, he became the first African American to be elected to statewide office. Only one other blackman, Ralph Cook (1993–2001), like Adams a Democrat, has been able to secure a statewide office (also Supreme Court membership, initially by appointment of Democratic governor Jim Folsom Jr.) by popular vote (in 1994).

Three African Americans have served by Democratic presidential appointment on the federal bench in Alabama. The first of these, Judge U. W. Clemon, the choice of President Jimmy Carter, decided to retire after twenty-eight years' service, but waited until another Democratic president, Barack Obama in 2009, was about to be sworn in, succeeding a Republican, George W. Bush.

Legislative Influence

Democratic control of the legislature was a boon to black Democrats, giving them the opportunity to fill high leadership positions, including the president pro tem position in the Senate and speaker pro tem in the House. They also served as the chairs of key legislative committees. Since there are presently no black Republican legislators, there are no black Republican leaders. This development is not unique to Alabama. The rise in Republican strength in southern state legislatures has meant a drastic reduction in African American influence. Before the mid-1990s, almost all blacks serving in state legislatures were in the (Democratic) majority. With Republicans in control of most southern lawmaking bodies, however, very few are, since African American Republican legislators are a rarity. Amendments to and strengthened interpretations of the Voting Rights Act have facilitated the election of black legislators, but they have done nothing to prevent Alabama's continued movement in a Republican direction. To preserve the gains they have previously

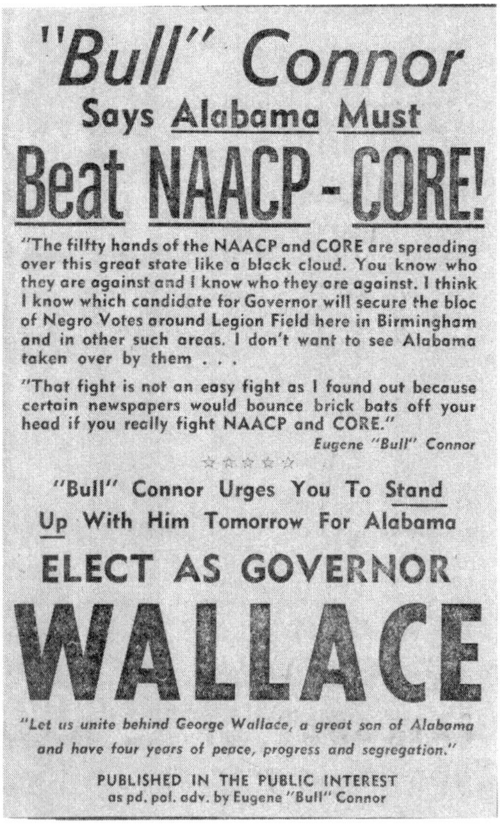

5.3. "Bull" Connor's Wallace for Governor poster. From the William H. Stewart collection

made as well as perhaps to encourage the formation of black-white coalitions with winning potential, blacks continue to look to the federal government.

Black Political Groups

As early as 1960, when blacks were still unable to participate unhindered in the political process, there was an Afro-American Unity Party. In 1965, the Lowndes County Freedom Organization was established locally as an alternative to the still white-supremacist Alabama Democratic Party.[21] The Black Panther Party was also founded in this Black Belt county.

Pioneering Groups

More important than these very small groups over a longer period of time was the National Democratic Party of Alabama (NDPA) that ran its chair, Dr.

John Cashin, for governor against the regular Democratic nominee, George Wallace, in 1970. Cashin was the first blackman to run for governor of Alabama. While losing badly against Wallace (Cashin polled only about 15 percent of the vote), the NDPA elected candidates for local offices in heavily black Greene County. Cashin led the NDPA until 1976, when African Americans finally were able to participate fully in regular Democratic Party activities.

The most significant African American political interest group, whose membership has not been confined to Alabama, is the Southern Christian Leadership Conference (SCLC) established by Dr. King and others in 1957 with the goal of "sav[ing] the soul of America."[22] In recent years the SCLC, now based in Atlanta, as had approximately ten thousand members and eighty chapters in seventeen states.

At its height, the SCLC had had about 100,000 members. However, the group's political influence has been weakened not only by declining membership but also by infighting among its leaders.

The NAACP is the oldest nationally affiliated black political organization, but others have eclipsed it since the 1970s. Decades earlier the NAACP was the primary representative of blacks as they waged their battles for equal rights in federal courts.[23] The NAACP was temporarily unable to operate in the state because the Alabama legislature passed a law (later declared unconstitutional) that required it to reveal its members. The NAACP is fully operational today, but it is usually not involved actively in state politics.

The Alabama Democratic Conference

The Alabama Democratic Conference (ADC) has been the most important black political interest group in the modern era of Alabama politics. Joe Reed leads this group (as he has for more than forty years). Reed was formerly president of the black Alabama State Teachers Association before it merged with the formerly all-white Alabama Education Association in 1969. Bass and De Vries give Robert Vance (later assassinated while serving as a federal district judge) credit for welcoming African American Alabamians to the Democratic fold, including making Joe Reed the vice-chair of the party for minority affairs. At this point the ADC started to operate as the party's black caucus.[24] Scher notes the ability of the ADC over the years to "deliver substantial blocs of votes to candidates of their choosing."[25]

One of the most important things Reed did was to initiate successful litigation that switched substate elective positions uniformly from at large to district (where there are sizable black populations) so that blacks would have a better chance of electing officials from their own ethnic group.

ALABAMA DEMOCRATIC CONFERENCE

Joe L. Reed
State Chairman

Tuscaloosa County

OFFICIAL GUIDE BALLOT

DEMOCRATIC PRIMARY ELECTION

June 1, 2010

This is the official Guide Ballot for State Offices recommended by the Alabama Democratic Conference (ADC). Local candidates were endorsed by the local leaders. Let us vote together, United we stand, divided we fall.

Paid for by the Alabama Democratic Conference, P.O. Box 6233, Montgomery, AL 36106

Curtis Travis
County Chairman

Joe L. Reed, Chairman

INSTRUCTIONS TO THE VOTER

TO VOTE YOU MUST BLACKEN THE OVAL (⬬) COMPLETELY! DO NOT MAKE AN X OR ✓.
USE ONLY THE MARKING DEVICE PROVIDED TO MARK THE BALLOT.
IF YOU SPOIL YOUR BALLOT, DO NOT ERASE, BUT ASK FOR A NEW BALLOT.

FOR GOVERNOR
(Vote for One)
- ARTUR G. DAVIS
- ⬬ RON SPARKS

FOR UNITED STATES SENATOR
(Vote for One)
- WILLIAM G. BARNES
- ⬬ SIMONE DE MOORE

FOR UNITED STATES REPRESENTATIVE, 7TH CONGRESSIONAL DISTRICT
(Vote for One)
- MARTHA BOZEMAN
- EARL HILLIARD, JR.
- TERRI A. SEWELL
- ⬬ SHELIA SMOOT

FOR ATTORNEY GENERAL
(Vote for One)
- ⬬ JAMES H. ANDERSON
- MICHEL NICROSI
- GILES PERKINS

FOR STATE SENATOR, DISTRICT NO. 5
(Vote for One)
- BILL 'J' CLEGHORN
- BRETT WADSWORTH

FOR STATE TREASURER
(Vote for One)
- ⬬ CHARLEY GRIMSLEY
- JEREMY SHERER

FOR DISTRICT ATTORNEY, 6TH JUDICIAL CIRCUIT
(Vote for One)
- ⬬ TOMMY SMITH
- ROBERT SPENCE

FOR STATE DEMOCRATIC EXECUTIVE COMMITTEE (MALE) DISTRICT NO. 70
(Vote for One)
- CHRIS CHIRINO
- MAXIE THOMAS

THESE OFFICES WILL NOT APPEAR ON ALL BALLOTS

"Shall the following Amendment be adopted to the Constitution of Alabama?"

PROPOSED AMENDMENT WHICH APPLIES TO THE STATE AT LARGE

PROPOSED STATEWIDE AMENDMENT NUMBER ONE (1)

Proposing an amendment to the Constitution of Alabama of 1901, relating to the promotion of propane gas by authorizing the Legislature to enact legislation providing for an assessment on the members of the propane gas industry for the purpose of financing promotion programs. (Proposed by Act No. 2009-547)

- STATEWIDE AMENDMENT NO. 1 YES
- ⬬ STATEWIDE AMENDMENT NO. 1 NO

This is a common ballot, however, these offices will appear only in certain precincts which will apply to your districts.

5.4. Tuscaloosa County, Alabama Democratic Conference ballot sample, June 1, 2010. From the William H. Stewart collection

The Alabama New South Coalition

The most significant challenge to the influence of Reed came with the founding of the Alabama New South Coalition (ANSC) in 1986. Its initial leaders included Richard Arrington, J. L. Chestnut, Michael Figures, and Hank and Rose Sanders. Its origin had been in a movement called the Campaign for a New South that had worked to elect black legislative candidates, most notably Sanders. The organization itself was a coalition of highly localized civic leagues.

Although they are frequently rivals, the ADC and the ANSC often endorse the same candidates. This has been especially true as the number of Democratic aspirants for statewide office with a realistic chance of winning has declined drastically. Of the two groups, the ADC has the most successful track record in terms of successful candidates.

Most recently there was a feud between Reed and former US Representative Davis, previously identified as an unsuccessful Democratic gubernatorial primary candidate in 2010. Reed had originally opposed Davis's election to Congress and continued to be at odds with him during his race to become Alabama's first black governor. He strongly criticized Davis for his vote against the Obama health care bill. Cynthia Tucker wrote a column in December 2009, urging: "Dethrone the kingmaker," meaning Reed.[26] The ADC endorsed Davis's white opponent, Agriculture commissioner Ron Sparks, who lost to Robert Bentley in the general election. At the time of the ADC's endorsement meeting, the senior Associated Press correspondent in Alabama, Phillip Rawls, found it ironic that "an organization that helped end all-white governments in Alabama [was] celebrating its [previous] successes without the first serious, well-funded black candidate for governor."[27]

Making Amends for Past Injustices

After racial barriers contained in the 1901 constitution were federally invalidated, blacks and whites (despite partisan differences) were sometimes able to work together, particularly on behalf of symbolic causes such as removing segregation provisions from the 1901 constitution.

Removing Jim Crow Language

When Alabama voters excised the federally invalidated ban on interracial marriage from their constitution in 2000, even the frequently pessimistic historian Wayne Flynt said, "The people decided in the eyes of the Constitution we are not black or brown. . . . I think this indicates race is receding as an issue in Alabama politics and that's good news."[28] A dozen years after repeal of the inoperative antimiscegenation language, it was reported that Alabama ranked seventh in the nation in terms of black and white marriages.[29] Marriages of this sort had been banned in Alabama and fifteen other states until the US Supreme Court's ruling in the 1967 case of *Loving v. Virginia*.[30]

In 2004 language related to segregated schools was put up for an excising vote, but the proposed constitutional amendment failed narrowly. Opponents, led by Republican jurist Roy Moore, contended that since the new language would remove the existing proviso saying that there was no right to education at public expense in Alabama, judges would be able to order tax increases to enforce adequate funding for the unitary system of public schools. As noted in chapter 6, a 2012 proposal to remove the racist language was also defeated, this one in a campaign supported both by AEA and the major black political organizations. Unlike the proposal of eight years earlier, it had left out the 1901 language guaranteeing an education at public expense. Since there is no consensus on how to get rid of the Jim Crow–era verbiage, it will undoubtedly remain in the Alabama constitution for the foreseeable future.

Despite the controversies just mentioned, there has still been enough black-white agreement to take other mostly symbolic actions that did not contemplate any economic sacrifices on the part of whites on behalf of the generally less affluent blacks.

Honoring Civil Rights Pioneers

Black History Month (February) has been observed in Alabama as elsewhere for many years. The University of Alabama Press published a book, *Alabama's Civil Rights Trail*, to highlight particular places in Alabama where historic civil-rights-related events had occurred.[31] Civil rights studies are part of the Alabama school curriculum, and the state was given an A in the fall of 2011 by the Southern Poverty Law Center for the thoroughness of the instruction that students receive.[32] Three of Alabama's neighboring states did not receive the highest rating. Georgia got a B while Mississippi and Tennessee each got C's.

Nationally, as well as in Alabama, Dr. King is honored annually in his January birthday month. Every four years this occurs on the same day as the gubernatorial inauguration, and the individual being sworn in makes appropriate reference to this in the inaugural address. Many Alabama communities have some thoroughfare bearing Dr. King's name, as do sections of interstate highways and public schools. Coretta Scott King was inducted posthumously into the Alabama Women's Hall of Fame the first year she was eligible to be included. Other pioneers such as Rosa Parks and Richard Arrington, the mayor of Birmingham from 1979 to 1999, are similarly honored.

In April 2009, the Alabama legislature passed a resolution paying tribute to the first African Americans to serve there during Reconstruction. Visitors to the Alabama Historic Capitol now see plaques with the names of these pioneers (numbering 100 between 1867 to 1878) in prominent places in the building and on the grounds.

Unlike in some other parts of the South, sentiment in Alabama has not been sufficient to cause the removal of names from buildings of those who may have been closely associated with the white supremacy doctrines of the pre–civil rights era and massive resistance. The Wallace names, for example, both George and Lurleen, continue to be attached to multiple community colleges and other institutions. The Sons of Confederate Veterans remains alert to real or imagined slights, and during the Bob Riley administration it publicly complained in 2009 that black legislators of the past had been honored, but Confederate History and Heritage Month had not been proclaimed. On June 24, 2015, Governor Robert Bentley ordered the removal of Confederate battle flags from the Alabama capitol grounds. This followed the murder of nine African American worshippers at a church in Charleston, South Carolina, by an avowed Confederate sympathizer.

Apologizing for Wrongs of the Past

As discussed in chapter 2, former Governor Wallace made the most famous apology to African Americans. On the thirtieth anniversary of the Selma-Montgomery voting rights march (March 11, 1995) he repented of his past militant opposition to black citizens' rights, most notably his pledge of "segregation forever" at the capitol and his "stand in the schoolhouse door" at the University of Alabama.[33] For its part, the university has restored the site of the stand and erected landmarks to honor the first African American students to be admitted to the institution. The anniversary of Birmingham's Sixteenth Street Baptist Church bombing of September 1963 is commemorated annually at the site where it occurred.

Taking place every March in Selma, the "Bloody Sunday" commemoration is the anniversary in Alabama that gets the most national publicity. In presidential election years, especially if there is a competitive contest for the Democratic nomination, major candidates can be expected to appear, as then-senator Barack Obama and then-senator Hillary Clinton did as they were vying to be the 2008 Democratic presidential candidate. Senator Obama spoke at the Brown Chapel church on March 11, 2007, to an overflow crowd.

Governors and mayors have pardoned large numbers of people (usually posthumously) who were convicted many years ago for challenging Jim Crow laws. The most famous was Rosa Parks, of Montgomery bus boycott fame.

The first gubernatorial pardon for an Alabama injustice had occurred when Clarence Norris, one of the defendants in the infamous "Scottsboro Boys" cases of the 1930s, was pardoned.[34] A museum was established at the site of their initial hurry-up trial. One local booster commented: "This is another example of Alabama celebrating landmark developments in civil rights and attracting tourists as well."[35]

Also, Alabama State University has been selected as an interpretive center for the Selma-to-Montgomery National Historic Trail. Students from the university who had been expelled decades ago for participating in sit-in demonstrations were officially reinstated.

The Alabama legislature has apologized for the institution of slavery. This occurred in April 2007, when both the House and Senate concurred in House Joint Resolution 321 denouncing the historic practice of it. This resolution did not pass unanimously, however. Some Republicans cautioned that in approving it, the legislature might be encouraging suits for reparations by descendants of slaves. To make it clear that reparations would never be paid, resolution proponents amended their original measure to expressly prohibit any suits seeking them. The House then passed the resolution on an unrecorded viva voce (voice) vote. The Senate did have a roll call vote, a party-line vote in which all the yeas (22) were cast by Democrats and all the nays (7) by Republicans. Governor Riley quickly signed the resolution when it reached his desk.

More than merely symbolic is the actual punishment of perpetrators of crimes against participants in the civil rights struggles of decades ago.

Reopening Cold Cases

Where feasible both federal and state authorities have reopened "cold cases" to determine if those believed to be guilty during the civil rights era could still be brought to justice. Early in the new century, two men were indicted and found guilty of murder in connection with the Birmingham Sixteenth Street Baptist Church bombing in a federal trial. At least two other subsequent cold case prosecutions were also made and guilty verdicts returned. One murder committed in 1965 was successfully tried in state court over four decades after it had taken place in a small town in the Black Belt. By the end of 2011, however, most witnesses and evidence were no longer available, so this approach to righting past wrongs is very difficult to pursue successfully.

Conclusion

Efforts to address injustices of the Jim Crow era have been discussed in this chapter. The general mindset of the politically active white has been so markedly changed that he or she would not want to be in any way associated with what is perceived to be a white supremacist group—whether because it would be wrong or because it would damage future political prospects (or both). The Southern Poverty Law Center identifies the League of the South, for example, as a hate group, and most politicians avoid any association with it. One letter to the editor writer observed that, "Whether we like it or not, the phrase 'Confederate History Month' and the symbol of the Confederate flag conjure up images of slavery, racism, violence and hate in a lot of people's minds. Why would we want to do anything to celebrate or glorify these evil aspects of our history?"[36]

Alabama is still governed by the constitution mentioned in the first sentence of this chapter, a document the principal goal of which was to reimpose, to the extent allowable, the values represented by the Confederacy on its black citizens. Although the state has moved significantly away from these values, the constitution written by Civil War veterans and their sons remains in place.

6
The Alabama Constitution

Alabama has had six constitutions since it entered the Union in 1819, and the current one, dating from 1901, may actually be "the longest constitution in the world." India is generally identified as the nation with the longest written constitution—it has *only* about 115,000 words.

The Notoriety of the Alabama Constitution

"We're No. 1 in the world."[1] This was the tongue-in-cheek boast of letter-to-the-editor writer Carl Dimick, who called readers' attention to a question on *Who Wants to Be a Millionaire?* From four alternatives the contestant was to choose the state that correctly matched this fact: "With over 350,000 words and over 800 amendments, this state has the longest constitution in the world." The answer was the state of Alabama.

In this chapter we will find out how Alabama came to hold its famous (or infamous) spot. Louisiana has had the largest number of state constitutions with eleven. Following are Georgia with nine and South Carolina with seven. Alabama's total of six is shared with Florida and Virginia.[2]

Constitutional Background

Alabama originally came in to the Union in 1819 based on "An act to enable the people of the Territory of Alabama to form a constitution and State government, and for the admission of such State into the Union on an equal footing with the original States."[3] The first constitution was written by a convention assembled in Huntsville. Attorneys who had migrated into the Alabama Territory, mostly from Georgia, North and South Carolina, and Virginia, controlled the proceedings.

An analogy could be made between Alabama's first constitution in 1819 and the document produced by the federal convention in Philadelphia in

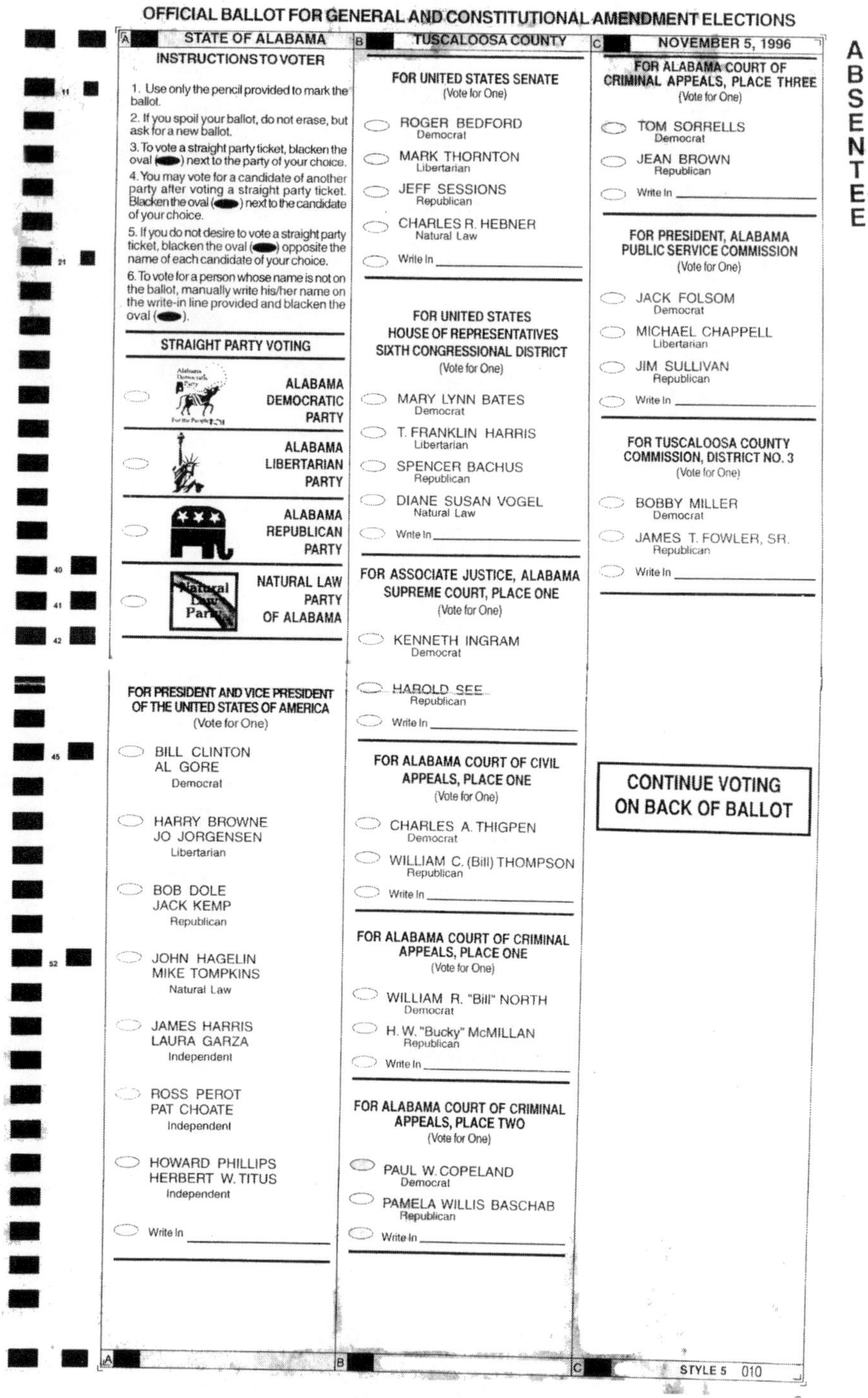
OFFICIAL BALLOT FOR GENERAL AND CONSTITUTIONAL AMENDMENT ELECTIONS

A STATE OF ALABAMA | B TUSCALOOSA COUNTY | C NOVEMBER 5, 1996

ABSENTEE

INSTRUCTIONS TO VOTER

1. Use only the pencil provided to mark the ballot.
2. If you spoil your ballot, do not erase, but ask for a new ballot.
3. To vote a straight party ticket, blacken the oval (⬬) next to the party of your choice.
4. You may vote for a candidate of another party after voting a straight party ticket. Blacken the oval (⬬) next to the candidate of your choice.
5. If you do not desire to vote a straight party ticket, blacken the oval (⬬) opposite the name of each candidate of your choice.
6. To vote for a person whose name is not on the ballot, manually write his/her name on the write-in line provided and blacken the oval (⬬).

STRAIGHT PARTY VOTING

ALABAMA DEMOCRATIC PARTY
ALABAMA LIBERTARIAN PARTY
ALABAMA REPUBLICAN PARTY
NATURAL LAW PARTY OF ALABAMA

FOR PRESIDENT AND VICE PRESIDENT OF THE UNITED STATES OF AMERICA
(Vote for One)

BILL CLINTON / AL GORE — Democrat
HARRY BROWNE / JO JORGENSEN — Libertarian
BOB DOLE / JACK KEMP — Republican
JOHN HAGELIN / MIKE TOMPKINS — Natural Law
JAMES HARRIS / LAURA GARZA — Independent
ROSS PEROT / PAT CHOATE — Independent
HOWARD PHILLIPS / HERBERT W. TITUS — Independent
Write In ______

FOR UNITED STATES SENATE
(Vote for One)

ROGER BEDFORD — Democrat
MARK THORNTON — Libertarian
JEFF SESSIONS — Republican
CHARLES R. HEBNER — Natural Law
Write In ______

FOR UNITED STATES HOUSE OF REPRESENTATIVES SIXTH CONGRESSIONAL DISTRICT
(Vote for One)

MARY LYNN BATES — Democrat
T. FRANKLIN HARRIS — Libertarian
SPENCER BACHUS — Republican
DIANE SUSAN VOGEL — Natural Law
Write In ______

FOR ASSOCIATE JUSTICE, ALABAMA SUPREME COURT, PLACE ONE
(Vote for One)

KENNETH INGRAM — Democrat
HAROLD SEE — Republican
Write In ______

FOR ALABAMA COURT OF CIVIL APPEALS, PLACE ONE
(Vote for One)

CHARLES A. THIGPEN — Democrat
WILLIAM C. (Bill) THOMPSON — Republican
Write In ______

FOR ALABAMA COURT OF CRIMINAL APPEALS, PLACE ONE
(Vote for One)

WILLIAM R. "Bill" NORTH — Democrat
H. W. "Bucky" McMILLAN — Republican
Write In ______

FOR ALABAMA COURT OF CRIMINAL APPEALS, PLACE TWO
(Vote for One)

PAUL W. COPELAND — Democrat
PAMELA WILLIS BASCHAB — Republican
Write In ______

FOR ALABAMA COURT OF CRIMINAL APPEALS, PLACE THREE
(Vote for One)

TOM SORRELLS — Democrat
JEAN BROWN — Republican
Write In ______

FOR PRESIDENT, ALABAMA PUBLIC SERVICE COMMISSION
(Vote for One)

JACK FOLSOM — Democrat
MICHAEL CHAPPELL — Libertarian
JIM SULLIVAN — Republican
Write In ______

FOR TUSCALOOSA COUNTY COMMISSION, DISTRICT NO. 3
(Vote for One)

BOBBY MILLER — Democrat
JAMES T. FOWLER, SR. — Republican
Write In ______

CONTINUE VOTING ON BACK OF BALLOT

STYLE 5 010

6.1a. Front of official ballot for general and constitutional amendment elections. From the William H. Stewart collection

D STATE OF ALABAMA

"Shall the following Amendments be adopted to the Constitution of Alabama?"

PROPOSED AMENDMENTS WHICH APPLY TO THE STATE AT LARGE

PROPOSED AMENDMENT NUMBER ONE (1)

Proposing an amendment to the Constitution of Alabama of 1901, to guarantee the right to hunt and fish in this state in accordance with law and regulations, the "Sportsperson's Bill of Rights." (Proposed by Act 96-569)

⬭ YES

⬭ NO

PROPOSED AMENDMENT NUMBER TWO (2)

Proposing an amendment to the Constitution of Alabama of 1901, to phase out the supernumerary system for public officials and to provide for the participation of public officials in the Employees' Retirement System of Alabama. (Proposed by Act 96-584)

⬭ YES

⬭ NO

PROPOSED AMENDMENT NUMBER THREE (3)

Proposing an amendment to the Constitution of Alabama of 1901, to remove the prohibition on guilty pleas to an information in non-capital felony cases within 15 days of arrest. (Proposed by Act 96-586)

⬭ YES

⬭ NO

E TUSCALOOSA COUNTY

PROPOSED AMENDMENT NUMBER FOUR (4)

Relating to Morgan County, proposing an amendment to the Constitution of Alabama of 1901, authorizing the governing bodies of the respective Cities of Hartselle, Falkville, and Decatur to provide for bingo operations for profit within their respective jurisdictions in the county; and providing that the Legislature, by local law, may authorize bingo operations in any other city located within the boundaries of Morgan County. (Proposed by Act 96-378)

⬭ YES

⬭ NO

PROPOSED AMENDMENT NUMBER FIVE (5)

Relating to Jefferson County, proposing an amendment to the Constitution of Alabama of 1901, to provide that the monetary amount of prizes for the playing of bingo shall be established by local law. (Proposed by Act 96-420)

⬭ YES

⬭ NO

END OF BALLOT

F NOVEMBER 5, 1996

HAVE YOU VOTED BOTH SIDES OF THE BALLOT?

D E F

6.1b. Back of official ballot for general and constitutional amendment elections. From the William H. Stewart collection

1787. This is because the end product was similar: a liberal document ("the most liberal of any state's at that time"[4]) that served the state well and probably would not have needed replacement by the constitution of 1861—*if* the Civil War never happened. The original delegates ratified their handiwork on August 2, 1819. Reception into the Union came on December 14 of the same year.

Four constitutions removed from the original one in 1819 is the current constitution of 1901, which mostly reflects its immediate predecessor, the constitution of 1875. This constitution had drastically changed the one it succeeded, the constitution of 1868 (Reconstruction Constitution).

African Americans and the Constitution

What the 1875 constitution made a start on, the 1901 constitution continued in an even more determined way—removing African Americans from Alabama politics. The men in charge of the convention that drew up the new constitution in 1900 used the discretion they had "to perpetuate their power and privilege through restricting the size and composition of the Alabama electorate."[5] The original provisions of the Alabama Constitution, according to political scientist Julie Novkov, amounted to "the most elaborate suffrage requirements that have ever been in force in the United States."[6] As we saw in chapter 5, the constitution formulated in Montgomery at this time was part of a southwide effort to perpetuate and strengthen the Jim Crow system that had begun in earnest with the end of Reconstruction.

On November 11, 1900, the Alabama electorate (including most notoriously African American voters who were "voted" to disfranchise themselves) ratified the constitution under which they and those who came after them have lived for 113 years. This is about two-and-one-half times as long as the original constitution lasted. Of all the southern states adopting new constitutions when the threat of federal intervention was safely past, Alabama was the only one to stipulate popular ratification. Historian Wayne Flynt says that this was a concession to "traditional Alabama democracy."[7]

Assessments of the Constitution

One of the few things that can be said in defense of the constitution is that it was not open to the charge of hypocrisy with regard to the dominators of Alabama politics. Its provisions clearly showed who would really hold political power in the Alabama of the new century.[8] Ironically, in this respect it was actually superior to the federal Constitution. The Constitution that emerged from the Philadelphia convention in 1787 indicated that the goal was primarily to establish a representative democracy. It is a fact, however, that its framers, as enlightened as they were, were more concerned with protecting property rights. A simple reading of the document would not immediately bring this objective to mind. In contrast, even a cursory review of the Alabama Constitution of 1901 would show without a doubt that its framers had as their overwhelming goal the perpetuation of the reestablished white supremacy.

The Alabama Constitution of 1901 was similar to others drafted in that era of southern state constitution writing (from the late nineteenth century down to the start of World War I) in its abundance of legislative details, but even more explicit in its framers' passion to prevent unwanted change in the future. The change least desired was the exercise by African Americans of any political power in Alabama.

The reader may find it remarkable that the United States still operates under an eighteenth-century Constitution with the primary goal of protecting property, but one never hears of any serious proposal to replace it. At the same time, Alabama is governed by a twentieth-century constitution that a governor (Emmet O'Neal) saw as outdated only a decade after its adoption. Just six years after it went into effect, in 1907, the editor of a multivolume work on state constitutions, pioneer political scientist James Quayle Dealey, noted that the Alabama Constitution with its 33,000 words was one of the nation's three longest. Rounding out the top three were Virginia and Louisiana.[9] In the same time period, a more famous political scientist, Charles A. Beard, pointed out that "the Legislature of Alabama must even buy its fuel according to the rules laid down in the fundamental law of the commonwealth."[10] It was that detailed.

"Dillon's" but Not "Home" Rule

In legislating for local areas as it does, Alabama is slavishly following the nineteenth-century dogma of Iowa Supreme Court Justice John F. Dillon and his rule (Dillon's Rule), which defines local governments as "creatures of the state."[11] That is, they owe their existence to the state and any powers they exercise must have been specifically delegated by the parent government. (Most other states do not follow Dillon's Rule to the extent that Alabama does.)

Only a few Alabama counties have been granted limited home rule by county-specific constitutional amendments. Part of the explanation for local governments, especially counties, not having any more home rule than they do at present was the fears of the 1900 white supremacist framers of "Negro domination."[12] This was especially true, as one would expect, among delegates from black-majority counties.

Most of the amendments to the constitution are local (applying only to a specific substate area), and a majority of the ordinary bills the legislature passes at each session are local as well. The *Montgomery Advertiser* editorialized a few years ago that, "Among the many flaws in Alabama's constitution is its centering of vast authority over local matters in the Legislature, rather than allowing local governments to make decisions on purely local issues." This "allows legislators to impose unsought and undesired decisions on local governments."[13]

Federal Intervention

State leaders tried repeatedly to circumvent federal moves to negate its original provisions aimed at denying the vote to blacks. In 1946, for example, Amendment 55, the Boswell Amendment (named for its state legislative sponsor, Senator Elmo C. "Bud" Boswell), altered the original Section 181 of the constitution. This amendment sought to evade the Supreme Court's decision banning the white primary.[14] It attempted (unsuccessfully as it turned out) to disassociate the state from the activities of the State Democratic Executive Committee in connection with primaries. Many years later blacks would come to dominate both the state committee and the primaries from which they had previously been rigidly excluded.

State Constitutional Comparisons

Unlike Alabama a few states still have the constitution they originally entered the Union with. Experts have found that the older the state constitution is, the better it is likely to be.[15] As state constitution writing proceeded from the eighteenth century onward, framers of constitutions tended to become much more detailed in what they wrote. And, the more date-specific material they included, the more amending would be needed later.

In literature concerned with what a constitution should be like, a brief framework for government is usually preferred. It is argued that since the constitution "is the basis of law, [it] should deal with basic concepts and fundamental issues."[16] While Alabama is an outlier example of the departure from this approach to constitution making, most other state constitutions are not brief statements of principles either—and also amount to much more than a short outline of governmental institutions, as political scientist Christopher Hammons points out.[17]

Alabama's "War and Peace"

The Alabama Constitution is generally not available in a printed version. If it were, using standard font sizes, it would be well over 1,500 pages in length. The typical state constitution could be reprinted about a dozen times in the space required to print the Alabama Constitution once. Vermont has the shortest state constitution, consisting of fewer than 15,000 words. Alabama's is the longest, with approximately 350,000 words.

The constitution is available on the secretary of state's website. A staff member in this office predicted that the number of constitutional amendments (893 at the end of 2015) would reach 1,000 by 2016 if new amendments continued to be approved at the prevailing rate.

While Alabama is the undisputed leader among the states in having a *very* long constitution, nationally syndicated columnist George Will also identified California's as "one of the world's longest constitutions," having "been amended more than 500 times by direct democracy."[18] Alabama doesn't have the initiative, so all of its 893 amendments have been approved by the legislature first. Then they go to the voters.

Recent Constitutional Referenda

A group known as the Callahan Commission, named after its Senate sponsor (originally a Democratic state legislator but later a Republican US representative from Mobile), Sonny Callahan, makes the determination as to how legislatively approved amendments will be submitted. They may appear only on ballots in the localities directly affected or they may be subjected to a statewide vote. (Amendment 555 provides that strictly local amendments are to be voted on only in the substate areas affected.) The commission is forbidden from distinguishing local from state amendments on racially biased grounds. Also, if there were any negative votes during legislative consideration, amendments are put on a statewide ballot even if their language specifies only a local area to which they will apply. Otherwise, the Callahan Commission has considerable flexibility in classifying proposed amendments.

Major Constitutional Provisions

Now, let's take a look at the constitution, beginning with the Preamble and Declaration of Rights and then examining several of the constitution's fourteen articles. Two of the 1901 constitution's original articles were replaced on November 6, 2012—that part of Article XII dealing with private corporations and Article III concerned with banks and banking. They were the products of the work of the currently operating Constitutional Commission (about which more later) as approved by the legislature and now the voters as well.

The Preamble

Like most state constitutions, Alabama's acknowledges God. This was part of Chief Justice Roy Moore's defiance of a federal court order to remove a Ten Commandments monument he had installed in the state judicial building. He had taken an oath to uphold the Alabama as well as the US Constitution and believed that his installation of the monument in the judicial building was consistent with the oath.[19]

Declaration of Rights

The equivalent to the federal Constitution's Bill of Rights is Alabama's Declaration of Rights. Law professor Bryan Fair argued for a new Declaration of Rights article for the constitution, primarily because it contained no equivalent to the US Constitution's equal protection clause.[20] Article 1, Sec. 2, of the Alabama Constitution does mention "protect[ing] all citizens in their privileges and immunities equally," and these words could be interpreted in the same way as the Fourteenth Amendment's equal protection clause. To do so, however, would probably be too risky politically for Alabama's popularly elected judges. Judges are more likely to be receptive to expanding positive rights claims if they enjoy some protection from possible voter displeasure—for example, if they were initially appointed to office in a merit-selection state. (The subject of merit selection is discussed in chapter 13.) Even though the Alabama Constitution, in its Declaration of Rights, has almost double the number of provisions guaranteeing the rights of people accused of crimes in comparison to the federal Constitution, new ground is infrequently broken in state courts in cases where defendants claim that their rights have been violated. Most deprivation claims have been made successfully in federal court.

Article 1, Sec. 11, of the Alabama Constitution, guaranteeing an individual the right to a jury trial, was initially seen as standing in the way of binding arbitration agreements when Democrats controlled the Alabama Supreme Court. This is not the situation now, however, when Republicans occupy all seats. The court has upheld legislation that has buyers routinely agreeing to arbitration when, for example, they are purchasing an automobile and problems later develop.

Some state constitutions have been amended formally—or informally through judicial interpretation—in recent years to provide new "positive rights" in addition to those traditionally included in bills of rights. For example, several states now explicitly commit to protecting the environment to advance a better quality of life for residents.[21] States with environmental bills of rights include Florida, North Carolina, and Virginia—the only southern states to have them.

Alabama's constitution has been more likely to be amended to prohibit behavior the majority of the population opposes, such as gay marriage (Amendment 774). (In February 2015 this "sanctity of marriage" amendment was ruled unconstitutional by a federal district judge, Callie V. S. Granade [2015 WL 736091], in the case of *Strawser v. Strange*.) Another negative response to positive rights claims was the constitutional amendment (509) declaring that English was the state's official language and the state had no legal obligation to make allowances for non-English speakers.[22]

Alabama is not unique in having a largely inconsequential bill of rights. One legal scholar, Robert Force, wrote in the late 1960s about state bills of rights that, he said, represented both "a case of neglect and the need for a renaissance."[23] More recently, there has been somewhat of a "renaissance" as far as state bills of rights are concerned. But changes, whether made formally or through judicial interpretation, have not always been in the direction of more individual rights.[24]

Separation of Powers

Like the federal government, the government of the state of Alabama is supposed to be based on a system of separated powers. In the US Constitution the separation of powers is implied from the existence of distinct constitutional articles for three governmental branches (legislative, executive, and judicial). In contrast, the Alabama Constitution, like its counterparts in many other states, has a separate article (3) enunciating this principle. Even though the Alabama Constitution bears little similarity to the New England model in most other respects, the Alabama separation of powers provision and that of Massachusetts (inserted in 1780) are actually about the same.[25]

In Alabama, this clause has been only symbolic. Each of the three branches regularly exercises powers supposedly reserved to the others.

Legislative Article

The legislature traditionally was the most politically powerful branch of state government. This explains why the legislative branch is typically dealt with first among the branches in state constitutions.

To ensure that Alabama's and other states' legislatures would be demographically representative, federal courts entered the highly political arena of legislative reapportionment beginning in the 1960s. As was true in many other states, Alabama's legislature was badly malapportioned. A small percentage of the state's population could elect a majority of its members. Although the constitution specified that legislative seats should be reallocated after each census, they never were until the federal courts ordered it.

Beginning with *Baker v. Carr* in 1962, the federal courts have required that state legislatures properly apportion themselves or have it done federally for them.[26] The malapportioned Alabama Senate provided the basis for a second important US Supreme Court decision, this one requiring that both houses of a state legislature be based on population.[27]

Most of the things the legislature was *not* to do, according to the constitution, had originated in the 1875 document. For example, the legislature was forbidden to "authorize lotteries" (Article 4, Sec. 65). Due to the inclusion of so many verboten activities, the committee on the legislative department's report in the 1875 convention made the legislative article nearly twice as long as the comparable one in the 1868 constitution (and its predecessors).[28] Even at this time there were critics of this approach to constitution making. The *Mobile Register* editorialized that the legislative minutiae lacked the "remotest relevancy to a State constitution" and were put in only because of Reconstruction-related experiences.[29]

One of the many race-related restrictions contained in the 1901 constitution forbade the legislature from sanctioning interracial marriage (Article 4, Sec. 102). As we saw in chapter 5, this prohibition, like many others with racist origins, was ultimately held to be in violation of the US Constitution.[30] When the vote was taken in Alabama in 2000 to expunge the inoperative antimiscegenation language from the constitution, it passed, but not by a wide margin.

The constitution as it emerged from the convention in late 1900 was certainly not "liberal" in most respects, but it did obligate the legislature to fund public education in this manner (even though this was never the case). (This mandate was contained in Article 14, Sec. 256.) In 1956, as the era of massive resistance to *Brown v. Board of Education* was gaining strength, this duty was amended, by Amendment 111, to eliminate the state obligation to furnish a publicly funded education.

When a constitutional amendment deleting inoperative language calling for segregated schools was defeated in 2004, the most commonly accepted explanation for this failure was that it had restored the right to an education at public expense. To secure this right, courts could (according to the line of reasoning that prevailed) order tax increases if necessary. When a similar amendment was put before the voters in 2012, but without the guarantee of a publicly funded education, it was overwhelmingly defeated. The AEA spent heavily to bring about this result, and the leading black political organizations were opposed to it as well. Since there is an obvious impasse regarding this issue of the "right" to a public education, the inoperative Jim Crow–era language relating to segregated schools (and invalid poll taxes also) will remain a part of the constitution for the foreseeable future.

Executive Article

The office of governor is provided for in Article 4 of the constitution. Comparing its provisions with comparable ones in the constitutions of other states, one finds the formal powers granted to be similar and, in some cases, greater in number. (These powers are identified at the beginning of chapter 12.) For an Alabama chief executive to dominate state government, however, he or she will need to exert a lot of personal influence as well.

Like many other states, Alabama has a plural rather than a single executive. The constitution provides in Article 5, Sec. 112, that, "The executive department shall consist of a governor, lieutenant governor, attorney-general, state auditor, secretary of state, state treasurer, commissioner of agriculture and industries, and a sheriff for each county."

Until 1968 (and the adoption of Amendment 282) neither the governor nor any of the other executive officials just named (except for the county sheriff) were allowed to succeed themselves in office. They were eligible for subsequent terms only after the lapse of a term. One positive aspect of the executive branch constitutionally is that administrative structure is not presented in a detailed way. For the most part, reorganizations have been taken through legislative act and/or executive order.[31]

Judicial Article

The judicial article of the Alabama Constitution is the only one pertaining to the three branches of government to be replaced since 1901 (by Amendment 323). A new foundation for the "judicial department," as the constitution refers to it, was approved in 1973 due to leadership provided by then-chief-justice Howell Heflin. ("The Courts as Political Institutions" will be our subject in chapter 13.) The organized legal community did not have sufficient clout to change the state from partisan judicial elections, as many of its members would have preferred. This meant that the Alabama appellate judiciary would likely not ever emulate its counterparts in what legal scholar Mirjan Damaska identifies as "highly interventionist states" where courts have "become instruments of state policy" in pioneering ways.[32] It was the 1868 constitution constructed by the most representative assembly ever to write an Alabama Constitution that first called for all state judges to be chosen by the voters from among party nominees. Former governor John Winston lamented following the 1868 convention that "Alabama had gotten a judiciary in no way independent of the people."[33]

In Massachusetts, where the members of the judiciary are appointed, a majority of the Supreme Judicial Court was willing to declare that the prohibition of marriage for two people of the same gender was unconstitutional.[34] This type of ruling would not be expected in a state where judges regularly run for popular election on partisan ballots. The opposite attitude prevails among Alabama appellate judges.

Alabamians interested in liberalizing change must still be reliant primarily on federal courts. Sometimes plaintiffs will "judge shop" to find a friendly US judge to hear their case and hope that his or her ruling, if favorable, will be upheld on appeal, maybe if only because appellate courts are limited in the number of cases they can review.

The Constitution and Taxes

The Alabama Constitution also includes both an article on (11) and numerous amendments dealing with taxation. For example, in 2012, voters in Tuscaloosa County approved an amendment to the constitution prohibiting local governments there from levying an occupation tax. One of the main characteristics of tax-related matters in the Alabama Constitution is earmarking. The Alabama Constitution does this to the extreme, earmarking a higher percentage of its revenues than any other state. The constitution is most notable for its restrictions on property taxes.

When the regular legislative session of 2011 established a new constitutional revision group, its supporters made it plain that current provisions of the constitution pertaining to taxes would be off limits.

Constitutional Reform

Efforts have been made to "reform"—or replace—the Alabama Constitution of 1901 dating from the next decade after it went into effect. For the most part, however, efforts to achieve any sort of comprehensive change have been unsuccessful.

The Courts and Reform

Constitutional reform in Alabama has mostly come about as a result of federal courts declaring unconstitutional race-related (but also other) provisions of the constitution of 1901. During and even before the modern civil rights era, the federal courts had begun to disallow Alabama laws aimed at disenfranchising black people. As we have previously seen, the most important step taken to prevent continued disenfranchisement was congressional passage of the Voting Rights Act in 1965.

The Alabama appellate judiciary has been more likely to be an impediment to than a facilitator of constitutional reform. More than a half century ago, in 1955, the state Supreme Court in a 4–3 vote issued an advisory opinion that said the state could not hold a limited constitutional convention.[35] Governor James Folsom Sr., was interested primarily in legislative reapportionment and knew that other politically sensitive subjects would be too difficult for a convention to deal with.

Twenty-eight years later (in 1983) the high court ruled that the legislature could not submit a new constitution to the voters for ratification in the form of a single amendment.[36] Lieutenant Governor Bill Baxley and Senator Ryan de Graffenried Jr., had taken the lead in drafting a cleaned up Alabama Constitution (divested of obsolete language) and secured its passage by both houses of the legislature. Voters were preparing to vote it up or down when the Supreme Court intervened to stop the referendum with its ruling in the *Manley* case.

Most recently, in 2010, the Alabama Supreme Court turned back a challenge to the 1901 constitution brought by nine black citizens who claimed that it was not legitimately ratified.[37]

Those filing the suit requested a revote on the 1901 constitution or a vote on a replacement. The plaintiffs charged that it was only because of massive fraud in a dozen mostly black counties that the constitution received more yes than no votes. The Supreme Court, however, dismissed the suit because the plaintiffs didn't have proper legal standing. They weren't alive at the time the constitutional referendum was held. None of them had lost *their* right to vote as a result of the constitution's discriminatory provisions. The attorney for those who filed the suit said, "We end up having this wrong without a remedy."[38]

Comparative Constitutional Reform

States normally don't engage in major constitutional reform activities in a vacuum. From time to time there have been national or regional movements afoot, and Alabama has been a part of them, as was the case when the 1901 constitution was adopted. The last such movement was in the 1960s and 1970s. Although Alabama did not implement a new constitution at that time, it did approve the new judicial article (1973) and adopted annual legislative sessions (1975). With so many other pressing problems, constitutional reform almost inevitably has a lower priority.

Each of Alabama's previous constitutions was drafted in the traditional way of achieving reform—through a convention of elected delegates. In recent years, resolutions to put the question of calling a constitutional convention have regularly been introduced in the legislature, but none has come close to passing.

The Alabama Citizens for Constitutional Reform (ACCR) is the principal interest group dedicated to the cause of constitutional reform, and it has regularly lobbied on behalf of resolutions to assemble a citizens' convention to draft a new constitution for voter consideration. Most Republicans voted against the most recent resolution in 2010, while most Democrats supported it. Even some African American legislators are opposed to a convention, however, despite the present constitution's racist origins. Like their white counterparts, black legislators also may enjoy the centralization of power in Montgomery. In the 2010 gubernatorial election cycle, only one candidate, Democratic US representative Artur Davis, supported a constitutional convention. He opposed a legislative revision because he said the legislature "was the center of special interest power in Alabama."[39] Davis also labeled the article-by-article rewrite approach as "a code word for let's do nothing." In contrast, his successful primary opponent, Ron Sparks, said that a convention was "a code word for raising taxes."[40]

The Constitutional Commission

A commission is now studying designated constitutional articles. This commission, set up in 2011, will periodically report back to the legislature, which will then decide whether or not to send the commission's recommendations on to the voters for their approval or disapproval. The commission has the assistance of the Alabama Law Institute, a legislative support unit that studies public policy problems possibly necessitating legislative action.

It was anticipated that the commission would complete its work by 2014. However, this deadline was not met. Ideally, unconstitutional language would be removed from the constitution and articles relating to private corporations, banking, the distribution of power, the legislature, representation, the Declaration of Rights, the executive branch, education, impeachments, exemptions, and miscellaneous activities would be studied, looking toward possible revisions (totaling nine constitutional articles). As noted earlier in the chapter, voters approved revised articles dealing with private corporations and banking in November 2012. Former governor Albert Brewer, who led in the formation of a similar commission during his administration (1968–71), is chairing the current constitutional study group. The public is generally unaware of the work of the commission headed by Brewer, however, and it would be accurate to conclude that this unawareness reflects very low public interest in constitutional reform.

Despite what some of them may occasionally say to the contrary, most Montgomery-based interest groups are quite satisfied with the present constitution, and the alleged defects that are of so much concern to reformers do not bother them. Many of these groups have sought at times to load the constitution with even more amendments to enhance their economic status, political power, or both. At this point we will turn our attention specifically to some of the interest groups involved in Alabama politics, those mentioned in previous chapters plus others that seek in multiple ways to influence what happens in the capital city.

7
Interest Groups

At a time when a party tie was virtually irrelevant in Alabama politics (because almost everyone was a Democrat), interest groups were filling an important vacuum. In today's Alabama they have a somewhat different but still very important role.

Overview

At the opening of each regular (and special) session of the Alabama legislature senators and representatives introduce many bills. Most of those dropped into the hoppers of the respective chambers will never be heard from again, however. Why is it that a select few proposals not only ultimately pass, but also may even pass fairly early in the legislative session? (In contrast, most bills die in the committee to which they were initially referred.) An important part of the answer to this question accounts for the presence of a chapter dealing with interest groups in this book. Some groups have been so powerful in the recent past that they could be reasonably sure that the legislature would quickly approve their high-priority bills. A few could be fairly confident that their bills would pass before the legislative session ended.

Accounting for Interest Groups

Interest groups generally emerge spontaneously in free societies, and their life span may be long or short. These associations are important components of the politics of every state. However, political science research has shown that group influence varies among them. Also, the actual number of groups is different in different parts of the country.[1] Obviously, we would expect that a state with a large population would have more groups than a sparsely settled area—and this is true. It is impossible to give the exact number of in-

Table 7.1. Official lobbying in Alabama (2008–12)

Year	Lobbyists	Employers
2008	663	775
2009	692	874
2010	654	751
2011	572	772
2012	67	771

Source: Alabama Ethics Commission, *Annual Reports* (2008–11 and Vicky Manning of the commission).

terest groups in a state, but we can know how many are actively involved in the policy process. Most states require groups that hire individuals who regularly lobby members of the legislature register, either with a legislative or some other designated office.

A large number of interest groups would constitute high density. High density is also reflected in a high lobbyist-legislator ratio. As of August 2011, Alabama had 603 registered lobbyists. Dividing the number of legislators (140) into this figure yields 4.3, or four lobbyists per legislator. The most populous of Alabama's neighboring states, Florida, had twelve lobbyists per legislator. Figures for the other adjoining states were: Georgia, six; Tennessee, three; and Mississippi, two.[2]

Characteristics of Interest Groups

In this chapter we will find the following to be true about interest groups as they operate politically in Alabama:

(1) There is little evidence that key political actors are motivated by a "general interest" that overrides more particularistic concerns;

(2) In Alabama politics, as elsewhere in the United States (at both the federal and state levels), the advantage lies with the group that has carefully defined goals that are regarded as legitimate in the larger society; furthermore, these goals should not involve significant changes in existing ways of doing things;

(3) Interest group influence tends to be greater when both costs and benefits are narrowly concentrated.[3] Another way of saying this is that in Alabama, unlike the situation in many other states, not only the major political decisions but also many minor ones are made at the capital in Montgomery. Interest groups don't necessarily have to be strong in every county and municipality; and

(4) Interest group activity in Alabama historically has been subject to very little regulation. More has been added recently, but whether it will change the Montgomery political culture (as was speculated in chapter 4) is very uncertain. When we use the term *special interest group* in these pages, it is not meant to be derogatory. It simply denotes the fact that a group has particular concerns of interest to its members that nonmembers may not share.

When candidates wage campaigns with the currently popular pledge that they will not be beholden to "special interest groups," their vows may resonate with voters because many voters believe that this is the way things work now. One disgusted citizen said that it was clear to "anyone familiar with Alabama politics . . . that our Legislature is run by special interest groups."[4] The view is also common that the large amount of money that interest groups give to legislative (and other) candidates amounts to "bribery thru campaign donations."

What to Look for in This Chapter

Based on what has been said in the previous paragraphs, this chapter has several objectives. We need to identify what an interest group is. How do interest groups differ from political parties and what are the relationships between them likely to be? Why are interest groups formed in the first place? In what respects are interest groups more or less important in Alabama than in other states?

In addition to coming up with some answers to these questions, we will see how and where interest groups operate as well as some of the methods they use to try to accomplish their objectives. Finally, we will assess the extent to which interest group activities are regulated.

Citizen Participation in Alabama Politics

If they are not already completely alienated from government, citizens have many ways of attempting to influence governmental policies aside from working through organized groups.

How Citizens Get Involved

Without reference to groups, they can contact public officials, speak out at public meetings, write letters to the editor (several of which are quoted in this book), post on blogs or other Internet sites, and, of course, go to the polls and vote on Election Day. There is, however, strength in numbers, and experience has shown that people who are organized are more likely to exert influence than amorphous, leaderless masses.

A dictionary definition of an interest group is that it is "a body of persons that seeks or receives benefits or privileged treatment, especially through legislation."[5] Years ago interest groups were primarily referred to as pressure groups, as in the title of the famous V. O. Key book, *Politics, Parties, and Pressure Groups*.[6] In current usage, *interest group* is regarded as a more objective, less loaded term.

Reasons Why Interest Groups Have Been Strong in Alabama

People working through interest groups in Alabama compete in a "market."[7] It is not a fair market because the "rules" favor some groups and work against others. These rules are not immutable, however, and the Alabama interest group system is fairer than it used to be, in part due to the great increase in the number of groups competing for influence in the public policy process. Historically poor states like Alabama tended to have a few strong interest groups but, as they have developed economically and socially, more groups have appeared. Although liberal-leaning groups like the Alabama Education Association (AEA) have been very important in state politics in recent decades, the most influential Alabama interest groups historically have been conservative. The same has been true for most southern states.

The process of *disaggregation* is a fancier way of saying dividing a whole, a system, into two or more parts. As the Alabama political system has become more complex, there has been a "disaggregation" of the state's system of interest groups—it is much more complex than it was during most of the twentieth century. Even in the middle of the twentieth century, it was common to speak of a relative handful of "big mules," urban industrialists who, along with their Black Belt planter allies, basically determined policy within the state. Now that we are well into the twenty-first century, the number of interest groups has vastly multiplied.

It is true that growth in the numbers of groups has advantages in terms of more participation, but, at the same time, in the absence of strong, disciplined political parties, it can also increase the likelihood for governmental stalemate. In the first regular legislative sessions following the 2010 elections, Alabama had a disciplined Republican Party in charge, and there were no stalemates. In the second, in 2012, the pace of legislative activity was much slower—more typical of the former days of Democratic control. Much of an accumulated Republican legislative plan had been adopted during the 2011 session. More importantly for the main concern of this chapter, interest groups, including the AEA, were able to reassert a measure of their former power and wean some legislators away from strict adherence to a party line. When Alabama was an overwhelmingly one-party Democratic state, interest groups functioned in place of political parties in the organization of legislative coalitions. They filled the vacuum the absence of strong parties left. It was sometimes even called a "no-party" state because, if nearly everyone was a "Democrat," being a Democrat conveyed very little information about one's individual political views. As Alabama developed into a two-party state, then into one with overwhelming Republican dominance in state government, this situation changed.

State leaders in one sense coordinate with interest groups as they make public policy. But using the term *coordinate* may not give enough weight to the power some interest groups have at times been able to exercise. It has not been unusual for groups such as the Alabama Farmers Federation (ALFA) to have a virtual veto over what was or was not passed by the Alabama legislature.[8]

Nearly sixty-five years ago, V. O. Key was calling attention to the "compelling" lobbying power of the Alabama Farm Bureau Federation (the former name of ALFA).[9]

The Centralization of Power

As we saw earlier, interest group influence tends to be greater when the centers of decision making are of a smaller rather than a larger number. This means that decision-making power is not widely diffused throughout a particular political unit such as a state like Alabama. To use one example, most of the funding for public schools is provided at the state level in Alabama. In New England states, in contrast, most public school funding is locally originated. The Alabama situation causes groups, such as the AEA, to focus most of their energies on influencing decision making in Montgomery. A group's task is thus easier than it would be if making the key decisions about allocating resources for schools was widely dispersed (as it often is elsewhere).

Political Power Variables

The attributes of interest group influence to be discussed in the following paragraphs obviously are not separate and distinct. Most overlap. For example, people of considerable wealth will likely have more access to decision makers and, because of this, will be able to exercise more influence.

Size

Normally, it would be expected that small groups would not be able to exercise as much influence as large groups. Many resources would be available to a group of large size that a small organization would not likely have, especially money. A large organization's endorsement in an election campaign would mean more than the backing of a small group unless the latter is composed of notably affluent people with high socioeconomic status.

In recent years AEA has had more than 100,000 members, active or retired teachers or education support personnel. All of them do not support AEA positions, but they are dues-paying members nonetheless. In the past, AEA has been sufficiently powerful that it did not have to worry about sending out dues notices and waiting for members to make political contributions if they wished. In late 2010, however, the new Republican legislature abolished payroll deductions. (AEA has challenged the ban on automatic deductions in federal and state court.)

Unity

Groups that are able to speak with a united voice tend to carry more weight than those that are divided. This would be especially true for smaller groups. Large groups like the AEA may be divided, but the AEA has collected dues from all members and spent the funds as the leadership saw fit, whether many members agreed or not.

Stability

AEA also has had a remarkable continuity of leadership. When the formerly all–African American Alabama State Teachers Association and the all-white Alabama Education Association merged more than four decades ago, the leaders of the respective organizations were Joe Reed and Paul Hubbert. It was only in late 2011 that these two powerful men finally retired. Reed also was (and remains) the head of the Alabama Democratic Conference (as we pointed out in chapter 5), one of the two most important black political groups in the state. The Alabama New South Coalition is the other. Until he resigned, Hubbert, like Reed, also served as a vice-chair of the Alabama Democratic Party.

Group and Public Relations

Groups are more effective when they keep in continual contact with members as well as the public. The heads of the Business Council of Alabama (BCA) and the Chamber of Commerce Association of Alabama cowrote an op-ed piece that appeared in the state's largest newspaper, the *Birmingham News*.[10] Not all groups would have prestige sufficient to ensure that their opinions would receive such generous publicity.

Legitimacy

Some groups would be ineffective because they lack legitimacy. Groups seeking to legalize marijuana, for example, might be influential elsewhere, but not in Bible Belt states such as Alabama.

Interest Group Techniques

Interest groups in all states are intensely concerned with getting particular bills passed in the legislature (or getting them defeated). In Alabama, unlike in some other states (particularly in the West), the legislature has a monopoly on lawmaking. Citizens can't bypass the legislature and put measures on the ballot by getting petitions signed by a designated percentage of registered voters. This was most recently demonstrated during the 2010 regular legislative session, the last under Democratic control. House members and senators, and the divided interests they represented, could not agree on an electronic bingo gambling bill to submit to the voters, so it died, even though its consideration had occupied most of the legislators' time during the session. (There were other reasons as well, as noted in chapter 4, dealing with corruption.)

Legislative Lobbying

Aspirants for the legislature learn quickly how important interest groups are in the state. In the first place, unless they are independently wealthy, they will need to have access to a lot of money if they are to mount campaigns that have a fair chance of success. The main source of funds, aside from affluent friends they may have, has been interest groups, frequently working through PACs (political action committees).[11]

This situation has changed somewhat. In the 2010 campaigns the state Republican Party leadership assumed a large (and ultimately successful) role in financing legislative races. They collected needed funds from wealthy donors and then spent them, mostly on behalf of the nonincumbent candidates they had recruited, with the vendors of campaign services.

Interest groups are, of course, also influential *after* the election. In late 2010, newly installed members of the Republican-dominated legislature were urged by party leaders to go ahead and designate those who would hold key legislative positions (well in advance of the January organizational session). The reasoning was that the longer these decisions were delayed, the more subject to interest group influence the newly elected or reelected legislators would become.

Groups regularly sponsor lobby days at the Alabama State House on which they ask group members to come en masse to Montgomery to lobby legislators on their behalf. "Higher Education Day" brings college and university administrators, faculty, and students to the capital in large numbers annually.[12]

Coalitions

Even a large group like the AEA at times needs assistance from other groups. During the controversy over charter schools that began in 2010, for example, AEA worked in coalition with associations of school boards and administrators—entities with which they are frequently at odds. Groups lacking legitimacy will find it difficult to form coalitions with other groups, which fear guilt by association.

Some companies, most notably Alabama Power, a part of the vast Southern Company, are so strong that they operate and lobby mostly on an independent basis. They work with business-friendly organizations, but alone have so much clout and so many resources that they don't need a group like BCA to be able to exercise influence. When ExxonMobil had plans to construct an LNG (liquefied natural gas) facility in Alabama in 2003, it did its own lobbying among politicians whose approval was needed to make the plant a reality.[13]

Other Techniques for Other Arenas

The legislature and the governor are not the only targets of interest group influence. Groups also attempt to sway the decisions bureaucrats and judges make. They will try as well to affect broader public opinion during the decision-making processes of the legislature, governor, and other officials. If there is to be a public referendum, groups will definitely seek to influence its outcome to accord with group preferences.

Important Interests in Alabama Politics

We have already had occasion to mention some of the most important associations in contemporary Alabama politics, but their significance (and that of others as well) warrants further emphasis.

Education and Other Public Employees

The Alabama Education Association (AEA), to which reference has been made frequently, is most often identified in the media as the teachers' union. It does primarily represent the interests of teachers and other education employees, especially at the K–12 level. Since Alabama law does not permit an organization of public employees to function as a union would in the private sector (for example, negotiating conditions of employment), the AEA works mostly through the legislature and administrative agencies to secure its goals.[14]

A writer for *Education Week* spoke of "the unusual relationship between politics and education that exists in Alabama."[15] To try to approximate the influence of AEA, Alabama's institutions of higher education started raising money to donate to friendly candidates in political campaigns as well as to maintain a continuing lobbying presence in Montgomery, mostly through the Higher Education Partnership.

AEA's A-Vote was the first political action committee created by an interest group in Alabama. Funds spent by A-Vote and other PACs to whom funds were transferred would total in the million-dollar range for a particular election cycle. The Alabama State Employees Association is the primary representative for noneducation employees who work in some aspect of state government.

Labor

Especially in the 1940s, genuine trade unions were politically strong in Alabama, and they helped elect progressive Democratic politicians like Governor James E. Folsom in 1946. Aspiring candidates who were sympathetic to labor causes sought the endorsement of labor political action groups like the CIO's Committee on Political Education (COPE).[16] Since the enactment of the state's right-to-work law more than a half century ago (1953), however, the influence of labor as a political force has been on the decline. Right-to-work laws have also been passed in twenty-one other states where business interest groups are strong, especially in the South, but also in the Midwest and Far West (with the notable exception of California).

As in the nation at large, a much smaller percentage of the labor force belongs to unions (10 percent) than was formerly the case. Even so, Alabama has a higher percentage of its work force organized than its neighboring states.[17] Their figures are: Florida, 6.3 percent; Mississippi, 5 percent; Tennessee, 4.6 percent; and Georgia, 3.9 percent. Private sector trade unions in Alabama continue to make endorsements in political campaigns, but they are usually not decisive in terms of producing winners and losers.

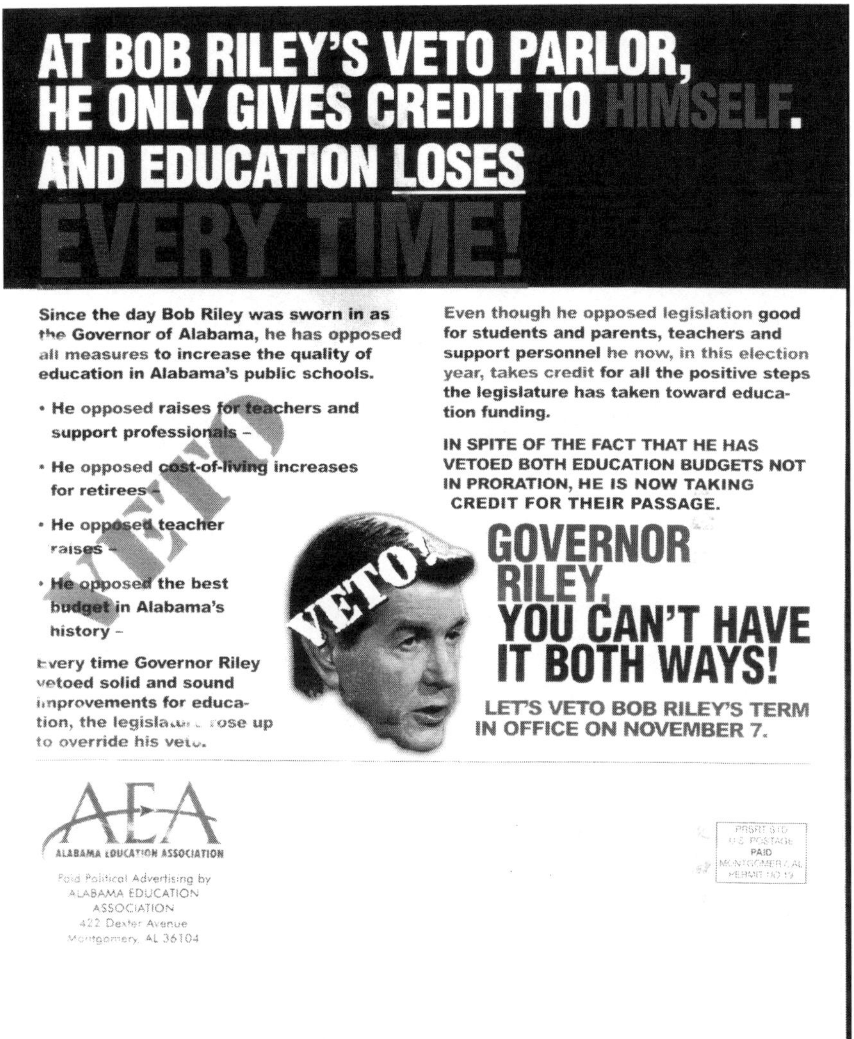

7.1. AEA mass mailing, political lobbying, 2006. From the William H. Stewart collection

Professions

Every professional group has its own most important interest group. For example, lawyers have the Alabama Bar Association. It is claimed that the unified bar group was the "pioneer experiment of its kind" and that other states patterned their bar associations after the 1923 legislative act that established Alabama's.[18] Like many other groups, the Alabama Bar Association is affiliated with a national group, the American Bar Association. But lawyers are not monolithic politically.

The Alabama Association for Justice, for example, represents the group of attorneys most frequently identified as trial lawyers (or *plaintiff's* trial lawyers). Their counterpart on the opposite side representing the interests of business is the Alabama Defense Lawyers Association.

Less prestigious occupational groups are also active politically. They have been especially influential in the creation of state licensing boards that regulate who can practice in Alabama and under what conditions.[19] Typically, if the regulated groups have not actually been responsible for the origin of these regulatory units, they will seek to capture them and shape their actions in the directions preferred by the interest groups—most frequently to discourage competition by other groups whose members perform similar functions.

Agriculture

A century ago Alabama was overwhelmingly a rural state. Only one citizen out of eight lived in an urban area. Much of its political history involves struggles by both plantation owners and small farmers to improve their economic fortunes. ALFA (the insurance arm of the Alabama Farmers Federation) is easily the most important general farm group, but almost every agricultural interest has its own promotional association (all kinds of fruits and vegetables, cotton, corn, and such).

Business

Of all the interests mentioned thus far, business is the most important in contemporary Alabama politics. The BCA, Business Council of Alabama, mentioned above, bills itself as "a nonpartisan statewide association that represents more than 4,000 member companies and 750,000 working Alabamians."[20]

Obviously, BCA cannot rationally claim that all of the people represented in its membership agree with its policy positions, but it is a powerful force in the legislature and elsewhere in Alabama government. The BCA is closely linked with the Chamber of Commerce Association of Alabama, composed of 126 local chambers that, in turn, count almost 60,000 businesses among their members. The Alabama Retail Association is another group that is identified as an element of the "GOP business establishment" (despite previous claims of nonpartisanship).[21] In election campaigns it works primarily through the Alabama Retail PAC. These and other groups are given substantial credit for the election of Bob Riley as governor both in 2002 and 2006.

Another very active business group is the Alabama Bankers Association. According to its website, the ABA has established its ALABPAC to provide its "member banks and bankers concerned with our industry's future a means for involvement and influence in Alabama politics."[22] The dominance of business groups is inversely related to that of consumers. Research in the 1980s showed that, among the states, Alabama and West Virginia had the lowest scores in terms of responsiveness to consumer interests.[23]

Civil Rights

Much of Alabama's political history from the middle years of the twentieth century to its conclusion was influenced by the activities of civil rights groups, especially the Southern Christian Leadership Conference. We discussed the SCLC and other groups composed primarily of African American Alabamians in chapter 5. Direct-action campaigns were frequently used by civil rights groups a half century ago, and they are still occasionally revived. For example, when Governor Bob Riley was working to close electronic bingo casinos in 2011, their employees, mostly African American, conducted mass rallies in Montgomery that were reminiscent of those held during the civil rights era of the 1960s. Mostly, however, the Alabama Democratic Conference and the Alabama New South Coalition represent the interests of blacks.

Although Alabama's population is still divided largely between black and white, as we saw in chapter 1, there are increasing numbers of Hispanics. They maintain a political presence through the Hispanic Interest Coalition of Alabama and keep members informed with the publication of the *Hispanic y Latino News*. Hispanics have not as yet been able to exercise significant political power in Alabama, however. Most undocumented immigrants are reluctant to be conspicuous participants. Hispanics have been most visible recently in demonstrating against the immigration legislation passed in 2011. Their principal allies in these protests have been leaders of mainline Christian churches, especially Catholic and United Methodist.

Native Americans were drawn into the political process a few years ago when the issue of gambling initially dominated the political agenda. Casinos are operated on Indian reservations, as noted in chapter 4, and the Alabama-Coushatta and Tigua tribes have worked in the manner of other interest groups to promote the profitability of their gambling enterprises.

Religion

Conservative religious groups mobilized to defeat the Don Siegelman lottery amendment (also a topic of chapter 4) in 1999 to an extent not seen since the days of Prohibition when churches, especially Protestant denominations, were even more politicized than they are now.

The Alabama Citizens Action Program (or ALCAP) and the Christian Coalition of Alabama, elements of the previously identified Christian right, are currently active religiously oriented groups. While John Giles, a prominent Montgomery political insider, still headed the Christian Coalition, it was one of Montgomery's more influential interest groups. After his departure, however, its influence subsided considerably.

Other Interests

A relatively new category of interest group, one representing crime victims' rights, has been active in Alabama recently. The leading group is Victims of Crime and Leniency (VOCAL). As noted in chapter 3, VOCAL is one of the strongest defenders of Alabama's practice of capital punishment. Primary credit for the formation of these groups in the states (and nationally) is given to law enforcement personnel.[24]

There are also groups that are not as influential as organizations seeking to improve the economic condition of their own members but that do generate publicity on behalf of what they believe to be good causes. Occasionally, with the assistance of the media, they may achieve some of their objectives. VOICES for Alabama's Children, for example, identifies itself as "a nonpartisan, nonprofit organization committed to improving child well-being in the state."[25] A group with a broader focus, Alabama Arise, says its "goal is simple, if ambitious: to speak to the Alabama Legislature."[26] Alabama Arise mostly consists of other groups, especially churches and civic organizations that are trying to improve the lot of the poor of all ages in Alabama. One ongoing effort has been to repeal the state sales tax on groceries.

Conservation interest groups have been on the scene for many years. The largest of these is the Alabama Wildlife Federation, which dates back to 1935. Groups focused on protecting the environment (which would be aspects of the green movement) are more recent. Specific environmental groups include the Alabama League of Environmental Action Voters, the Sierra Club (and subgroups such as the Cahaba Group within the larger club), and an assortment of river-keeper and bay-keeper associations.

Think tanks, especially the Public Affairs Research Council of Alabama (PARCA) and the Alabama Policy Institute (API) are sources of ideas for new public policies. Research has shown a recent trend of these officially nonpartisan entities to become more partisan.[27] The Alabama Policy Institute definitely appeals overwhelmingly to the Republican Party, and the growth in its influence has coincided with this party's advancement in recent Alabama politics. In 2014 the head of the API, Gary Palmer, was elected on the Republican ticket as a member of the US House of Representatives.

Illustrative of ad hoc groups that are formed for a particular purpose and then may disband is the Rescue the PACT group, whose title indicates its mission of protecting the Prepaid Affordable College Tuition Program created in 1990 but which was forced temporarily to suspend new enrollments in 2009.

Interest Groups and Political Parties

Interest groups are to be distinguished from political parties. Interest groups typically do not officially run candidates for public office, although (as we are seeing frequently here) they do take an active interest in political campaigns—most often expressed monetarily. Some, like the AEA, have been very closely associated with the Democratic Party, while others, like the BCA—the Business Council of Alabama—are identified as quasi-components of the Republican Party. The prefix "quasi" is appropriate because they sometimes endorse Democratic candidates, as was true in 2010 when the BCA threw its support to the (unsuccessful) reelection effort of Lieutenant Governor Jim Folsom Jr. As is true in many other states, in Alabama businesses have demonstrated an impressive ability to mobilize on behalf of their public policy preferences.

Still, interest groups have a narrower focus than political parties. Some are single-issue groups (for example, abortion) while others have a multiplicity of concerns (as the BCA does). No interest group, however, has the diversity of issues it takes positions on as either the Republican or Democratic Party. Further, even with the Alabama Democratic Party's great loss of identifiers in recent years, it is still much larger than any interest group.

Some interest groups are strong enough to "warn" political parties if they appear to be deviating too much from the positions the groups expect them to take on political issues. ALFA, for example, in 2010 cautioned Republicans that if they took positions on insurance that went contrary to ALFA views (it is one of Alabama's largest insurance companies), they risked losing the organization's political support.[28] The recent growth in Republican political power in Alabama may, however, tilt the locus of power slightly more toward elected officials and political appointees while decreasing the power exercised in the past by some interest groups such as ALFA. It is too early to tell if this informal regulation of interest group influence will actually occur over the long term.

Regulation of Interest Groups

Interest groups are not subject to a lot of regulation in Alabama. There are, however, several requirements that organized interest groups in Alabama must meet, most recently updated in late 2010. Alabama did not operate in a vacuum. There was a general movement in southern states, which had seen numerous public officials indicted for alleged corrupt activities. States vary in the extent to which they regulate lobbying and other interest group activities, and political scientists have been working on trying to explain the reasons for the differences.[29] Obviously, the more powerful interest groups currently are, the better they will be able to prevent unwanted restrictions on their activities.

Under the new Alabama laws, individuals must register if they receive compensation to lobby any aspect of state government, the executive and judicial as well as the legislative. In terms of lobbyist entertainment, there are now eighteen hospitality rules that must be adhered to. The most debated ethics question in recent years, the permissibility of PAC-to-PAC transfers, which worked against transparency in campaign finance, was dealt with by forbidding such monetary shifts. In a federal case brought by the Alabama Democratic Conference, a federal judge suspended the ban on transfers to that group for its GOTV (get out the vote) activities.

The Ethics Commission was given subpoena power for the first time in the 2010 ethics legislation. As previously noted, the power of the AEA was dealt with by forbidding the deduction of dues and political contributions from employee paychecks. Further, education employees are forbidden to run for public office. All lobbyists now receive mandatory training in what they can and cannot do. The new laws are considered to be weak as regards expenditures by nonlobbyists.

Conclusion

Despite the recent dramatic growth of the Republican Party, interest groups remain very powerful in Alabama, as they have always been. As the Alabama economy and milieu generally continue to diversify, more groups are being formed regularly.

As we saw in the preceding discussion, the Republican unity following its landslide legislative victories in 2010 has tended to diminish since that time, and its members do not vote as solidly for the positions endorsed by party leaders as they initially did. In the next chapter the focus will be specifically on parties, and we may assess the importance of groups from the parties' perspective. Parties have a formal role in organizing the major institutions of government that interest groups don't. The discussion of parties and the elections in which voters choose from among the candidates presented by the parties will provide the major foundation for an examination of these institutions.

8
Political Parties

Do you consider yourself to be a member of a political party? In Alabama you are accepted as a "Democrat," "Republican," or as a member of some other party (or no party at all)—it's whatever you say. (Registering to vote is discussed in chapter 10.)

What Are Political Parties?

Political parties may be defined by different people in different ways. One respondent said that, "A political party is a group of people wanting to take hold and maintain power within government."[1] Another definition, found in a Thesaurus, described it even more simply: "an organization to gain political power."[2] If you looked it up in a third source (this one strictly in the mind of the author) it might go something like this: "A political party is an organization that collectively represents a political ideology." The first two definitions are typically more accurate as far as American parties are concerned over the long span of the nation's history.

A century ago the Alabama Democratic Party did represent a political ideology—the belief in white supremacy. Today it mostly consists of people with moderate to liberal views comparable to those of Democrats in other places. The Republican Party in modern times has been a more homogeneous group and has had a more consistent ideological core of beliefs. Even so, people identify with parties for many different reasons, and all Republicans definitely don't agree on everything. In the late years of the nineteenth century there was sharp conflict within the Republican Party between white and African American identifiers.[3] Among the white Republicans were "mountain Republicans," residents of areas such as Winston County who had opposed secession and opportunists in other areas who converted to Republicanism in hopes of enjoying patronage and other spoils of office. Bass and De Vries comment that "to be a Republican in the South [in this era] meant an opportunity to share in patronage if the party was in power in Washington, or to hobnob every four years with the leadership of a national political party at a convention."[4]

Political Party Systems

For many years, the Alabama Democratic Party was a "big tent," which included virtually all white groups except for the minority just identified. A contrasting model is desired by many Republicans today—the church model. As in a church, loyal communicants faithfully hold to a particular set of beliefs that distinguishes them from nonbelievers or members of other churches. One contemporary Republican activist, rather than celebrating, reacted negatively when the member of Congress representing his north Alabama district (Parker Griffith) changed his party affiliation from Democrat to Republican before the latter's 2010 primary. The switch was made, so he contended, simply for opportunistic reasons. "Are we going to be a bottom-line political party or are we going to be just a random aggregation of individuals?" he asked rhetorically (making it obvious what his own answer to the question would be).

A chair of the Alabama Republican Party was quoted as saying shortly after taking this job: "By golly, if you say you are a Republican, you better act like a Republican."[5] He then named a committee whose mission was to see how Democrats could be kept from voting in Republican primaries and otherwise influencing Republican decision making. Twenty-nine states and the District of Columbia, unlike Alabama, have party registration laws.

Distinguishing Political Parties from Interest Groups

In chapter 7 we discussed interest groups and saw how a large number of very diverse and specialized associations have been organized to influence public policies. As we found in the previous chapter, interest groups typically have a narrow range of concerns and are constantly struggling for political advantage with other groups. Even though they lack the cohesiveness of European parties, American parties—including their Alabama affiliates—still have enough unity to bring together a larger number of people for the purpose of organizing government than would be possible for any interest group.

The Historical Background of Parties in Alabama

Parties, even if not in their current, more mature, form, have been evident in Alabama politics since the earliest days of statehood. These were for the most part not formally organized parties but factions composed of settlers who had come from other states such as Georgia, Virginia, and North and South Carolina.[6]

Reconstruction

With the defeat of the southern states in the Civil War, the Democratic Party was temporarily rendered impotent, and most political battles during Reconstruction were fought between factions of the Republican Party. Alabama Republicans held their first convention in Montgomery on June 4–5, 1867. African Americans were strongly represented. In the 1868–69 session of the US Congress, Alabama's delegation was all Republican. It was split between the "black and tan" and "lily white" factions, however.[7]

White Supremacist Democrats

As the Democratic Party grew stronger in the late nineteenth century and early twentieth, and less fearful of federal intervention on behalf of former slaves, they made their white supremacist sentiments increasingly clear. Party leaders did this by placing a crowing rooster at the top of the Democratic ballot, accompanied by the motto: "White Supremacy for the Right." These identifying marks were removed only in 1966 when the Democratic donkey replaced the rooster and the racist slogan was deleted. In the 2012 general election Democrats substituted "Alabama Democrats" in block letters for the donkey.

For about a century, Alabama was grouped into the category of one-party states. Anyone who wanted to be taken seriously as a political candidate (except in a few isolated localities) ran in the Democratic primary. Being successful in the Democratic primary amounted to being elected, and the vote in November was just a formality. Sometimes Alabama in this political era is referred to as a "no-party" state due to the inclusiveness of the Democratic Party (with the notable exception of African Americans).[8] The term *no-party* suggests a lack of party organization, and this is true. V. O. Key's pioneering research posited that Democratic strength was not essentially attributable to superior organization and discipline but instead was based on long-continuing anti-Republican sentiments.[9] There was tacit agreement that when Democrats were in power in Washington they would let southern whites in their states handle race relations as they saw fit. Republicans were associated with what secession apologists called the "tragic decade" of Black Reconstruction rule.

Evolution of Alabama's Modern Parties

Beginning especially in the 1950s what was referred to as split-level realignment began to occur as larger numbers of Alabamians would vote Republican in the presidential election and Democratic for lower-level offices.[10] This phenomenon occurred even more strongly in other southern states such as Virginia and Florida. Also, in the years 1920–60 more urban southerners were likely to vote Republican in the presidential election than their rural and Black Belt neighbors.[11]

Early Republican Successes

At this time the Republican Party was divided between the Old Guard and the New Guard. The Old Guard was primarily interested in patronage while, as political scientist Norman Parks pointed out, the New Guard wanted the party to actually begin putting economically conservative Republicans into public office.[12]

The first big success for the modern Alabama Republican Party came in 1964 when the GOP presidential nominee, Senator Barry Goldwater of Arizona, carried the state with 69.5 percent of the popular vote. Harold Stanley notes that the southern vote for Goldwater in 1964 represented the first time that a larger number of southerners had cast Republican instead of Democratic ballots.[13] Bernard Cosman found that the perception of Goldwater's conservatism as based primarily on race caused the urban presidential Republicanism noted above to decline outside the Deep South.[14] There, Goldwater ran strongly, however, and, in Alabama, the GOP also elected five members of Congress plus other candidates where they had bothered to recruit them. Alabama previously hadn't elected a Republican to Congress in the twentieth century.

The developments just mentioned occurred a year before the long shutout of blacks from the state electorate would end with passage of the Voting Rights Act of 1965. President Johnson's preferred slate of regular Democratic elector candidates was not even represented on the Alabama ballot in 1964. The only option mainstream Alabama Democrats had was to vote for a slate of unpledged electors who might, in the unlikely event Johnson won the state, vote for him when electoral votes were cast in December. Ironically, in this same momentous year when President Johnson signed the Civil Rights Act, ultraconservatives seized control of Republican Party organizations throughout the South from Eisenhower-oriented moderates, and, according to Bass and De Vries, "blacks were virtually read out of the party."[15]

Causes of Democratic Decline

As long as George Wallace commanded state politics, Alabama was unable to mature politically. He was the presidential candidate of a third party in 1968 but mostly stuck with the Democratic Party both at home and in his national campaigning. Alabama elected its first Republican to a statewide office in 1980 (two years before Wallace was elected to his fourth and final term). He was Admiral Jeremiah Denton, a heroic figure from the Vietnam War, when he suffered for many years as a POW. At the same time Denton was winning a US Senate seat, Ronald Reagan was taking the state's presidential electoral votes away from incumbent Democratic presidential candidate Jimmy Carter, who had won them four years earlier (the last Democratic candidate to do so). Just as Goldwater had represented a milestone as far as southern presidential voting was concerned, Reagan was a benchmark for party identification. His era was one in which many more southern whites than previously identified themselves as Republicans, not Democrats. Earl Black and Merle Black say they were willing to make this change because "Ronald Reagan's presidency legitimated the Republican party for many white southerners."[16]

The Goldwater and Reagan victories in the South were not signs that the region was proceeding unhindered in the Republican direction. In 1978, two years before Reagan was elected, the most important executive offices in Alabama, governor and attorney general, were won by men (Fob James and Charles Graddick) who had switched from Republican to Democrat, not the reverse. And, as Scher points out, the handful of Republican senators elected along with Reagan (including Alabama's Denton) were defeated by Democratic challengers after just a single term.[17]

In the 1980s state developments competed with national political changes to promote the continued demise of the Alabama Democratic Party. In the process of holding a court-ordered special reapportionment election in 1983, party leaders opted to handpick Democratic nominees instead of leaving this decision to the voters in a primary. Many longtime Democrats were outraged. An even bigger state Democratic miscalculation occurred only three years later, in 1986. In that year, Democratic gubernatorial frontrunner Charles Graddick was denied the nomination because he had encouraged Republicans to cross over and vote in his runoff against Bill Baxley despite the fact that Democratic Party rules forbade this. When a federal court ruled that the crossover ballots had depressed the influence of African American voters, the Democratic Party was ordered to hold a new primary or award the gubernatorial nomination to the second-place finisher (Baxley). The party chose the latter course, which once again angered many Democratic identifiers throughout the state.

In the 1986 general election, virtually unknown Republican Guy Hunt was elected as Alabama's first governor from that party in 112 years. Early in Hunt's second term, as we saw in chapter 4, he was prosecuted and convicted for taking money from an inaugural fund (a felony). This meant automatic expulsion from office. Once again a Democratic initiative, this one to get rid of the state's first GOP governor in the modern era, was viewed by many as a partisan conspiracy, and more damage was done to the party. In the next quadrennial election that occurred after Hunt's ouster (1994), seven Republicans were elected to statewide office. In the race for chief justice of the Alabama Supreme Court, Republican Perry Hooper Sr., narrowly edged incumbent Democratic Chief Justice Sonny Hornsby. Federal judges deliberated for nearly a year before holding that Democrats had sought to alter absentee ballot rules to assure Hornsby's reelection. Hooper had won the office.

The Turn toward Republicanism

It was in the mid-1990s, Stanley points out, that "the politically ambitious began to switch parties" in large numbers.[18] The most notable switcher was US senator Richard Shelby, who had earlier prevented Denton from serving more than six years. By 1996, a majority of southern state executive offices were occupied by Republicans. This hadn't been true since Reconstruction days. Both Alabama US Senate seats were in Republican hands, also not the case for well over a hundred years. Lamis feels that 1996 was the year in which "Alabama appears to have reached such a 'critical mass'" as would stimulate "yet more forward movement" toward being a strongly Republican state.[19]

The New Century

In 2000, state races were notable because Republicans won all contests for the chief and associate justice positions on the state Supreme Court. By 2009 Alabama was ranked by the Gallup Poll as the seventh most Republican state in the nation and ahead of all other southern states.[20] In the 2012 elections, a perennial never-elected candidate who filed for Supreme Court chief justice was initially the party's only statewide candidate except for Lucy Baxley, who was running for another term as Public Service Commission president. (The judicial candidate was later disqualified for injudicious statements and replaced by one with many more credentials.)

When he had affixed his signature to the Civil Rights Act in 1964, President Lyndon Johnson is reputed to have commented that his Democratic Party had "lost the South for a generation."[21] So far his prophecy has proven

8.1. Mass mailing from Alabama Republican Party for Tuscaloosa candidates from the November 2006 election. From the William H. Stewart collection

to be correct. In the 2008 presidential election, white voters in the neighboring states of Alabama and Mississippi supported Republican John McCain at an estimated rate of 90 percent. White Mississippians continued their disdain for Barack Obama by about the same percentage in 2012, while Obama's percentage of white Alabamians' votes rose by a modest 6 percentage points in his race against Mitt Romney.

The southern strategy of Johnson's successor, Richard Nixon, had involved both exploitation of white opposition to federal racial integration initiatives and publicizing liberal Democratic stances on a variety of other domestic issues. Evangelicals had not previously taken leading roles as Alabama continued its shift toward being a primarily Republican state. Economically motivated conservatives had taken most Republican initiatives.

The Democratic Response

Democrats in Alabama in recent years typically have pursued a coalition strategy, but it has become increasingly unsuccessful. This is "identity politics." Its most important elements are left-leaning interest groups and African American voters.[22] Illustrating its lack of success was when north Alabama's Fifth District became the last part of the state to be represented by a white Democrat—Parker Griffith, who switched to Republican as he neared the end of his first (and only) term. (He lost a Republican primary bid to retain his seat.) The Tennessee Valley had been represented by a Democrat since the end of Reconstruction. Before his switch, Griffith was identified as a "Blue Dog," a congressional Democrat who was generally more conservative than the majority of his fellow Democrats in the US House of Representatives. Succeeded by Republican Martha Roby, Bobby Bright also was elected as a Blue Dog Democrat in the southeast Alabama district (the Second) in 2008. However, he too served only one term before being defeated for reelection by a Republican. This district had previously been in Republican hands since the 1960s. In the 2010 midterm elections, nineteen southern House members and one senator were defeated, along with Bright, thus greatly decimating Blue Dog ranks. Only one white Democrat won a congressional election in five Deep South states. The 2012 elections produced no changes in the Alabama congressional delegation. In 2014 retiring Republican representative Spencer Bachus was succeeded by another Republican, Gary Palmer. In the Mobile area, former Republican gubernatorial aspirant Bradley Byrne replaced Republican representative Jo Bonner, who had resigned to take a position with the University of Alabama System.

Showing the nationalization of politics in Alabama, many of the Democratic constituents of Alabama's one-term Blue Dog representatives were reported to be dissatisfied with their voting patterns. Loyal Democrats in Alabama typically share more in common with Democrats elsewhere in the nation than they do Republicans. One mainstream Alabama Democrat commented critically on Facebook: "Pass the word! Bobby Bright's running on the DEMOCRATIC ticket—even if he doesn't want you to know it!" Another asked rhetorically: "And WHY are we supposed to vote for Mr. Bright? If he's ashamed to be seen with us, why should we continue dating him?"[23]

Continuing Democratic Decline

In the 2012 presidential election Republicans got the overwhelming majority of white votes (84 percent according to exit polling) in the Romney-Obama race, while Democrats were receiving 95 percent of ballots cast by blacks.[24] African American Alabamians have come full circle in Alabama politics. From being totally excluded by the Democratic Party in the Jim Crow era to finally being allowed to participate when the federal courts voided a whites only policy, they had now become its most loyal constituency.

Whites and blacks historically in Alabama have identified with different parties. When blacks could initially participate freely in Alabama politics, practically all were Republicans while native whites were overwhelmingly Democrats. Now just the opposite is true. Democrats have been unable to prevent the exit of most whites from their fold, and Republicans have been unable (and unwilling seriously to try) to construct a genuinely biracial party. When Ron Sparks was campaigning as the Democratic nominee for governor in 2010, he reminded voters: "You've got a chance to vote for a millionaire or a working man."[25] Many white working-class voters (who were also conservative in their faith) were turned off, however, by Sparks's heavy emphasis on the expansion of gambling as the answer to Alabama's economic problems.

Those who find it irrational that poor people would vote Republican are fond of quoting novelist John Grisham: "They live poor and vote rich."[26] But this argument ignores the importance of noneconomic values. According to Bartley and Graham, "many rural and lower-income whites saw themselves threatened more by social change than by economic exploitation."[27] Southern whites, oftener than northerners, these two scholars found, were "more likely to use their ballots in state and local politics to express personal beliefs or prejudices rather than socioeconomic self-interest."[28]

Republicans continue to use the unpopularity of the Democratic Party to maximum advantage. The successful Republican lieutenant governor candidate in Alabama in 2010, Kay Ivey, said that, "Democrats all across Alabama are running from their Party label . . . we are seeing literature touting Democratic candidates that say things like, 'an independent voice,' or 'fresh face with new ideas,' and even 'It's not about party affiliation.'"[29]

A former chair of the Republican Party stated a political fact in 2004: "When business and evangelicals get together, we're unstoppable."[30] Evangelical voters were more likely to be mobilized on the basis of "wedge issues" such as gay marriage as opposed to just economic issues.

Republican Schisms

The Republican Party in Alabama has in very recent years grown to the extent that it can afford dissent within its ranks and still be, in the former chair's words, "unstoppable." When tape recordings were played in the first gambling trials discussed in chapter 4, they were said to "hint at a world of GOP infighting and political frnemies [*sic*]—allies on the surface who say nasty thing about each other in private."[31]

Former Chief Justice Roy Moore's March 2012 winning of his party's nomination to return to the position from which he had previously been removed (confirmed in the November general election) was said by a stanch Demo-

8.2. Map of Alabama counties from the 2012 presidential election. Source: United States Election Atlas

cratic partisan, former US district attorney Doug Jones, to have "signal[ed] a change in what base of the GOP is in control of the party." Jones continued, "The corporate side of the party, the Bob Riley, Bradley Byrne, Business Council of Alabama, establishment side of the Republican Party [has] lost control to the Tea Party, values voter side of the party. It's that side right now that is dominating and they are happy with Roy Moore and they don't care what the perception of this is across the rest of the nation."[32]

Moore himself said his March 2012 victory was a defeat for "the big business wing of the Republican Party who [*sic*] has never been able to buy me or control me. They don't want me back."[33]

Regardless of what "they" want, however, Moore was back in January 2013.

GOP Demographics

Other prominent groups in the Alabama Republican Party today, besides those just mentioned, include retirees, some of whom prefer to reside where fellow senior citizens share their own partisan values. One retiree told a reporter, "I just wanted to say that I live in Hoover, Alabama."[34] The affluent

Birmingham suburb of Hoover is one of the strongest areas of Republican support in the state.

Demographically, the largest numerical loss to the Democratic Party has been white males. Paul Hubbert, at the time still executive secretary of the Democratic-oriented AEA, said: "White males are almost non-existent in the Democratic Party. Democrats, I think, have paid more attention to . . . issues affecting seniors and young people. I think white males tend to be more attuned to the economy, probably to the cultural climate, those sorts of things."[35]

In the 2012 presidential election, 84 percent of white males are believed to have supported Romney over Obama. (This was virtually the same as the figure reported for white women, 83 percent.)

Following the 2010 elections, one news story said Alabama had been painted a "deep red" as a result of the election outcomes in the state.[36] A national conservative magazine, the *Weekly Standard*, proclaimed: "The wildest dreams of Republicans have come true."[37]

With such success as the Alabama Republican Party has experienced in recent years will come growing pains. Party leaders will try to hold together a larger (and more diverse) group of followers.

Future Prospects

Alabama Republicans are in the driver's seat at present, but just like the Democrats' prior dominance, this will not continue "forever." Alabama's rural population, at present majority Republican (54 percent combining whites and blacks in the 2012 presidential election), will continue to decline. As Susan MacManus notes, all southern states except Louisiana have seen growth in foreign-born residents that exceeds the national average. While Alabama does not now have any metropolitan areas that are leaders in the acquisition of newcomers who were born in other countries, this could change in the future. Also, the phenomenon of blacks returning back to the South has been notable in Alabama already. This will increase the Democratic vote and decrease the Republican. In terms of voting on the basis of age cohorts, as older voters pass away and are succeeded by younger generations a greater affinity for the Democratic Party, especially on the basis of its social liberalism, will be demonstrated. In the 2012 presidential election, 52 percent of Alabamians age eighteen to twenty-four supported Romney. In contrast, 69 percent of those sixty-five and over did so.

MacManus observes that, "When compared with their older counterparts, younger voters in today's South are more racially/ethnically diverse, more concentrated in urban areas," and "more likely to be racially tolerant."[38] Finally, "the influx of more highly educated, moderate-to-liberal, mostly white retirees from the Northeast and Midwest" will, over the long haul, reduce "the political clout of older, native-born, more conservative southern white voters," even if not at present, in Alabama.[39]

Party Organization

Key, surveying the southern political scene in the late 1940s, said the Republican Party was in many places so weak it "scarcely deserved the name of party."[40] In fact, he found it to be a genuine party in only three states—North Carolina, Tennessee, and Virginia. The situation is much different today.

Party Leadership

Both the Alabama Republican and Democratic parties have permanent headquarters in Montgomery, the state's capital city. These facilities are open continuously and operated by small staffs. Their operations expand during campaign cycles with the addition of volunteers.

In 2005, Twinkle Andress Cavanaugh was elected chair of the Alabama Republican Party by the party's executive committee. Informally, she was the choice of the titular head of the party, Republican governor Bob Riley. Typically, the party chair serves for a few years. If the party does especially poorly, as the Democrats did in 2010, a change will likely come. Mark Kennedy, the son-in-law of the late governor George Wallace, was named the new Democratic chair on January 29, 2011. Even though an African American chair could have easily been selected for this position, the black vice-chair, Joe Reed, said he was "under no illusion. White Democrats want to hear from a white leader."[41]

The Republican Party also got a new chair after the 2010 elections when the previous chair, state representative Mike Hubbard, became speaker of the Alabama House of Representatives. He was succeeded by a former legislator, Bill Armistead, who was the choice of the new Republican governor, Robert Bentley.

Party chair is not a full-time job. The supervising boss at the headquarters is the executive director. He or she would be selected by the party chair and governor (in the case of the in-power party). As will be noted in chapter 10, "Elections," both parties will use the services of attorneys who are committed party members. In a litigious society many controversies involving the parties end up in court. Volunteers for the parties are frequently recruited through social network websites. The College Democrats and College Republicans are also good sources.

The Party Network

In addition to chapters of the College Democrats and College Republicans, the party network includes women's groups such as the Alabama Federation of Republican Women and, at the local level, the Madison County Democratic Women, to give another example. There are also party organizations outside the regular party framework such as the West Alabama Republican Assembly, which identifies itself as being composed of "Reagan Republicans."[42] In March 2011, a new Republican group, Alabama 2014, was formed to help the party hold on to its 2010 legislative gains as well as "to make sure true Republicans are elected in the primary."[43] They were especially interested in the credentials of Democrats hoping to run as Republicans ("RINOS" or Republicans in Name Only) in order to improve their chances of winning.

It is unlikely that Republican leaders will have any more success in preventing people with widely varying beliefs from running as Republicans if they so choose than was the case when Democrats dominated state government. In the mid-twentieth century the Democratic Party attempted to achieve a semblance of party unity by putting an oath (a "loyalty oath") on its ballots pledging voters to support primary winners in the general election, but this was unenforceable.

Patronage

The awarding of the perks that come with holding office is one of the oldest means of instilling party loyalty. Even though it is not as important as it used to be, it can still be a divisive issue.

Following the inauguration of President Barack Obama in 2009 there was a struggle between Alabama's ranking Democratic US House member, Artur Davis, and the regular Democratic Party organization. The party chair (Joe Turnham) established a committee to recommend loyal Democrats to the president when he had political appointments to make while Representative Davis formed his own committee. It was composed mostly of retired judges and law school deans while the party committee was made up mostly of party officials and activists. Davis said the party group was "acting presumptuously" and that it "had no legitimacy."[44] This intraparty conflict would later work against Davis succeeding in his bid for the Democratic gubernatorial nomination. On the Republican side, when the new legislative leadership hired two Democrats to fill patronage positions after the 2010 elections, activist Republicans complained bitterly, and they were forced into declining the jobs.

Democratic Rebuilding

Both loyal Democrats and more neutral observers have offered their opinions on what the party can do—if anything—to reverse the dramatic declines noted in the preceding pages.

"A Vision for Our State"

Natalie Davis, both a political scientist and a former Democratic US Senate candidate, said that her party "ha[d] tired leadership and it offers voters nothing that speaks to their daily concerns and needs." She continued: "Until the leadership of the party steps aside or is forced out, the Alabama Democratic Party exists in name only." She further predicted that "the Alabama Democratic Party [was] dead, at least for a number of election cycles[,] as a true competitive party."[45] Davis said that, regardless, her party needed to develop "a vision for our state." "Getting serious," she continued, "means crafting a message which reclaims the rural white vote, reminds seniors of the traditional responsiveness of the Democratic Party to them, and attracts compelling candidates who want to run as Democrats."[46]

Party Principles

Even the new post-2010 chair of the Alabama Democratic Party, former state Supreme Court Justice Kennedy, remarked that he could identify Republican principles, but not those of his own party because the opposition had done "a good job of delivering its message to voters." His own party, he believed, had "neither developed a cohesive message nor learned to deliver it in memorable sound bites."[47] Kennedy planned to change this by adding media experts to the Democratic staff, using social media more extensively, and reaching out to college students who, like their elders, were now preponderantly identifying as Republicans rather than as Democrats.

No Separation

The strategy Natalie Davis suggested rules out an unrealistic attempt to separate state and national parties. The outgoing chair of the Alabama Democratic Party, Joe Turnham, lamented that, "You used to be able to separate

Alabama Democrats from national Democrats, but with the advent of cable TV and the Internet, it's hard to separate them."[48] The continued Democratic success following the Goldwater-Republican sweep in 1964 is attributable to the fact that at least for a few decades afterward it *was* still possible for voters to make a distinction between Alabama partisans and their fellow Democrats nationally. It was surprising in 2012 when the block letters "Alabama Democrats" were substituted for the national Democratic symbol, the donkey, on the November general election ballot. Democratic leaders in the state were not verbally attempting to separate Alabama Democrats from their fellow partisans elsewhere. As of November 7, 2012, Republicans filled all thirty-one Alabama statewide offices. (This was the date on which the last Democrat, Public Service Commission president Lucy Baxley relinquished her position to associate commissioner Twinkle Cavanaugh who had defeated her in the previous day's voting.)

Conclusion

Total Democratic despair over their current position in Alabama politics is unwarranted. Despite Republican supermajority rule, they do not have the almost complete control that Democrats had during the Jim Crow era. Also, at the state level, the 2012 and subsequent legislative sessions showed that Republicans were no longer able to operate collectively with machinelike precision. (This subject will be discussed more fully in chapter 11.)

The majority-minority districts continue, as do majority white counties where Democrats still dominate courthouse offices. In west Alabama, for example, in 2010, in three counties (one majority white and two majority black) there were no Democrat versus Republican races. Democrats captured every local office on the ballot.

County courthouses have been identified as "the Democrats' last stronghold in Alabama."[49] In an e-mail aimed at eliciting generous financial contributions, the party told potential donors that Democratic courthouse control was "the only thing standing in the way of complete Republican dominance in Alabama."[50] "Complete Republican dominance" was not achieved in the 2012 elections. In a post-2012 election statement, Democratic Party Chair Kennedy noted that, "Alabama Democrats still maintain a majority of local offices in Alabama."[51] In the state's largest county, Jefferson (Birmingham), even though it is not black majority, Democrats won every contested local race.

Alabama voters, like voters elsewhere, generally have no well-developed ideologies and are not likely to follow rigidly ideological leadership. Yet Alabama politics has matured to the extent that neither party can be a sufficiently big tent that it can successfully appeal in their campaigns over the long term to all groups in the society.

We now turn specifically to the subject of political campaigns. In the discussion that follows we will want to see how present-day Alabama electioneering differs from voter appeals of former times. We may find some aspects of continuity, however. There is valuable research both from Alabama and southwide perspectives that we can bring to bear on this subject.

9
Campaigns

How do politicians seek to persuade enough voters to cast their ballots for them so that they can win elections? The settings in which Alabama political campaigns are waged are in most respects markedly different from those of former times.

Traditional Southern Campaigns

Political scientist Richard Scher has observed that the "demagogue" model of political candidacy "may represent, in the popular mind, the stereotypical southern politician: portly, sweating, wearing red galluses and a broad-brimmed Panama the demagogue was noted for his oratorical skills and his ability to mesmerize his audience as he spoke, whether from a stump in a hot, dusty courthouse square or in a more formal setting. Here could be found the 'essence' of southern gothic politics—fire and brimstone oratory, rabble-rousing, fighting words, an emotionally charged message."[1]

Campaigns Alabama Style

Bartley and Graham point to the "magnetic appeal" that "Big Jim" Folsom had beginning in the 1940s for "voters residing in the backwoods." They appreciated his "splendid ability to bait the metropolitan newspapers, millionaires, Big Mules, and monopolies."[2] W. J. Cash, in the classic *The Mind of the South*, viewed the demagogic politicians as "the natural expression of the people who elected them and who looked to politics as a theater 'for the play of the purely personal, the purely romantic, and the purely hedonistic.'"[3] Any serious discussion of economic and social issues was conspicuous by its absence.

9.1. Governor Don Siegelman. From the William H. Stewart collection

Why the Change?

In sharp contrast to the traditional demagogue, Scher notes, the business-person, the modal high-level southern politician of today, whether campaigning for or in office, is "quiet and low key."[4] This type of campaign was always likely to be preferred by "the more genteel middle and upper classes" who were "appalled at the vulgarities and incivilities of the Demagogue."[5] In time, with "increasing education and sophistication of the population, increasing urbanization and industrialization, [and] a more affluent economy," the more subdued style came to be preferred by the electorate generally. Also, since race baiting and demagoguery had been closely linked for most (excluding Jim Folsom), black enfranchisement meant the end of both phenomena. Finally, Scher points out that "the coolness and detachment of television . . . discourage the flamboyant style of the older Demagogue."[6] Missing from cur-

9.2. Albert Brewer for Governor pamphlet, 1970. From the William H. Stewart collection

rent campaigns in Alabama besides demagogic speeches are what Scher called "hokey activities, like the hillbilly bands 'Big Jim' Folsom used in his gubernatorial campaigns."[7] Rather than rely on PACs (which did not exist in their present form), Folsom passed the suds bucket to collect donations from those who attended the multiple rallies he held every day throughout the state.

Presidential Campaigns

As we saw in chapter 8, Alabama was formerly a part of what was the Democratic Solid South in the period after Reconstruction up to 1964 when Alabama voted for Republican Barry Goldwater. (In 1948 the state had cast its electoral vote for the Dixiecrat candidate, Strom Thurmond.)

Reliably Republican

Presidential elections were unexciting in the Solid South era just as they are now when Alabama is one of the most reliably Republican states in the Union. Due to its relatively small number of electoral votes (nine), Alabama would not usually expect to be a crucial state in presidential elections. And,

9.3. George Wallace for Governor pamphlet, 1966. From the William H. Stewart collection

since it is noncompetitive, Alabama voters would normally not see presidential campaigning but for TV or their computer screens. One political junkie lamented: "There is no presidential campaign in Alabama."[8] An Alabama-based political scientist said: "How would [you] know there is a presidential election in Alabama? Have you seen any ads on TV, do you see a lot of bumper stickers? Alabama has been written off by the campaigns."[9]

Presidential Primaries

Alabama is a possibility for major campaigning in the presidential primary stage of the nomination process. In 2008 all of the Democratic and Republican presidential aspirants campaigned in the state prior to its primary on Super Tuesday (February 5, 2008). The legislature had moved the presidential primary to a prime spot on the calendar, confident that the state would be able to have a somewhat more influential role in the selection process. The state economy was fairly robust before the onset of the Great Recession, so funds were available to finance the change.

On primary day in 2008, 1.1 million voters, or about 40 percent of those registered, participated. Due to the closeness of the race between Senators

9.4. James E. (Big Jim) Folsom for Governor mailing, 1962. From the William H. Stewart collection

Barack Obama and Hillary Clinton, Obama's win in Alabama did help to produce his ultimate victory in Denver. As we saw in chapter 3, in the Republican race in 2012, the three candidates remaining at the time of the Alabama presidential primary on March 13—Mitt Romney, Rick Santorum, and Newt Gingrich—each campaigned in Alabama prior to the day the voters went to the polls. As they did in 2008 when they gave more of their votes to former Arkansas governor Mike Huckabee, in 2012 Alabama Republicans preferred the candidate who was perceived as socially most conservative, Rick Santorum. Extensive campaigning also occurred before the party's March 1, 2016, presidential primary.

The Art and Science of Campaigns

Campaigns require candidates, and what causes some people to run while most others have absolutely no interest in doing so warrants consideration.

Sources of Candidates

As the Republican Party has developed in Alabama in recent years, state party leaders have enlisted men and women to run, especially for legislative seats. Large interest groups such as AEA also have recruited mostly Democratic candidates and then supplied them generously with the financial and technical resources needed to wage winning campaigns.

In Key's time, in sharp contrast, "The entire [campaign] machinery [was] in the counties and in the precincts [and had to] be set up anew for each primary."[10] Also characteristic of the era of one-party democracy in Alabama was a candidate-centered campaign politics. It was a given that all credible candidates would run under the rooster (the party symbol), but the party played little or no role in helping candidates enhance their electoral chances. Members of the party's chief policy-making body, the Democratic Executive Committee, were also elected in the primary. Candidates for this group were slated by the leaders of the "loyalist" and "states' rights" factions, but alliance with one or the other faction was generally not significant in candidacies for state elected offices.

Running Alone—and Behind

In one-party Alabama, Key found coordinated campaigns to be rare. "Joint campaigns [were] not feasible in an atomistic individual politics," he explained. Thus, "Campaigns for governor steer[ed] scrupulously clear of formal connections with other state races and races for Federal and local offices."[11] In the Republican-dominant Alabama of today joint campaigning occurs frequently.

The reasons why some people enter campaigns are hard to discern. For example, in 2010, four white Republicans sought their party's nomination in the Seventh Congressional District that was specifically constructed to strongly encourage (if not actually to guarantee) the inclusion of an African American in Alabama's US House delegation. All of the Republican candidates combined did not draw as many votes as the last-place finisher in the Democratic primary, which also had four entries. At the time qualifying was in progress for the spring 2012 primaries and no Democrat had turned in papers to run for state Supreme Court chief justice, a former statewide candidate, James Anderson, predicted "someone will qualify, but I hope it's not just a throwaway candidate."[12] Unfortunately for his party, that is exactly what happened when a perennially unsuccessful candidate secured the Democratic nomination for the state's highest judicial position unopposed. This candidate was later disqualified for making inflammatory social network statements, and a Jefferson County circuit judge, Robert Vance, was named to run against Republican nominee Roy Moore. (Moore defeated Vance by 52–48 percent.)

Campaign Variables

Here are personal attributes that may make some candidacies potentially more successful than others. They are not offered as advice. This list, grounded in southern politics research, refers primarily to a candidate's individual qualities. Considerations of party and constituency are relevant, of course, but many of these have already been presented in chapter 8 or will be discussed in chapter 10. Candidates of unusual ability may sometimes be able to overcome unfavorable circumstances in these categories, however:

(1) Candidate's commitment—Running for high elective office is not a casual affair or cannot be if the candidate is to have a hope of being successful. When former governor and lieutenant governor Jim Folsom Jr., explained his decision not to run for governor in 2010, he said: "It has to be a decision where you feel like you're fully committed to running, you have the fire in the belly. To do less, you would be . . . [doing] a disservice to your supporters."[13]

(2) Candidate's appearance—Different political eras have different preferences. In 2010 Democratic gubernatorial aspirant Ron Sparks shaved off the moustache he had worn for years—no candidate with facial hair had won the governorship in nearly one hundred years.

(3) Candidate's Alabama ties—Unlike New York, there is no precedent in state politics for someone to be chosen for high office who is not either an Alabama native or who has not lived in the state for most of his or her adult life. Census figures for 2010 as tabulated by *Governing* magazine indicated that approximately three-fourths of those who live in Alabama are

natives of the state. This computation placed Alabama in the top ten of states with a preponderance of native-born residents.[14]

(4) Candidate's marital status—Probing questions in this area are generally not asked of candidates, but the higher the office one seeks the more marital status seems to matter. Most candidates like to have family pictures on their campaign material. Neither Democratic candidate was able to do this in 2010, however, since Ron Sparks was divorced and Artur Davis had only recently married.

(5) Candidate's education—If a candidate has been to college out of state this will be omitted or de-emphasized on campaign materials. Also, Alabama has no tradition of electing the "overeducated" (master's or PhD degrees).

(6) Candidate's speaking ability—Even though political rallies and the stump speeches of the old southern politics are relics of the past, the candidate for state office will be invited to participate in forums sponsored by party, interest, and civic groups. Also, the candidate will be asked to appear on talk and other radio programs and to field a variety of questions from sometimes-hostile listeners.

(7) What a candidate says—Not only speaking ability but what is said (or not said) is important. The candidate can never be sure that what she says is not being recorded or otherwise taken down. In the 2010 Republican gubernatorial primary campaign, candidate Tim James made an offhand, joking comment about possibly firing University of Alabama football coach Nick Saban or reducing his salary that some observers felt cost him a runoff position—the difference between his vote and that of Robert Bentley (who ultimately became governor) was only a few hundred votes. Also, the candidate should say "we" instead of "I" when discussing the campaign. This emphasizes the collective nature of any winning electioneering effort.

(8) Candidate's ability to identify with the "average Alabamian"—One of Alabama's oldest political traditions is its disdain for elitism, and we have already pointed out how candidates exploited this. In historian Wayne Flynt's *Poor but Proud*, the author says that in Alabama's earliest days "the key to election was . . . to convince the plain folk of one's genuine claim to be a common man in a state with universal manhood suffrage."[15]

(9) Candidate's religious beliefs—As noted in chapter 3, most Alabamians are classified as conservative Christians to whom, in larger numbers than is the case in many other states, their faith is very important. They frequently vote for candidates who indicate that they have a strong religious commitment as well.

(10) Candidate's political ideology—Election to high state office will not be

feasible for otherwise highly talented men and women who are left leaning in their political beliefs. James Folsom was the last openly liberal candidate to be successful in Alabama, and his time in office ended well over half a century ago.

(11) Candidate's support for gun owners' rights—No serious candidate of either party supports additional gun control.

(12) Candidate's ability to separate himself or herself from the other candidates in the field—The winner of the 2010 Alabama gubernatorial election, Robert Bentley, wanted to be known as the doctor who wouldn't accept a paycheck until the state reached full employment (which he defined as 5.2 percent).[16] At the time he made the pledge, unemployment was in the double digits. (Well into his second term he still had not been able to accept a salary.)

(13) Candidate's ability to maintain an image of consistency on issues—One of the most frequently criticized aspects of a candidate's campaign by opponents is alleged flip-flopping. Changes in position need to be subtle and, when made, be capable of satisfying explanation. The biggest change one may have to explain in an Alabama campaign is the reason for switching parties.

(14) Candidate's ability to remain positive despite evidence that his or her campaign is not doing well.

(15) Candidate's ability to grasp onto an up-ballot candidate's (especially gubernatorial) coattails—This would apply primarily to state legislative candidates. (We will illustrate this point with a specific example from a recent campaign in chapter 10.)

(16) Candidate's ability effectively to shift strategies once his or her party nomination is secured—The electorate expands from the party base in the primary to a much larger slice of the voting population in the general election. It will still be conservative, however.

(17) Candidate's ability to lose with grace—Assuming the above tasks have not been performed successfully enough, the candidate must not be a sore loser. This would likely prevent him or her from rebounding in a subsequent election. Artur Davis, an unsuccessful gubernatorial aspirant in 2010, was widely regarded as a poor loser since he both left the state and joined the Republican Party, taking a prominent role at its 2012 national convention. (He later switched back to the Democratic Party.)

Campaign Resources

For a successful campaign, in addition to a generous amount of funds (the acquisition of which was discussed in chapter 7 but is addressed again following this section), the candidate will need to have quick access to the following, among other resources:

(1) Research on issues and his or her opposition;
(2) legal advice to ensure that all laws related to a political campaign are fully complied with. Not filing required reports in a timely manner could lead to disqualification;
(3) focus groups to gain insights on how the candidate's persona and message are coming across to representative cross sections of the voting population;
(4) polling and survey research data on how his or her message is resonating with the voters;
(5) latest methods for political involvement, including social networking;
(6) direct mail, advertising space, and time-buying expertise;
(7) travel and communication planning;
(8) mechanisms for coordinating with student groups; and
(9) an experienced campaign manager plus consultants and advisers who are capable of assisting with multiple aspects of the campaign, including development of a cohesive agenda.

Campaign Finance

To do all of these things (plus many others) and do them well it is necessary for the campaign to have ample funding. Raising needed funds will be the candidate's most time-consuming activity unless the party does it for him or her as the Republican Party did, especially for nonincumbent legislative candidates, in 2010.

How Much Is Enough?

Some of the variables that will influence how much money will be needed include the extent to which the candidate is known statewide, whether he or she is an incumbent or is facing an incumbent, and the current cost of the things for which money will need to be spent. One former Democratic candidate said that "candidates for the Legislature will have more difficulty raising money because affluent people [would] rather give to races for governor and Supreme Court, for example."[17] Thus the Republican approach was especially helpful to House and Senate candidates in 2010.

Campaign expenditures have increased dramatically in recent years—most dramatically, of course, in general elections. Larry Sabato found that Wallace had spent $930,000 in his successful 1970 Democratic gubernatorial primary campaign but only $96,000 in the general election.[18] The statewide candidate of today will need to raise the very large contributions his or her campaign will require through both personal visits and telephone conversations. Since the focus here is primarily on statewide campaigns, it is assumed (something that will not always be the case) that the candidate has previously run at the substate level and has begun to build a foundation of support among Alabama's political elites, including corporate executives.

Political allies developed over a period of years within the party will be helpful in this. It has been accurately stated that, "The search for campaign cash makes 'dialing for dollars' one of the most time-intensive parts of any political campaign."[19]

Why and How People Give

Prior to beginning intense fund-raising, the candidate will need to have studied why people give and tap into these motivations. Probably the most important thing that can be communicated by the candidate to potential donors is the access that they have to him or her. They will have this regardless of whether a contribution is made or not. During the first set of gambling corruption trials in the summer of 2011, an attorney for one of the defendants said that his client made contributions only to those candidates who supported his favored causes: "You don't support people who don't support you."[20] (No defendant was convicted in either the first or second set of trials—the latter in February–March 2012.)

The candidate will host a series of fund-raisers around the state. Invitations will be sent to people previously identified as party supporters (at least some of the time) and affluent enough to make contributions of more than just a few dollars. Unless the candidate personally knows national party VIPs and can get them to make appearances in the state on the campaign's behalf, he or she will have to depend on the party to share funds raised on occasions when such appearances are made. In the spring of 2010 an appearance by Karl Rove raised approximately $40,000 for the Alabama Republican Party. The candidate may have friends and contacts in the opposition party who will donate to him or her in some legal fashion without attracting publicity. In the 2010 race for attorney general a fund-raiser for incumbent Republican Troy King (who lost out in the primary) had "indirect Democratic fingerprints."[21]

Some of the legitimate areas of campaign expenditure have been identified. Others aren't appropriate. The candidate, for example, should not pay for endorsements. In 2010 it was claimed that Democrat turned Republican US representative Parker Griffith had paid for an endorsement from a group known as the Minutemen. Seeking money in return for an endorsement is known as "shopping" an endorsement. Endorsements so obtained, when exposed, do a campaign serious harm.

It is illegal to commingle funds collected for federal and state races. Prior to his successful race for governor, then-US representative Bob Riley was reported to have given all of the campaign contributions he had collected while campaigning for and serving as a member of Congress to a campaign committee for Republican gubernatorial candidates. This committee then donated these funds to the Riley gubernatorial campaign.[22] There is no Alabama law that regulates how much money a candidate's campaign may receive from PACs or individual donors. A corporation is allowed to give only $500 to a candidate in a given election cycle, but it can donate to as many PACs as it desires.

Alabama is identified by the National Conference on State Legislatures as one of seven states with only "minimal" restrictions on campaign contributions.[23] Six states have no upper limits.

Fund Transfers

During the 2010 alleged gambling corruption trials a lobbyist who pleaded guilty and testified against other defendants said he told one lawmaker that he, the lobbyist, could make him a "rainmaker" by furnishing him with money that he could then give to fellow Republicans.[24]

Less controversially, prominent incumbent Alabama federal and state politicians have frequently shared their largesse with less generously endowed candidates. In 2010, US senators Richard Shelby and Jeff Sessions not only donated surplus funds to (successful) attorney general candidate Luther Strange, they also authorized the use of endorsements from them in a Strange campaign brochure. (In the previous election they had supported the incumbent, Troy King.)

Sometimes candidates will attempt to make an issue of not accepting funds that are nonetheless legal. In the 2010 primary race for the Democratic attorney general nomination, one of the aspirants, Giles Perkins, pledged not to accept gambling-originated campaign funds and also challenged other candidates to do likewise. Many years before, Key had laid it down that a candidate "must not accept support that will alienate more important influences."[25] But this was before PACs and PAC-to-PAC transfers (although historically it was possible to hide sources of campaign financial support). Perkins's opponents didn't accept his challenge and, with PAC-to-PAC transfers still legal at the time, it would probably have been impossible to determine if candidates had received gambling contributions or not. Legal scholar Terri Day has said that bans on such political phenomena as PAC-to-PAC transfers are examples of efforts of state legislatures to "gentrify" political campaigns.[26]

Self-Financed Campaigns

Personally affluent candidates may be able to draw from their own wealth to supplement or supplant the need for funding from other sources. US Representative Griffith, campaigning for reelection as a Republican, was able to do this, but he still lost. Funds that a party can donate to its candidates traditionally have been very limited. Once again a Democrat, Griffith also lost the 2014 gubernatorial election to incumbent governor Robert Bentley.

The PAC Phenomenon

Large sums of money may be spent by groups (both national and state) in a candidate's behalf. Typically, both PAC and super PAC ads praise one candidate while criticizing another. They do not specifically urge voters to support the candidate they commend.

The Growth of PACs

The main instrument for the accumulation of campaign funds is the PAC. PACs registered with the Alabama secretary of state's office totaled 785 active groups in the 2010 election cycle. That figure represented an increase of 597 since 1988.[27]

One Montgomery lobbyist, John Teague, alone was credited with forty-eight PAC registrations. Another PAC entrepreneur, Rudy Davidson, created multiple PACs with names that would not evoke images of selfish politics (for example, Children's PAC). His PACs donated a half-million dollars to state and local candidates at the start of the 2010 election cycle.[28] The money had been received from a variety of other PACs.

Money Laundering

As we saw in chapter 4, the practice of transferring funds from one PAC to others was banned by ethics reform legislation passed in December 2010. Unless campaign operatives are able to find ways to get around the ban, it will now be possible to know who is contributing to whose political campaign, there being no more money laundering by PACs. For the 2010 election casino entrepreneurs "cleansed" money through 134 PACs, some of it being spent for voter mobilization efforts.[29] The Alabama Democratic Conference has thus far successfully challenged the transfer ban as it relates to its own GOTV ("get out the vote") activities.

Recent Use of PACs

The most notorious use of PACs during the 2010 gubernatorial election cycle involved the activities of PACs with the names of True Republican PAC and Conservative Coalition for Alabama PAC. Donors to both of these PACs vehemently opposed one Republican aspirant in particular, former postsecondary education chancellor Bradley Byrne. The source of funds for these "Republican" and "conservative" PACs was the Alabama Education Association, which has been closely associated with the Alabama Democratic Party. The PAC paid for numerous TV ads attacking Byrne.

TV Ads

The main (and most expensive) instrument for contemporary Alabama statewide political candidates is the TV ad. More than half a century ago, John F. Kennedy pointed out that, "TV has altered drastically the nature of our political campaigns."[30]

This could not be truer as it pertains to Alabama today.

The "hokey activities" as mentioned by Scher early on in this chapter are now only a distant memory. Radio ads are still used extensively in Alabama campaigns, however, and some of the most targeted messages from candidates will be aired on stations that statistical data show to have the listener demographics particular candidates seek.

From "Feel-Good" to "Feel-Bad"

Many decisions must be made as the candidate and his or her advisors plan their TV ads. Presumably they will start with "feel-good" positive ads ("family pictures, walking through the woods and eating at a picnic table") and "go negative" at the appropriate time.[31] One of the most creative ad firms, Film Ladd, is based in Huntsville. This company is one reason why the claim is made that, "Ads in Alabama are already unique to politics."[32]

Negative TV ads are perhaps the most controversial aspect of contemporary political campaigns in Alabama and elsewhere. With regard to those from the "heart of Dixie" that achieved national notoriety during the 2010 election cycle, Ben Smith of *Politico* identified them as "the amazing campaign ads of Alabama."[33]

It is common in political discussions to hear people say that the main thing that makes them dislike politics is its negativity. It is negative campaigning, however, that appears to activate the small amount of interest that people have in politics to start with.[34] Alabama politicians, like politicians everywhere, want their ads to be seen (especially on YouTube) by as many people as possible—in modern parlance "to go viral." Achieving this goal generally means attacking someone or something.

One upset voter, presumably not versant with the First Amendment and its guarantee of freedom of speech, wondered "why the party doesn't step in on negative ads."[35] Just because they are legal, however, doesn't mean that ads in which one candidate attacks another's character are a good thing. An opposing view to the one emphasizing the effectiveness of negative ads is the belief that attack advertising further alienates voters from politics and makes them even less trusting of electoral institutions. The result is that they don't vote.[36]

An Alabama-based analyst, political scientist David Lanoue, observed that, "If you're funny enough, controversial enough, clever enough, you can get loads of free publicity that would have cost you hundreds of thousands of dollars 10 years ago."[37]

This free publicity may not always translate into a winning total of votes, however.

Viral Ads

One of the 2010 campaign ads that got the most attention both in Alabama and across the nation was Republican gubernatorial aspirant Tim James's driver's-license-in-English-only commercial (titled "Language"). In the thirty-second ad, James looked directly at the camera and questioned why "our politicians make us give driver's license exams in 12 languages."[38]

When "Language" went viral in April 2010, James became one of the Republican gubernatorial frontrunners. "Left-wingers" beyond Alabama's borders were shocked by the xenophobia of the ad, but it gave James the opportunity to separate himself from the rest of the field as "a man who irks out-of-state liberals."[39] As noted earlier, however, James failed to make the runoff, possibly because an off-the-cuff remark of his that alienated part of the electorate. Sometimes negative advertising, if too extreme, may hurt not only the candidate using it but the party of the candidate as well. In 1996, Democrat Supreme Court incumbent Kenneth Ingram used an ad comparing his general election Republican challenger, law professor Harold See, to a skunk. The sympathy aroused for See was so widespread that several Democrats who besides Ingram also lost their races that year blamed the notorious "skunk ad" for their defeat.[40]

The Ground Game

All of the campaign activities discussed in this chapter will be performed simultaneously. The candidate will maintain a full schedule of attendance at events throughout the state or substate district. Shortly before the 2010 general election, it was reported that in the Fifth District successful Republican US House nominee Mo Brooks "over the last year . . . ha[d] attended every tea party, gun show, football game and open-air cultural event in North Alabama."[41] Candidate outlays to participate in activities such as this are referred to as ground-game spending.

The unsuccessful Artur Davis gubernatorial campaign in 2010 has been pointed to as one that lavished money on Internet and social media activities but was very lethargic when it came to answering attacks on the candidate. Also, the campaign infrastructure was incompletely developed. Mary Orndorff explained: "It was that lack of a ground game, the kind of face-to-face network of advocates in small towns and coffee shops that allowed the campaign attacks against him to take hold. . . . Even after seven years as a congressman, he did not have a grassroots organization."[42] Although much of what V. O. Key wrote about many years ago is out of date, some of it isn't. This famed scholar had cautioned in 1949 that, "To launch a successful operation in a county require[d] knowledge of local points of sensitivity and familiarity with politicos of potency."[43] Neither Davis nor his campaign staff had this.

Some politicians seem to campaign continuously, although they would prefer not to identify it as such. US Senator Shelby, for example, visits each of Alabama's sixty-seven counties at least once each year to hold town meetings. In addition to Christmas cards, former secretary of state Beth Chapman sent Thanksgiving greetings to a supportive mailing list (e-mail or regular).

The Internet

Despite the fact that Alabama is still a relatively unwired state, political candidates are placing an increasing emphasis on Internet campaigning. The most used social networks are Facebook, Twitter, and YouTube. Former US representative Spencer Bachus had a YouTube channel on which viewers could see his speeches in the House.

In the 2010 gubernatorial race, candidate websites usually had "get involved" sections where supporters could offer their services to the campaign, become a member of a Facebook group, and sign up for Twitter feeds. In 2010, it was estimated that probably a larger number of Alabamians got their news about campaigns from the Internet than newspapers. This estimate seemed high, however, since only 36 percent of Alabamians had broadband access. Close to 20 percent went online with the slower, dial-up system. Another consideration relating to the political significance of the Internet is that those most likely to vote (the middle aged and above) are also least likely to be Internet knowledgeable and engaged.

The Big Day

As Election Day nears, the candidate's campaign will print sample ballots with his or her race and name highlighted. The main emphasis will be placed on getting the candidate's supporters out to vote. Prior to this time the candidate and his or her staff (or party vendors) will have become experts on what campaign operatives can do to motivate supporters to go to the polls. A UAB communications scholar, Larry Powell, speaking specifically of a municipal election, said "candidates worked the phones, identifying voters early on in the campaign, then calling back those who indicated support to make sure they got out to the polls."[44] Before the first voting of 2010, one newspaper story headline proclaimed: "Candidates close in on primary elections with millions of phone calls."[45] Personal phone calls from volunteers and recorded calls (robocalls) from candidates were the main ways campaigns used to get supporters to their polling places.

Typically, on the day before the election gubernatorial candidates will make a statewide blitz, flying to each major city in Alabama to hold a press conference and pump up supporters to get the maximum vote out.

We will now turn to a discussion of the politics and mechanics of the elections toward which the campaign activities identified in this chapter are directed. The way they are structured may influence outcomes as much as electioneering.

10
Elections

The great majority of people don't get involved in politics to the degree that they would ever actually campaign to get elected to a public office. Voting is the key form of political participation for most people. And frequently (but certainly not always) a majority will vote at election time—especially if it's to decide on who will be president. Of course, people can and may talk about politics with their family, friends, and workmates, but it is through the act of voting that people can be officially recorded on the side of the parties and/or candidates of their choosing.

Districting

Most candidates are elected by people voting within territorial units smaller than the state as a whole. These units are called districts. Some of the smallest would be city council or county commission districts. The largest would be the congressional districts. State executive officials (chapter 12) and appellate judges (chapter 13) are elected from the state at large, as are US senators.

"One Person, One Vote"

Decisions of the federal courts, especially the US Supreme Court, require that the population of districts be as nearly equal as feasible.[1] Since population is continually moving and numbers are increasing or decreasing, a regular reapportionment of districts is necessary to see that they maintain population equality. The US Census Bureau makes available the data necessary to do accurate districting. The most recent census was taken in 2010.

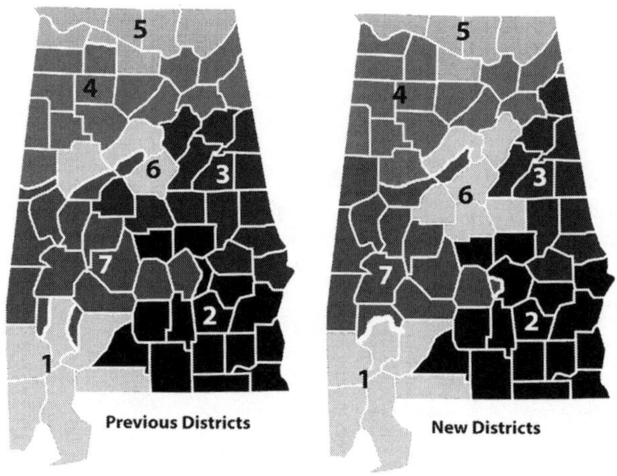

10.1. Alabama congressional redistricting. Source: http://en.wikipedia.org/wiki/Alabama's_congressional_districts

Legislative Politics and Procedures

The Alabama legislature has a standing Committee on Reapportionment consisting of twenty-two members, most belonging to the majority party, now the Republican Party. The committee consists of a senator and representative from each of the seven congressional districts plus four members apiece appointed by the lieutenant governor and House speaker. For the most recent round of state legislative redistricting in 2011–12, the joint committee working on it decided that its goal would be to have a total deviation of 5 percent between the smallest state House and the largest state Senate district. For school board districts, the goal would be 2 percent, and for congressional districts the objective would be exact population equality so far as possible. Dividing Alabama's 2010 population (4,779,736) by the seven US House seats yielded 682,819 as the ideal district population.

Redrawing congressional district lines following the 2010 census was necessary to add population to some while subtracting from others. The majority African American Seventh District, for example, needed about 80,000 more people to reach the ideal. The legislature approved a new congressional redistricting bill in its 2011 regular session, and the US Justice Department accepted it on November 21, 2011. (The department also certified the new state board of education districts then.) African American leaders would have preferred to have the "black district" not so heavily packed with African Ameri-

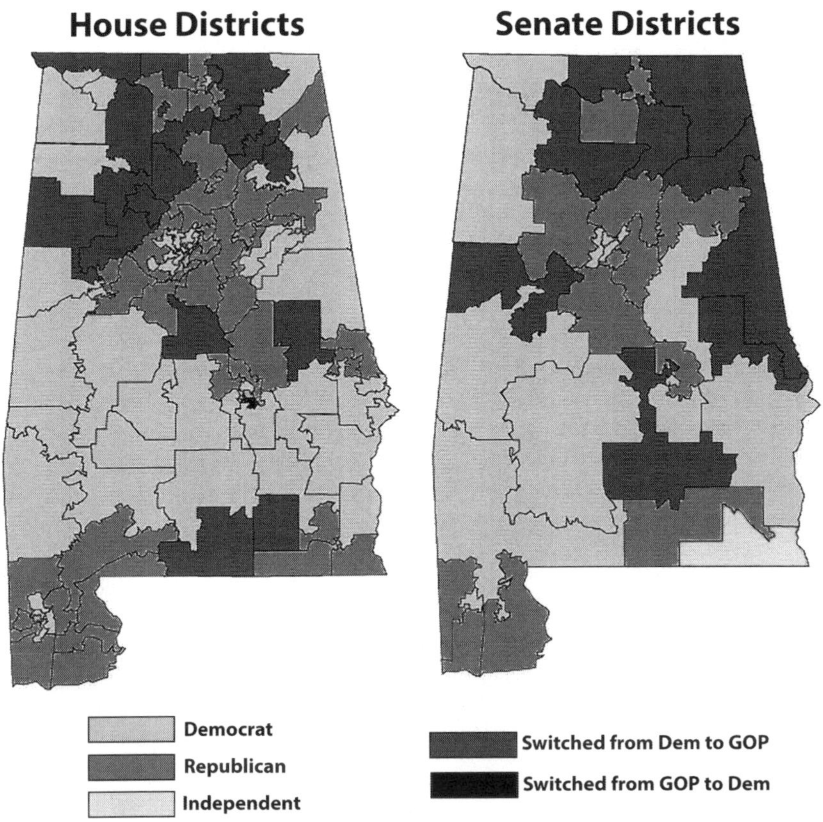

10.2. Changing legislature in Alabama. Source: http://ballotnews.org/state-legislatures/republicans-gain-control-of-the-alabama-state-legislature-for-the-first-time-in-136-years/

cans. Had some of them been diffused to other districts it would have provided black Alabamians, along with whites who still retain their Democratic loyalties, more opportunities to form coalitions to influence future elections.

Following public hearings throughout the state and private discussions among legislators and affected interests, districting bills are drafted representing the majority's views and filed as other bills are. The bills are then referred to committee where they are considered at length and afterward reported back to the originating chamber, presumably with amendments. This process is also followed in the Senate, assuming the bills originated in the House. Probably the versions of the reapportionment bills as passed by the House and Senate will be different and neither may initially agree on the

10.3. *Birmingham News* election/redistricting cartoon. Source: *Birmingham News*

other chamber's changes. If so, this necessitates the creation of conference committees that will draft unamendable compromise bills to be sent back to the House and Senate. Assuming they pass, they are referred to the governor who can sign or veto them. Since the legislature and governor are both under Republican control, it is likely that the governor has already had significant input on the legislation and will sign the bills. Unless successfully challenged in court, the new redistricting plans will go into effect the next time members affected by the set of districts involved are elected.

The federal courts recognize protection of incumbents as a legitimate consideration in redistricting in order to promote continuity in government so racial fairness and population equality are not the only criteria used in making decisions regarding approval of new districting arrangements. Republicans were able to take control of the legislature for the first time in 136 years running in districts that had been created by a Democratic majority following the 2000 census. New districts based on the 2010 enumeration should not deter a Democratic comeback if public sentiment wants this to occur. Some states use bi- or nonpartisan commissions to do their redistricting work, but most commonly this task is assigned to the legislature, as it is in Alabama.

Gerrymandering

Gerrymandering refers to gross partisanship in redistricting. Racial gerrymandering at least to the extent necessary to produce a majority-minority district is required in Alabama district construction to achieve racial fairness. Other motivations for redistricting may be subtler. When Alabama's Third District, which includes much of eastern Alabama, was redrawn preparatory to the 2012 elections, the white percentage was increased from 65 to 71 and the black percentage decreased from approximately one-third to one-quarter of the population. These changes made a safely Republican seat even safer. The Second District, temporarily snatched by a Democrat in southeastern Alabama in 2010, had its black percentage slightly reduced (from 30 percent to 29.5 percent). Although its white percentage was lowered from 68 percent to 65 percent (with the rest being mostly Hispanic), the Republican architects correctly expected that this would not jeopardize freshman Republican US Representative Martha Roby's reelection prospects. (Like the other Alabama US representatives, she won reelection handily in November 2012.) A former Alabama congressman, Democrat Ronnie Flippo (1977–91), noted that "once you get elected the first time, you get all the power of the incumbency and if you take care of business back home, it is much easier to get elected to future terms."[2]

The best opportunity for a party to pick up a seat comes when, for whatever reasons, an incumbent is not running again. Long congressional tenure has not always been the norm, however. During the Reconstruction era (1868–74) Alabama politics were so turbulent that four of the five members were in office for only a single two-year term.[3]

Due to the fact that there are so many overlapping constituencies for districted state and local officials, multiple ballots have to be printed for voters at every precinct. In Tuscaloosa County in 2010, seventeen ballots were necessary—thirteen Republican and four Democratic to accommodate the different districts for the offices on which voters balloted. Originally, a state Senate district consisted of three House districts, but this "nesting" practice is not followed now.

Registering to Vote

In order to vote in Alabama, one first must be registered. This process could be made easier than it is, but it is still much simpler than it was many years ago.

The Jim Crow Era

In the old Jim Crow days, when the emphasis of the white governing elites was on minimizing rather than maximizing the electorate, it was much more

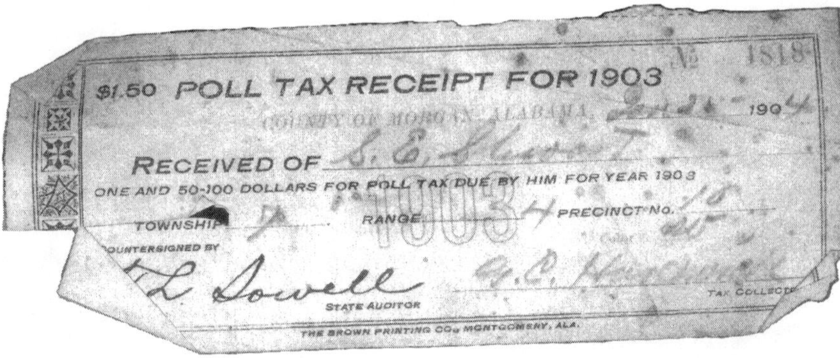

10.4. 1903 Alabama poll tax receipt. From the William H. Stewart collection

tedious to register to vote than it is now. Until they were declared inherently discriminatory, those who wished to sign up had to take a twenty-page test on the US and Alabama constitutions and the structure of state and local government. Such literacy tests, as they were called, were not fairly administered between blacks and whites.

In the Jim Crow era voters also had to pay a $1.50 per year poll tax to become eligible voters. If someone did not start voting until he or she was forty-five, for example, accumulated back poll taxes would have to be paid in addition to the current year's tax. The total bill would be $36 (covering from age twenty-one to forty-five). This sum was prohibitive for many Alabamians. In November 2012 Alabama voters declined to remove obsolete provisions related to poll taxes (as well as segregated schools) from the state constitution. As previously noted, the most vocal opposition came from the teachers union and black political organizations who objected that the original 1901 constitution's right to an education at public expense, taken out during the era of massive resistance to racial integration, had not been restored.

While sympathizers with African Americans outside the South frequently focused their concerns on the poll tax, V. O. Key's research in the 1940s was notable in showing that the tax actually kept more whites than blacks from voting.[4] Historian Barbara Fields noted that, at the time the Alabama and other southern state constitutions were being drafted, "Poor whites tended to oppose [black] disfranchisement, despite the trappings of white-supremacist ideology with which it was proclaimed." This was because, "They understood that they were to be its unstated secondary victims and so they became."[5] The primary victims were blocked in harsher, more personalized ways. As Richard Scher notes, southern blacks were victimized by "exploitation, manipulation, and oppression by the white community" that fully dominated the Jim Crow society to which they were confined.[6] The state ended the cumulative poll tax in 1953, and federal constitutional and judicial initiatives in the 1960s terminated the poll tax altogether.

Registration Today

At present almost anyone who is at least eighteen and is a resident of the area in which she or he lives at the time of registration can be added to the voter rolls. One can get a mail-in voter application at the secretary of state's website, at library branches, at the Department of Human Resources, and at numerous other governmental offices. Many young people register at school when they turn eighteen. Registration should be attended to at least ten days prior to primary or general Election Day. Some states such as New Hampshire allow Election Day registration, but Alabama doesn't. In most other democracies people don't have to take the initiative to register to vote. Some government agency does this based on numerous records indicating one's presence in a particular governmental jurisdiction.

Felon Disqualification

Alabamians who have been convicted of certain felonies said to involve "moral turpitude" are not eligible to register to vote unless they receive a pardon. Matthew Itkin cited research showing that, "about thirty-one percent of the state's adult, black male population has lost the right to vote" as a result of felon disqualification.[7] A former chair of the Alabama Republican Party, Marty Connors, was quoted as saying: "As frank as I can be, we're opposed to it [felons' voting rights restoration] because felons don't tend to vote Republican."[8] In his second term, Governor Riley was appointed by federal district court to be chief of elections. In this capacity, his office generated an inventory in excess of four hundred voter-disqualifying felonies. This was regarded by critics as too many.[9]

The Voter Rolls

Three registrars have the formal responsibility for voter registration in most Alabama counties. The governor, state auditor, and commissioner of agriculture and industries appoint them. In his unsuccessful campaign for governor in 2010 Democratic commissioner Ron Sparks noted that he named African Americans to the boards of registrars in twenty-seven Alabama counties. These registrars are supposed to keep voter rolls up to date.

In some cases, voter rolls are grossly in error, however. In 2008 the voter rolls in six Alabama counties contained more names than there were voting age citizens. Greene County, for example, had 7,540 registered voters near the time of the 2008 presidential election, but the Census Bureau's estimate for the county's adult population then was only 6,834. It is outdated voter rolls that are more likely to lead to voter fraud, especially in the casting of absentee ballots, more so than in-person deception at the polls.

Party Registration

In chapter 8 it was noted that in twenty-nine states, registering to vote calls for one to indicate a party or independent status. In Alabama this is not the case. One simply registers and, when primaries are held, decides which party to participate in, if either. The Democrats have a party rule stating that if one participates in the Republican Party's original primary, he or she shouldn't vote in the Democratic runoff. This rule is largely unenforceable. The Republicans had no such rule and, in 2010, it is widely believed that Republican aspirant Robert Bentley's runoff winning total was significantly enlarged by people who had earlier voted in the Democratic primary. The AEA, a strong opponent of the other Republican gubernatorial primary runoff candidate (Bradley Byrne), made robocalls to members reminding them that the Republican runoff was freely open to them, even if they had voted Democratic earlier.

The only way of knowing how many Republicans and Democrats there are in Alabama is through accurate polls. Survey findings fluctuate markedly. Even at times when Republicans have held a great majority of state offices polls have shown party identifiers to be fairly evenly distributed among the populace. In the 1990s political independents were pointed to as "a critical swing group" in the Alabama political system.[10] This was because neither self-identified Democrats nor Republicans constituted a majority of the electorate. At the time of the 2012 general election, 43 percent of Alabamians surveyed said they were Republicans. Democrats totaled 34 percent. The number identifying as independents or "other" was a substantial 24 percent. A 2010 study that ranked the states ideologically found Alabama to be the most conservative. Mississippi and Louisiana rounded out the top three conservative states.[11]

In the old Jim Crow days, state law gave southern parties the right to determine their own members. Basically, this meant keeping blacks out of Democratic primaries. In the mid-1940s, however, the white primary was outlawed by the US Supreme Court, one of a long series of steps leading to full black voting equality with whites.[12]

The Active Electorate

Bartley and Graham characterized what they called "the traditional twentieth-century pattern of southern politics" in this way: "The higher-status whites voted; the lower-status whites sometimes voted; and the blacks voted little at all."[13]

Alabama scholar Donald Strong found that, in his state, a decade before the Voting Rights Act was passed only about 55,000 blacks had their names on the voter rolls.[14] However, black voter registrations in the seven states targeted by the Voting Rights Act as initially passed in 1965, including Alabama, soon increased by more than 100 percent (to 2.4 million voters).[15]

Ironically, the white electorate expanded by a much larger actual number of voters, enabling such demagogic southern politicians as George Wallace of Alabama and Lester Maddox of Georgia to win the governorships in their states. While the 1960s had resulted in the addition of in excess of six million new names to the voter rolls, only 30 percent of these were African American while 70 percent were white.[16] Bartley and Graham cite the success of Wallace and Maddox as evidence that "the galoots were loose over much of the region" following passage of the Voting Rights Act.[17] For this reason they point to "the long-awaited and largely simultaneous enfranchisement of lower-income whites and blacks [as] a mixed blessing."[18]

At the time of the March 2012 presidential primary, Alabama had 2.63 million registered voters.[19] This was up modestly (two-tenths of a percent) from the 2010 total of 2.58 million. In the November 2012 presidential election, 2.10 million participated. This was identified by the secretary of state as 72.3 percent of "active" registered voters. Based on the Census Bureau's estimate of Alabama voting age population in 2011, the 2012 percentage would be 57.03. Whatever interest a particular election may hold, the voter rolls have not grown markedly, in part because Alabama hasn't experienced the in-migration of more highly educated and affluent people that such states as Virginia and North Carolina have. These two demographic groups have very high registration percentages.[20]

Primaries

The general election always comes in November (in 2016 on November 8), but it is up to the legislature to decide when party primaries are held. Primaries have occurred from as early as March before the general election in November to as late as September. In 2012, the primaries were on March 13, with runoffs (if needed) following on April 24. The federal Help America Vote Act of 2002 (HAVA) has provisions related to runoffs. They require states holding them, as southern states traditionally have since the (Democratic) primary nomination was "tantamount" to election, to schedule them at least six weeks after the first primary. Instead of the three weeks that was customary, the six-week interval allows more time for people in the military stationed abroad to vote.

As we saw in chapters 3 and 9, Alabama also has a presidential primary during which voters express preferences among candidates. The most recent one occurred on March 13, 2012. (For 2016 the primary date is March 1.) Unlike 2008, the Democratic presidential primary was uncontested. Showing that not all moderate-to-conservative voters have shifted to the Republican side, "uncommitted" received more votes than President Barack Obama in seven counties. Approximately 17 percent of the Democratic vote statewide was tabulated as uncommitted. In the Republican primary, Rick Santorum, Newt Gingrich, and Mitt Romney finished one, two, three.

Some states have gone so far as to virtually abolish party primaries. California has passed a proposition allowing candidates to enter the primary of the opposite party. The top two candidates, regardless of party, face each other in the general election. This voting innovation was spurred on by increasing concern about polarization between the parties and the hope that the new system would benefit moderate Democrats and Republicans.[21] Closer to Alabama, Louisiana has a "top two" system in which candidates from both parties compete together in one initial primary. If no candidate receives a majority of the votes cast, the first- and second-place finishers, regardless of party, run it off to determine the election winner. Democrats there implemented the "top two" system as they were becoming increasingly concerned about the rise of Republicanism. In 2016 this system facilitated the election of a Democratic governor in Louisiana.

The evolution of the party system in Alabama has had the effect of reducing the number of candidates running in the primaries, especially in the Democratic primary. The more likely a party is to prevail in the general election, the greater the prospect of primary races. Even so, it is frequently the case at present that both Republican and Democratic primary nominations go uncontested. The Republican candidates are more likely to be safe-seat incumbents, and the Democratic nomination may not be worth much since whoever emerges with it will be the underdog in the general election. Democrats had only two candidates up for statewide positions in November 2012, and both of them lost. In 2016, in Morgan County, a traditional Democratic bastion in north Alabama, that party offered no candidates for county offices.

The Ballot

The ballot is printed at state expense in the form designated by the legislature.

Candidate Listings

Candidates are listed on primary and general election ballots by the name they normally use without title or nicknames. In 2010, Dr. Robert Bentley, the man who ultimately became governor, officially changed his name to in-

10.5. Top of ballot showing political parties participating in the 1972 state general election. From the William H. Stewart collection

clude his title. The party executive committee would not allow this designation, however. (Its absence obviously did not prevent Dr. Bentley from winning the election.)

Even a candidate's usual name may generate publicity for his or her candidacy, however. This was the case in 2010 when Young Boozer was first nominated (over George Wallace Jr.) and then elected as state treasurer. The host of the *Tonight Show*, Jay Leno, made jokes about Boozer's name. Some states, such as Louisiana, allow the use of nicknames on ballots.

Ballot Access

In order to be on the Alabama ballot, parties not currently listed most recently had to collect the signatures of at least 5,000 active voters as verified by the secretary of state's office. This represented 3 percent of the votes cast in the last general election governor's race. In the November 2012 presidential election Alabama voters had the opportunity to choose not only between the presidential candidates of the Democratic and Republican parties but also from among those of the Constitution, Libertarian, and Green parties as well. The minor party that achieves representation through petition will have ballot access through the next election cycle. Afterward, if one of its candidates did not attain at least 20 percent of the vote in a statewide race it will have to repeat this process. In contrast with Alabama, Minnesota allows a new party to be placed on the ballot if it can collect 2,000 signatures. (Minnesota has about a half-million more residents than Alabama.)

Voting

In times past African Americans were discouraged from voting, even if they had somehow managed to get their names on the voter rolls. Today this is not the case, and federal observers are sometimes on hand to make sure of it.

Voter ID

At the polls on Election Day the registered voter will be asked to show photo identification. Photo ID has been a contentious political issue because many Democrats believe that this stipulation deters likely Democratic identifiers, African Americans and poor people especially, from voting. They charge that voter ID is essentially a "solution" to a problem (in-person fraudulent voting) that does not exist.

Fourteen states now require a photo identification before someone is issued a ballot at the polls. Alabama's law stipulates that the secretary of state will furnish a free photo ID to voters who don't have a driver's license.

Straight or Split Ticket?

In casting a ballot in Alabama today, the voter typically colors in circles by the names of preferred candidates and feeds the ballot into a computer that reads all of them when the polls close. One can also vote a straight party ticket in the general election by coloring in the circle under the party name and symbol on the ballot.

When Alabama was a one-party Democratic state, most people cast straight party tickets. As Republican strength started to increase, many began splitting their tickets, voting Republican for president and Democratic for other offices. (Frequently there were no Republican candidates for these offices.) This was split-level party realignment, and the term "presidential Republicans" was used to describe these voters.[22] As the Republican Party has become Alabama's dominant party, many people are apt to cast straight Republican tickets. One winning Republican legislative candidate in 2010 commented that he owed his election in part to the coattails of the Republican gubernatorial candidate, Robert Bentley.[23] Ironically, the candidate, state representative Daniel Boman, rather quickly switched to the Democratic Party after taking his seat.

In the November 2012 general election, Republicans cast 574,011 straight-ticket votes and Democrats cast 509,790. An additional 23,564 ballots were reported by seventeen counties as straight-ticket votes but without a party identification. These figures show that totaled, slightly over half (52.55 percent) of the votes cast in the most recent general election were of the straight-ticket variety. In contemporary Alabama, approximately a third of voters have been identified as "yellow dog" Democrats who would vote for their party's nominees regardless.[24] (In 2012, only 24 percent of the total vote was straight Democratic.) In general elections, people are also permitted to cast write-in votes. Voters are not obligated to vote on all races on the ballot. Most of the time there is a considerable drop-off between the top of the ballot—president or governor—to the bottom, for example, constable. One unsuccessful Republican primary candidate in 2012 feared that voters in her race (president of the public service commission) would "just get tired" and wouldn't want to keep voting until they reached the flip side of the two-sided ballot where this office (a "down race") was located.[25]

Absentee Ballots

Someone who was unable to go to the polls on Election Day could previously have cast an absentee ballot. Applying for an absentee ballot needs to be done with the county circuit clerk at least five days prior to the election. To have a ballot mailed, application is made at www.alabamavotes.gov.

It is absentee voting that is more likely to be associated with fraudulent activity than in-person voting. One county circuit clerk told a reporter: "You've got people controlling multiple ballots when they go out and solicit people to vote absentee." The official continued: "People are using them to control votes. If a person goes to the polls, you have no control over that. Through the absentee process you do."[26]

Absentee voter fraud works this way: Campaign activists ask for ballots for people and, after they are confident they have arrived, go to their homes. There they observe the absentee voters casting their ballot for the "right" candidates.

Typically in Alabama elections about 3 percent of the total ballots cast represent absentee votes. In some counties, however, the percentages have been much higher. This has been particularly true in such Black Belt counties as Greene and Perry. The controversial voter ID laws do not deal with the problem of possible absentee voter fraud since they only apply to persons who present themselves to vote personally at the polls.

Since the enactment of voting rights legislation in the 1960s, the US Justice Department has regularly monitored Alabama elections to deter or detect possible illegal denials of the right to vote. Closest scrutiny is paid to majority-black areas such as the Seventh Congressional District.

Voter Turnout

Even though the result in the presidential election has been regarded as a foregone conclusion in Alabama since 1980, this is still the election that brings out by far the largest number of voters. About 61 percent of the voting age population participated in the 2008 presidential election. As we saw earlier, the comparable percentage for 2012 was approximately 57 percent.

The big state elections in Alabama are held in what are referred to as "off years"—years in which a president is not elected. This is when Alabama chooses the governor, all members of the legislature, all single-headed state agency leaders, one-third of the state appellate judiciary, and many county and circuit court officials. Municipal officials are elected on nonpartisan ballots at times designated by the legislature (generally in August of presidential election years).

Research has long shown that ethnicity and income are associated with the level of voter participation, African Americans and lower income people voting less frequently than whites and the more affluent. Also, Republicans tend to turn out in higher percentages than Democrats. Of course, these factors are related since blacks have lower average incomes than whites and overwhelmingly vote Democratic. With the removal of racial barriers, voting by blacks and whites of the same economic status has been about the same. Also in terms of voter demographics, it is generally well known that older people (up to the very elderly) vote with greater frequency than do younger people. In Alabama, there was a 40 percent-plus higher probability that voters in the fifty-five to sixty-four age bracket would cast ballots than would those eighteen to twenty-four. In the 2008 presidential election, 66 percent of female registered voters participated as opposed to 58 percent of male.

Generally, the greater the number of elections, the smaller the turnout. In Alabama, participation typically drops off in runoffs after primaries. The primary runoff is really an anachronism since it is based on a one-party Democratic system that no longer exists. Voting is also typically low when constitutional amendments are up for ratification (at times in the single digits).

Normally, a large number of candidates depresses turnout since more information is necessary for voters to make choices among the field. Very bad weather would suppress turnout. Just the opposite used to be true. In the Alabama of long ago it was said that heavy rain meant a higher turnout because it was "too wet to plow." National variables such as increased public cynicism toward government depress turnout. Factors such as holidays and elections being held right after also may discourage it. One local official, trying to explain why his heavily Republican suburban county had only 19 percent of its voters go to the polls in the June 2010 primaries commented: "I think a lot of it was voter dissatisfaction. A lot of people just say 'I'm not going to vote for any of these bums.'"[27]

Republican growth has been encouraged in Alabama by the fact that the party's identifiers, as noted, are generally more affluent (and educated), and are more likely to vote than people who label themselves as Democrats.[28] In the gambling corruption trials in the summer of 2011, the fact that Republicans had worked feverishly to prevent the passage of a gambling referendum bill in the legislature was emphasized repeatedly. They were said to be fearful that this would attract an above-average number of African American voters who, as a group, supported expansion of gambling in larger numbers than whites. A large black turnout also would work against Republican efforts to capture control of the legislature because most blacks would presumably be voting for Democratic House and Senate candidates.

Showing the political change that has occurred in Alabama in recent years, in the 2010 primaries the Republican set attracted more voters (492,480) than the Democratic (318,984). In 2006, Republican voters had totaled 460,019 while Democrats totaled 466,537. This meant a 7.1 percent gain for Republicans and a 31.5 percent loss for Democrats. The year 2010 was only the second time a larger number of voters had participated in the Republican than the Democratic primaries. This initially had occurred in 1998 when the Republicans had a hotly contested gubernatorial race and Don Siegelman was a prohibitive favorite for the Democratic nomination. In the March 2012 primary combining the presidential primary with the few state and local races being voted on in "off years," the Republican turnout was three times greater than participation in the Democratic primary. There were no contested Democratic races for offices balloted on statewide and incumbent President Barack Obama ran unopposed. Voter turnout was calculated at 31.2 percent of those eligible. (Figures for voter turnout for November 2012 have previously been presented.)

Results

Results of elections are available shortly after the polls close. Alabama has uniform opening and closing poll hours, 7:00 A.M.–7:00 P.M. The website of the secretary of state offers up-to-the-minute election results as do al.com and other news organizations.

In the case of very close elections, such as in 2002 with the Siegelman-Riley gubernatorial race, state law now provides for automatic recounts when any candidate has a winning margin of 0.5 percent or less. At the time of the 2002 election the state had no effective recount law. A 2010 recount confirmed Robert Bentley's second-place finish in the Republican primary.

We now turn to an examination of the Alabama governmental institutions that are led by the winners of the elections. How the functioning of the major institutions of Alabama state government has been impacted by the end of Jim Crow should be evident after we have looked at politics in the legislative, executive, and judicial arenas. This includes a discussion of the politics of taxing and spending in chapter 14.

11
Legislative Politics

The role of the legislature in Alabama politics is a crucial one. It is not by chance that among the three branches of government, the legislative branch was put first in the constitution. Historically, American state legislatures were more important than state governors. As a reaction to royal governors in the colonial period, the first state constitutions provided for weak governors and, even though some measure of balance was provided for in the next wave of new state constitutions written when Alabama came into the Union, legislatures still exceeded governors in power. According to constitutional theory, the three branches of government—legislative, executive, and judicial—are equal in power. We will defer judgments on actual power until we have examined the legislative and executive institutions in greater depth.

Understanding the Alabama Legislature

A reviewer of a textbook published in the 1930s seemed puzzled by the fact that since the Alabama legislature was so badly malapportioned in favor of rural interests, it was nevertheless still possible for "the economic interests in the cities [to] exercise considerable influence over state policy making and execution."[1] The explanation lay in the Big Mule–Black Belt alliance, about which Key would later write in his classic *Southern Politics*.[2] That alliance of Birmingham industrialists and Black Belt planters has long since faded away, and the new critical elements for understanding the legislature are the political parties and a much wider assortment of interest groups (as we saw in chapters 7 and 8).

The Legislative Image

The reputation of the Alabama legislature has tended to be on the poor side, not only in the state but among outsiders as well. Scholars believed legislatures in Alabama and other southern states mirrored "a traditionalistic political culture [that] saw little need for government in society beyond defending the status quo."[3] Then, in the years just after World War II, it was explained that the southern legislatures (unfortunately) "reflected the race-based, rural-dominated, one-party, low-output politics" of this period of the region's history.[4]

A 1971 study by the Citizens Conference on State Legislatures rated most southern state legislatures as poor except Florida's—Alabama's was identified as the worst of all.[5]

Bob Blalock, an editorial writer for the *Birmingham News*, lamented that "getting anything done in the Alabama Legislature requires an Act of God."[6]

The Republican Takeover

In sharp contrast with the final phase of Democratic dominance, during the first Republican-majority regular session in 2011, when legislation was passing more frequently than ever before in modern political history, there were concerns that errors would occur due to too hurried consideration of bills. When unanticipated problems cropped up with the new immigration law these fears seemed to be confirmed. The totality of the "Handshake with Alabama," the name Republicans gave to their program, was passed in ten legislative days (only one-third of the number allotted by the constitution for regular sessions). In the 2012 and subsequent regular and special sessions, however, the pace of legislative policy making slowed down considerably. As we saw in chapter 7, the revived power of interest groups had a lot to do with this.

How the Legislature Is Organized

Normally the atmosphere in the legislature is relatively tranquil. On occasion it isn't. The most publicized instance of a breakdown of decorum in the Alabama legislature occurred in 2007 when a Republican senator "slugged" a Democratic senator, an event interpreted in the media as giving not only the legislature but also the state as a whole a black eye.[7]

Bicameralism

Like all but one of the American state legislatures (the exception being Nebraska) the Alabama legislature is bicameral, with a Senate and a House of Representatives. The Senate consists of thirty-five members and the House of 105. A representative needs to be at least twenty-one and a senator twenty-five at the time of election. In most states the lower house members serve two-year terms while the senators serve for four years.

11.1. Alabama House in session. Source: Photo a derivative of Alabama House of Representatives Transmercator Projection (https://www.flickr.com/photos/exothermic/3463372369/) by exothermic/CC by http://creativecommons.org/licenses/by/2.0/. Desaturated from original

Two other Deep South states, Louisiana and Mississippi, also have four-year lower house terms, however. Service in the smaller Senate is generally seen as more prestigious than in the House, so it is common for House members to "move up" to the Senate. Newly elected members take office immediately after their elections are certified.

The State House

The legislature holds its sessions in a facility known as the "State House." Many years ago it was the headquarters of what was then known as the Highway Department. From 1851 to 1985 the legislature met at what is now referred to as the Historic Capitol. The necessity of major renovation of the State House was indicated when its two bottom floors flooded during a torrential rain in 2009. Public support for providing more adequate legislative work facilities has been virtually nonexistent, however.

Who the Legislators Are

Legislative membership in 2012 included a number of African Americans (solidly Democratic) roughly proportionate to their presence in the total Alabama population. All Republicans were white. Blacks make up a majority of state House (twenty-seven of thirty-nine) and Senate (seven of eleven)

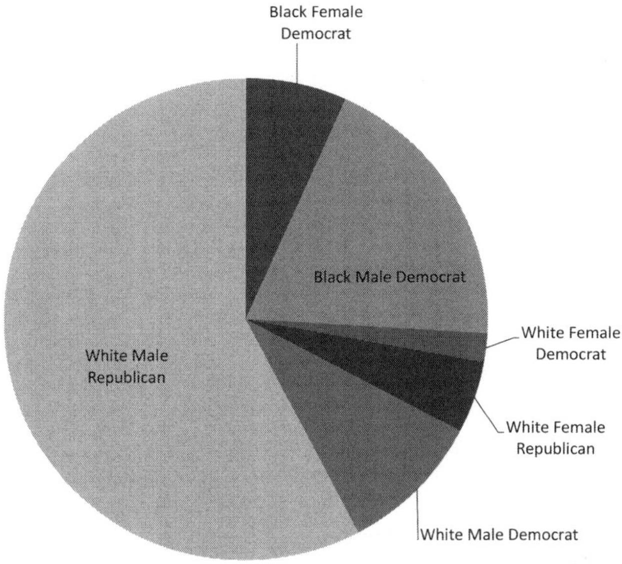

11.2. Alabama House breakdown. Source: http://legislature.state.al.us/aliswww/Representatives.aspx

Democrats. This is also the case in Alabama's neighboring states of Georgia and Mississippi: Most Democrats are black. Since Republicans now control a majority of southern state legislatures, this means that only about 5 percent of black members are part of legislative majorities. Out of 318 black southern state legislators, only three have Republican Party identification.

The Alabama legislature includes nineteen women (not in proportion since women amount to 51.5 percent of the total population). In 2011–12 rankings, Alabama was in the bottom group of states (5–14 percent women in the legislature) among the fifty states in terms of the percentage of female legislators.[8] (The only other states in this group were Mississippi, South Carolina, Oklahoma, and North Dakota.) In the Alabama legislature in March 2012, 86.3 percent of the members were men while 13.7 percent were women. The Republican supermajority (defined as two-thirds or three-fifths of a whole number) was composed overwhelmingly of men (95 percent). Most legislators were married (84.2 percent). In 2006 the first openly gay member of the Alabama legislature was elected. The median age for legislators is fifty-four years, nine months. A majority of the legislators are college educated, 86 percent possessing a bachelor's degree or more.

The legislature also includes a wide variety of occupational groupings. The fact that formerly about a fourth of the legislators worked for one of the com-

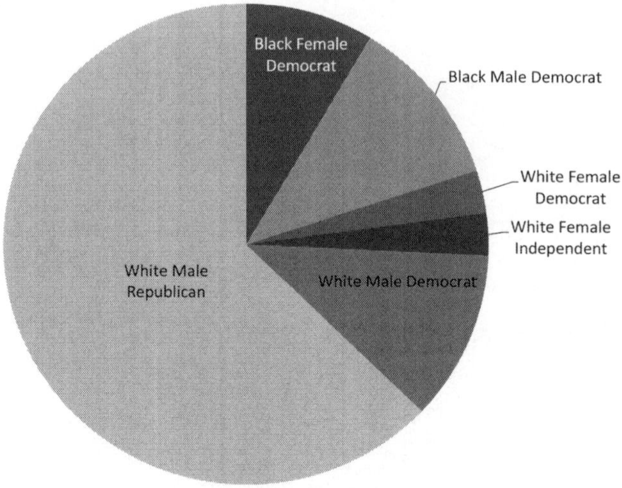

11.3. Alabama Senate breakdown. Source: http://www.legislature.state.al.us/aliswww/Senators.aspx

munity colleges (referred to as double-dipping) was one of the bigger controversies in Alabama politics in recent years. These relationships were valuable to the institutions because they depended on the legislature collectively to pass favorable budgets. One legislator confessed to using his job as a college administrator to launder state appropriations for his benefit and that of family members. He resigned his position and went to jail. At Governor Bob Riley's urging the State Board of Education ruled that legislators could not simultaneously hold community college jobs. The new Republican legislature made this ban a part of statutory law in 2011.

Most legislators are not novices. A majority of the members in 2012 already had served at least two previous terms. Turnover in the Alabama legislature has declined during the past several election cycles. Due to the typical absence of massive turnover it has been classified "hybrid professional."[9] Despite higher than usual anti-incumbent sentiment in 2010, thirty-nine sitting House members and six senators ran unopposed in both the primary and general election.

Following the 2010 elections in the country at large, Republicans were the majority in twenty-six states, including Alabama. Counting Alabama legislators, 53 percent (3,890) were Republicans nationwide, the largest percentage in more than eighty years. Alabama was actually tardy in joining its southeastern neighbors to have at least its upper or lower house with a Republican majority.

Legislative Sessions

In a unique experiment among state legislatures, the Alabama Constitution of 1901 originally called for the legislature to meet only quadrennially (that is, every four years). The framers were obviously not contemplating much being done. This arrangement never worked and frequent special sessions were called. In 1939 the constitution was formally amended to provide for biennial sessions (Amendment 39) and the move was made to annual sessions in 1975 (Amendment 339). The legislature meets for thirty legislative days within a calendar period of 105 days. In 2015 the regular session convened on March 3, 2015, and adjourned on June 4, 2015. In gubernatorial inauguration years (which 2015 was), regular sessions begin in March; in all others, in February. California provides a sharp contrast since in that state the legislature is in continuous session.

Early in January after their election, before the governor and other state officials take office, there is an organizational session of the legislature. These sessions are limited to a maximum of ten calendar days.

Special sessions may be called by the governor and meet for no more than ten legislative days within a period of thirty calendar days. Other states besides Alabama also put limits on the length of regular and special sessions. A special session may normally consider only items included in the governor's call. The legislature cannot call itself into special session. (These are known as self-starter sessions.)

Limitations on the Alabama legislature reflect the historic distrust of government to which we have previously called attention to in this book. In terms of constitutional specifications related to legislative structure and procedure, Alabama ranked second among the states in 2009.[10]

The Work of the Legislature

The Alabama legislature has certain fundamental tasks. How it performs them will have a lot to do with what the public thinks of the legislature.

Passing the Budgets

The main legislative task is to pass two budgets so the government can operate. Unlike the practice at the national level and in most other states, Alabama operates under two annual budgets rather than just one. Forty-seven states have a single unified budget. The governor submits the annual budgets shortly after the legislature begins its regular session. Even though changes to these budgets overall may be only incremental, in individual areas they may be altered markedly. When Republican Governor Bentley submitted his financial spending plans to the Republican legislature in early February 2012 they were said to be "dead on arrival."

According to the constitution (Amendment 448), passage of the education and General Fund budgets takes priority over all other legislation. A three-fifths majority is required for any bill to be considered ahead of the budgets. Since it has been most common for the budgets to be considered at the tail end of a legislative session, despite Amendment 448, this means that a three-fifths vote in each house of the legislature frequently is necessary just to take up a nonbudget bill. These measures are called "BIRs" (budget isolation resolutions). Groups such as AEA, the Business Council, and ALFA have had a much greater likelihood of getting the required BIR passed than less powerful groups.

Reapportionment

The other major legislative duty is to reapportion itself after each census. Since the 1960s, the legislature and the people of Alabama have learned that if the legislature shirks this duty (or doesn't perform it in an acceptable way) federal judges will perform it for them.

Legislative Compensation

Legislators are paid the same whether they serve in the Senate or House. The original 1901 constitution provided only the pittance of five dollars daily while the legislature is in session. For many years, most of the money members have received for their service came from statutes that greatly increased their expense money. By 2012 the legislative expense allowance amounted to about 95 percent of members' total pay.

Pay as a Political Issue

Regulating their actual pay was undoubtedly one of the most controversial things the legislature did. People who might otherwise seem oblivious to what was transpiring in the legislature paid close attention to pay raises; the news media made sure of it. The legislative vote for a 72 percent increase at the start of the 2008 quadrennium was especially controversial and helped Republicans in their bids to take control of the House and Senate in 2010.

Recent Changes

While there was no consensus in the Republican-dominant legislature to repeal the 2008 pay raise, members did approve and voters ratified in November 2012 a constitutional amendment (Amendment 845) setting legislative pay at the median household income in Alabama. The amendment would be effective in 2014 and remain unchangeable by legislators. It was estimated that the average legislator's pay would decline from about $55,000 (based on attendance at legislative sessions plus committee work) to $46,921, the median family income.

When the base family income rose, so would that of legislators. The State Personnel Board—not the legislature—would be responsible for establishing members' pay and expenses annually.

A 2009 National Conference of State Legislatures pay survey, prior to adoption of the new constitutional amendment, had Alabama in the middle range of states in terms of legislative pay. Looking only at the Southeast, however, Alabama legislators were found to be the most generously compensated.[11]

Key Leadership Positions

The legislature has both constitutionally provided as well as party leadership position. Politically, these sets of offices are closely connected.

Lieutenant Governor and President Pro Tem

The lieutenant governor presides over the Senate. Prior to the election of the first Republican to this office in 1998 (Steve Windom), the lieutenant governor actually set up the committees and determined the legislative agenda, frequently with strong gubernatorial supervision. In many instances the governor actually organized the Senate through the lieutenant governor just as the House was organized by the speaker whom the governor informally designated. This gubernatorial role was weakened in tandem with George Wallace's own physical condition.

In twenty-five states the governor and lieutenant governor (if provided for) are elected as a ticket on the federal model. In Alabama's recent political history, it was not unusual to have a Republican governor and a Democratic lieutenant governor. Due to Wallace's debilitated physical circumstance following the 1972 assassination attempt, the informal duties of the lieutenant governor expanded. By law, the lieutenant governor frequently serves as an ex officio member of state boards and commissions and is an appointive authority for others.[12]

Being governed by a Republican was something a still Democratic-majority Senate could not accept, so the rules were changed before Lieutenant Governor Windom took office in 1999 to shift the office's major powers to the president pro tem, always a member of the majority party. In spring 2011, when female senators protested the fact that a third of the Senate's most important standing committees had no members of their gender, this complaint was taken not to the lieutenant governor but to the president pro tem, who subsequently appointed women to six Senate standing committees. The pro tem is the presiding officer of the Senate when the lieutenant governor is not available.

The contemporary lieutenant governor's function is mostly to assure orderly debate in the Senate. Both Republican Lieutenant Governor Kay Ivey and her Democratic predecessor Jim Folsom Jr., were accused by the opposition party of bias in the recognition of senators wishing to speak.

Speaker of the House

Even before the Republican transformation, the legislature mostly selected its own leaders regardless of the governor's preferences (if expressed). In November 2010, it was a foregone conclusion that Mike Hubbard, who along with outgoing Governor Bob Riley was primarily responsible for the Republican legislative sweep, would be speaker. Hubbard was the consensus choice of the Republican House members. Like Hubbard, the previous (Democratic) speaker (Seth Hammett) had also served as party leader in the House prior to his elevation to the speakership. Committee chairs owe their positions to the speaker who names them at the beginning of legislative terms.

Partisanship in the Legislature

In the era of one-party Democratic rule, partisanship was irrelevant to the work of the legislature. The larger the number of Republicans became in recent decades (until they achieved majority status in 2010), the more important the tie of party became.

Caucuses

Collectively the legislators are members of either the Republican or Democratic House and Senate caucuses (except in the case of the occasional independent). The Senate Democratic caucus is officially known as the conference. It collects money to support the election of Democrats to the Senate. Since most Democratic members of the legislature are African American, there is considerable overlap between the Black and Democratic caucuses.

Committee Chairs

In 2010 the House Republicans selected their top leaders (speaker and speaker pro tem) based on a consensus among the membership as a whole. The speaker then selected the committee chairs. Senate Republicans used a committee on assignments that designated committee chairpersons. It has the authority to make changes at any time. For example, in November 2011 Senator Scott

Beason (R-Gardendale) was removed as chair of the Senate Rules Committee by his Republican colleagues. He had referred to African Americans as "aborigines" in a taped conversation used in the previous summer's first set of gambling trials, and this aroused intense opposition to Beason, especially among black senators.

In the 2010 regular legislative session, the Democratic House majority leader (Ken Guin) also served as the chairman of the House Rules Committee, which constructs priority calendars that specify when committee-approved bills will be called up for debate, if at all. In the Republican legislature different representatives selected by the speaker fill these positions.

As just noted, up until fairly recently party considerations were irrelevant to the legislative decision-making process. The Alabama legislature was like that of Texas in that prevailing votes were constructed through coalition formation.[13]

The Governor *in* the Legislature

Before the Republicans achieved their legislative majorities in November 2010, Governor Bob Riley had made unsuccessful attempts to form a majority coalition of more conservatively oriented Democrats with Republicans in the Senate. Despite this failure, unlike the situation at the national level, the governor may literally work with the legislature as it deliberates on bills. In April 2010 Governor Riley visited the House and Senate for several hours in hopes of getting legislative assent to an executive amendment to a bill to rescue the financially strapped college tuition program.

Governor Bentley, who only a couple of years back had been a House member, worked on the floor of the legislature in February 2012. The House minority leader, Craig Ford (D-Gadsden), said, however, that the governor had "relied too heavily on Republican leaders to come up with bills" during his first year in office, including the actual composition of the immigration bill.[14] (Bentley had advocated strong measures against undocumented immigrants during his successful gubernatorial campaign.) In July 2012 Representative Blaine Gallier (R-Rainbow City) resigned his House seat to become Bentley's legislative affairs director.

The Legislative Workload

The number of bills filed in a typical regular legislative session would be about 1,500. In 2007 the number was 1,470; in 2008, more than 1,600.[15] In 2012, 1,370 bills were introduced—785 in the House and 585 in the Senate.[16] There is no way, given its mandated short meeting time and its limited staff, that the Legislature could adequately consider this large number of bills.

How Bills Are Handled

It is more efficient if identical bills are introduced simultaneously in both the House and Senate (called "working both tracks"). Whichever house considers the bill first (and presumably passes it) can send it to the other one. If by chance there are no changes, the bill is ready for the governor's signature or veto. The ALISON legislative website enables the public to track the progress (or lack of it) of bills with which they are concerned. Those interested can also listen to a live feed from committee meetings by going to the legislature's website.

Generally, the House and Senate meet on Tuesdays and Thursdays with committee meetings on other days. Counting days on which they are at the State House for committee meetings, a legislator can expect to be in Montgomery for about 150 days each year.

Local Legislation

Many of the bills introduced in the legislature are local in nature and will be routinely passed according to the rule of legislative courtesy. If the local delegation supports a bill, generally the legislature as a whole will approve it. Alabama has been noted as one of eight states in which hundreds of local bills are on each session's agenda.[17] Local leaders need to have a good working relationship with their local legislative delegations in order to get state authorization for things they want to do. For many reasons, such as having representatives who also represent parts of several other jurisdictions, this may be difficult.

In the 2011 session, a Jefferson County senator (Scott Beason) put a "hold" on a local bill that would have increased the county's taxing authority, and it did not pass. In part due to the lack of needed legislative support, the county subsequently filed the largest bankruptcy petition in US local government history. Twenty-six legislators represented parts of Jefferson County. This total included seven senators and nineteen representatives, mostly white Republicans and black Democrats. Alabama has been identified as one of two states with county governments that lack substantial home rule and are therefore dependent on advance state legislative approval for many minor as well as most major county initiatives.[18]

Committee Work

As in most other state legislative bodies, but to a somewhat lesser extent than in the US Congress, the main work of the Alabama legislature is done in the standing committees of the House and Senate. What makes Alabama legislative standing committees less powerful than many of their counterparts elsewhere, however, is the fact that often bills are perfunctorily referred favorably out of committee even though there is a general consensus that such bills will never receive final legislative passage. In contrast, in the US Congress there is a significantly greater likelihood that committee-approved bills will ultimately become law. Years ago, American state legislatures were roundly condemned for having an excessive number of committees, many of them never meeting. In recent years, in Alabama as elsewhere, what Sabato identified as "the heart of the legislative process"—the committee system—has been "thoroughly overhauled."[19] Major Alabama legislative committees are made up of fifteen members each, ten Republicans and half that many Democrats.

Assignment of Bills

The committee to which a bill is assigned may have no relevance to the presumed jurisdiction of the committee. For example, in the 2010 regular session the usual bills to ban PAC-to-PAC transfers and authorize the Ethics Commission to subpoena witnesses were assigned to the Senate Economic Expansion and Trade Committee. When asked about the bill, the chair of the committee replied: "I didn't read it."[20] Logically, these matters would be the province of the Constitution, Campaign Finance, Ethics, and Elections Committee. In the Republican-dominated legislature, bills continue occasionally to be assigned to committees other than those expected to have jurisdiction over the matters dealt with in the measures. If the speaker is sympathetic with a particular bill, he may take the wishes of its sponsor into consideration when referring a bill so as to increase the likelihood that it will be reportedly out favorably. Also, a bill doesn't have to be assigned to a committee immediately after it is introduced. In 2009 the PAC-to-PAC ban bill was not referred to a Senate committee until twenty-one of the thirty legislative days had come and gone. (It was never reported out.)

Committees and Interest Groups

The inaction or outright hostility of committee chairs to many of the bills they receive is often very satisfactory to the conservative-dominant interest groups. During the time when Black Belt whites enjoyed a disproportionate amount of influence in the legislature due to malapportionment, these long-serving members were said to be "learned in the ways of getting the fewest bills passed in the longest possible time when that strategy suits their purpose."[21]

The committees meet when the chairs send out notices. Voice votes are frequently used. The House Tourism and Travel Committee passed a gambling measure in April 2010 on a voice vote. Sometimes news media covering hearings have to report that there were certain members "appearing to vote for it [a particular bill], but several 'no' votes were heard."[22]

There is no requirement that hearings be held on bills that committees consider. In January 2010, the leader of the committee to which a PACT ("prepaid affordable college tuition") rescue bill had been referred held a hearing because AEA asked for one.[23] Until the 2010 elections, Paul Hubbert, then head of AEA, was easily the most influential single individual in determining whether a bill would pass the Alabama legislature or not. One critic said that "the super-powerful Alabama Education Association owned more than half the state Senate, lock, stock, and barrel."[24] Reflecting on his time in the legislature, the present governor of Alabama (Robert Bentley) observed that during the period in which Hubbert was recuperating from heart surgery, the legislature was "a totally different place."[25]

A newly elected senator, Paul Sanford (R-Huntsville), said he was "stunned at some of the antics in the Senate, especially in committee hearings." He found most committee discussions of bills to be perfunctory, with little substantive discussion prior to their being reported out to the full Senate.[26] As the new senator assessed this situation, the Democratic chairs of the upper house committees (prior to late 2010) "moved bills out to the full Senate and then Democrats [the leadership] cherry-picked bills they wanted to take up. Attendance at committee meetings was often poor."[27] One legislator said that he absented himself from a meeting of the House Tourism and Travel Committee when it was considering a gambling bill both "because he was troubled by the measure" and because "the committee had become a rubber stamp for pro-gambling bills."[28]

Sometimes bills have been "walked out" of House committees. "Walking a bill out" means to circumvent the usual committee meeting to consider a bill in a public meeting. Instead, the chair of the committee circulates among the committee members and tries to persuade them to sign off on it.[29] This procedure is not used now in the House or Senate.

Floor Debate

Just as in the US Congress, the ways in which bills are considered differ as between the Senate and House.

Filibustering

Filibustering is one of the commonly identified attributes of the Alabama legislature, especially the Senate. Senate rules traditionally have bestowed considerable power upon members to prevent the passing of bills by talking them to death. Cutting off debate (cloture) requires the approval of twenty-one of the thirty-five members. Cloture has become much more common since Republican control of the legislature began. The bill to alter the teachers' retirement program was passed after debate was terminated following just a few hours' discussion. Hubbert, the former AEA executive secretary, likened the Senate's action to a "freight train."[30] In the 2011 regular session of the legislature Senate cloture petitions were filed on forty-four occasions and approved in all but five subsequent votes on them. This was an increase of 1,000 percent from the frequency of such successful petitions in recent Democratic-dominated sessions.[31]

Partisanship

In the last year in which the legislature was majority Democratic, Senator Sanford complained that his side was usually kept in the dark about the agenda for a particular legislative day. When they did find out they frequently had less than an hour to review bills scheduled for votes.[32] There is apparently a correlation between the treatment Republicans as a minority received and the Republican discipline noted since they became the majority. Research in five southern states, including Alabama, showed that GOP legislators were more likely to vote together when they had been subjected to what they regarded as mistreatment at the hands of their previous majority Democratic colleagues.[33]

Partisan politics has often not been shown in the biggest items that come before the legislature (measured in terms of the amount of money spent). There frequently have been unanimous votes both in committee and on the floor on appropriations bills. Given a combination of heavily earmarked revenues (to be identified in chapter 14) and severely constrained financial resources, there may be little or no slack over which Democrats and Republicans may do combat.

Republicans were able to demonstrate their partisan clout before they became the majority. During the 2010 regular session, the forty-four House Republicans in disciplined fashion voted solidly to prevent constitutional amendments that would take away from the governor's power to fill vacancies in local offices. This superseded the usual custom of local courtesy previously mentioned with respect to bills applying to one named substate area.

When the bill relaxing teacher dismissal regulations passed the Republican legislature in 2011, fifty-six of sixty-four House Republicans voted "yea." Every Democrat except one voted "nay." So party discipline was not total. One of the Republicans who sided with AEA against the bill (Daniel Boman) soon after switched to being a Democrat. Party-line voting in the 2010–14 legislature was less likely to be insisted on in voting on amendments to bills as opposed to the bills themselves. Thus when the House Democratic minority leader offered an amendment to weaken the teacher dismissal bill it was defeated, but only by a close 54–48 vote. A dozen Republicans did not join their GOP colleagues in supporting the stronger teacher tenure bill.

The Republican Party chair, Bill Armistead (a former legislator), the choice of Republican Governor Robert Bentley, said he "[would] keep watch and [would] confront any legislators who consistently vote[d] the wrong way. If they persist[ed], he said, [he would] go public with his criticisms."[34] This approach did not work when the present Republican governor was a novice legislator, however. Bentley recalled: "They told me, really I think it [was] about my first or second week down there in Montgomery, that I wasn't voting like I was supposed to be voting. As a matter of fact, the chairman of the party, who was Marty Connors at the time, called me on the phone and he said, 'You are not voting like we would expect you to vote.'" Bentley continued, the tone of voice turning stern. "I said, 'Marty, I want to tell you something: Nobody tells me how to vote and that includes you.'"[35]

Only a very skeletonized version of what goes on during floor consideration will be found in the legislative journals. Unlike the *Congressional Record*, there is no record of debates.

Getting Legislation Passed

The "Shroud Award" is presented annually to the "deadest" piece of legislation introduced that year—the one that had the least chance of passage. In the 2010 regular session this award was given to the author of a bill to change the state's official song to "Stars Fell on Alabama."

For small groups that have legislation that they would like to see passed, persistence probably will be the quality that members will most need in order to achieve success. The most notable example of this in recent years was a group called Free the Hops: Alabamians for Specialty Beer, which, through patience and hard work, was able in time to achieve its specific objective out of the legislature. When the group began its work Alabama's maximum beer alcohol content of 6 percent was one of the lowest of all states. This percentage prevented ninety-eight of the world's leading beers from being sold in Alabama.

The Free the Hops group located an influential sponsor for their bill, employed a lobbyist, and assembled information packets that responded to concerns legislators might have related to stronger beer. Members themselves communicated with their legislators through every means available. They also invited imbibing legislators to private beer tastings. After all of this activity, the high-alcohol beer bill passed the legislature in 2009. The bill that passed was not exactly like the one originally introduced. Free the Hops compromised to lower the alcohol limit to 13.9 percent (down from 14.9) and prohibit sales by convenience stores. The head of the group said: "If you don't compromise, you don't get the ideal, you get nothing."[36]

Resolving House-Senate Differences

Conference committees are used when the House and Senate pass bills in different forms and the originating house will not accept changes made to the bills by the second house.

Typically, conference committees consist of three House members and three Senate members.

Constituent Relations

In a political culture such as Alabama's, where citizens don't have the habit of frequently contacting their elected representatives, most are basically unaware of what is going on in the legislature except for the occasionally highly charged issue like a pay raise.

The Impact of Public Opinion

Many citizens don't feel their opinions count for much anyway. To the statement "Officials in Montgomery do not care what people like me think" only 30 percent of respondents expressed any kind of disagreement, according to a recent survey.[37]

Despite the job security members of the legislature seem to enjoy most of the time, members still worry about being reelected. When a sentencing reform bill was being considered in the 2010 regular session, legislators who previously had been supportive backed off when voters back home saw a newspaper story interpreted to mean that the state needed to release thousands of prisoners due to overcrowding.[38] Members tend to reconsider their support for a bill when it attracts negative publicity such as this and when their colleagues also are turning against it to the extent that it seems certain to be defeated.

Legislative Pork

Another way to counteract possible unfavorable reactions to votes they might cast, in addition to or besides switching sides, legislators have resources that they can take back to their districts. Legislative pork barreling is by no means unique to Alabama. (We discuss the same practice by Alabama national legislators in chapter 14.) When the legislature passed the Education Trust Fund budget in early April 2010, Governor Riley expressed regret that it contained $8.4 million for special grants for legislators to make, but the bill's critical nature made a veto risky. (He didn't want the legislature to adjourn without passing the budgets.) Combined, the Education Trust Fund and General Fund budgets had $12 million for what the news media generally referred to as "pork projects."[39]

Help for the Legislature

Full-time legislative staff totaled 154 in spring 2011. The most important member of the upper chamber's workforce is the Senate secretary. The secretary has an expert knowledge of all Senate rules and parliamentary procedures and assists the lieutenant governor or others who may be presiding in conducting the chamber's activities in accordance with past practices. (The comparable lower house official is the House clerk.)

Probably the most important in-house source of expertise for the legislature is the Legislative Fiscal Office (LFO). It seeks to predict revenue collections so that legislators can do their part in assuring the mandatory balanced budgets. The work of the LFO is consistent with reforms made elsewhere to keep state legislatures from being so dependent on the governor or interest group lobbyists for the information they need in the consideration of bills.[40] The oldest of the legislative staff agencies is the Legislative Reference Service, which members may ask to actually draft the bills they want to introduce (if interest groups haven't previously done this).

We turn now to the most important single official in Alabama politics—the governor. We have seen in this chapter how the governor relates politically to the legislature. In the next we will also see how the governor operates in many other settings and will make further assessments related to the respective power positions of the governor and legislature.

12
Gubernatorial Politics

The southern governor was traditionally viewed as a very weak figure, hardly worthy of being called the "chief executive." He (and all governors were males in the immediate post–World War II period) was not seen as a strong leader.[1]

Evolution of the Southern Governorship

The trend toward a stronger southern governorship became most noticeable in the 1960s. Although federal judicial reapportionment intervention primarily improved the image of the legislature, it impacted positively on all of state government, including the governor. As a result, more capable people were motivated to seek the office. When he published his influential book on the governorship in the 1970s, political scientist Larry Sabato pointed to "the emergence of a new type of executive—younger, more experienced, and better educated."[2]

In this chapter we will focus specifically on the Alabama governorship. Even though Alabama has been frequently pointed to in this book as lagging behind other states in many respects, in the case of an institutionally strong governorship this was not the case. As we will see shortly, when we enumerate formal powers the Alabama governor possessed, this state's "chief magistrate" (a constitutional designation) already had several of the powers deemed most important and that were only belatedly given elsewhere. Besides Sabato's, another influential book initially published in the 1970s, Bass and De Vries's, assessed the Alabama governorship as "institutionally . . . one of the strongest in the country."[3] Finally, in the study by Joseph A. Schlesinger of formal gubernatorial powers in all the states, only Virginia ranked in the top ten. Alabama ranked a respectable fourteenth, next down among the southern states.[4]

Table 12.1. Formal powers of southern governors

Power	Location
Four-year term of office	Alabama and all others
Self-succession	Alabama and nine others
No maximum tenure	Alabama and eight others[1]
A cabinet created by governor	Alabama and three others[2]
Full responsibility for budget making	Alabama and two others
Special majority to override veto	Seven states (not including Alabama)
Item veto on all bills	Alabama and two others
Other elective administrative offices	Alabama, 7; average, 7
Administrative offices filled by governor	Alabama, 17; average, 18

[1]The Texas constitution permits unlimited self-succession.
[2]In Alabama and Louisiana, the Cabinet is also created by statute.
Source: Multiple sources related to American state and local government.

Formal Gubernatorial Powers

Nothing written down can guarantee that anyone will be an effective leader. However, formal powers provide a foundation on which a capable woman or man can build a successful administration. The following are an Alabama governor's most important formal powers:

(1) Serving a four-year term with succession permitted (and no limit on the number of terms so long as no more than two are consecutive). The constitution has always provided for a four-year term. Succession was authorized in the late 1960s (Amendment 282);
(2) submitting the two annual budgets under which the state operates (these budgets were discussed in chapter 11 and will be referred to again in this chapter as well as chapter 14);
(3) ensuring that the state always has a balanced budget by prorating funds during the year if necessary (Amendment 26);
(4) giving a state of the state address annually that includes not only an assessment of conditions but also a gubernatorial legislative program (which southern governors have felt was their most important responsibility)[5];
(5) vetoing bills passed by the legislature, including individual items in appropriation bills (the limits on this power will be noted in the section dealing with constraints);
(6) amending legislatively approved bills (in the mid-twentieth century Alabama was one of only four states that gave their governor this power. Still much less than half do);

(7) calling special legislative sessions and fixing their agenda without extramajority votes;
(8) usually appointing heads of agencies created by law and always doing so in the case of agencies gubernatorially established;
(9) appointing replacements when vacancies occur in local offices;
(10) issuing executive orders and proclamations that may be either ceremonial or order citizens to take actions contrary to their own wishes; and
(11) commuting death sentences to life imprisonment.

Informal Powers

The governor also has informal powers (some of which may be implied in law but are not as clearly stated as those just mentioned). The following is a sample of these powers:

(1) Literally working with the legislature on the floor of the House and Senate as they consider bills;
(2) appealing to party loyalty as a motivation for others to go along with gubernatorial wishes;
(3) dispensing federal grant money, money appropriated as block grants and to assist state residents in recovering from natural disasters;
(4) making decisions that become expansive precedents for his or her successors (such as Bob Riley leading criminal investigations in 2010); and
(5) responding to public expectations that always seem to be in the direction of widening rather than contracting gubernatorial authority (Sabato wrote that it was the governor who "is the focus of the people's expectations" as "the commander-in-chief of state government"[6]).

Restraints on Gubernatorial Powers

But the portrait of the contemporary Alabama governor would be incomplete without also noting continuing constraints on the exercise of leadership from this position. The following are illustrative:

(1) Heading a plural executive branch, the most notable members of which—the lieutenant governor and the attorney general—are independently elected;
(2) no longer possessing the power to organize the legislature (as recently as the early 1970s);
(3) having a veto that can be overridden by a majority of the members in each legislative house;

(4) having an item veto on appropriations bills that can only be exercised if the legislature is in session to have the opportunity to override it (an unlikely situation for reasons identified later);
(5) facing possible legislative rejection of the budgets the governor has submitted; and
(6) coping with the economic downturn in recent years that has prevented governors from exercising leadership through costly new public policy initiatives.

The Attorney General

The existence of the plural executive branch was noted in the preceding section as a principal constraint on the exercise of gubernatorial power. While some of the other elected executives have important duties, they do not set policy. The attorney general does, however, have an important role in this respect.

Recent political conflict between the governor and the attorney general warrants examination. It illustrates some of the likely problems with the plural executive branch. In addition to making policy with respect to law enforcement, the attorney general slot is also notable for having the best possibilities for being used as a stepping-stone to a higher position. In 2004 Attorney General William Pryor was appointed to the US Court of Appeals. Governor Bob Riley then named his legal advisor, Troy King, to serve until the next election. Don Siegelman, who was elected governor in 1998, had a term as attorney general on his resume (1987–91). Another attorney general, Jeff Sessions, was elected US senator in 1994 and still serves.

The Troy King–Bob Riley turf battle provides a valuable illustration of the consequences of constitutional vagueness. King was probably accurate in saying: "No governor wants an independent attorney general."[7] He attributed his and Riley's original falling-out to his refusal of a request Riley allegedly made of King to issue an advisory opinion, one of the attorney general's main functions, affirming that state law required annual rather than four-year reassessments of property values for tax purposes. Riley implemented annual reappraisals on his own that, in a time of rising property values, meant more state revenue without the tax increases voters had decisively rejected in a 2003 referendum. (This shows the impact of gubernatorial decision-making precedents as mentioned earlier.)

Attorneys general sometimes get extensive news coverage for their activities. This was true, for example, in the tobacco litigation of the 1990s. Legal scholar Michael DeBow said it was "hard not to reach the conclusion that the [tobacco] cases were an audacious attempt by the states' attorneys general to impose a totally unforeseen liability, retroactively, on the defendant tobacco companies, without the benefit of legislative action."[8]

In the most publicized dispute between Governor Riley and Attorney General King, to be discussed later in this chapter, Riley made it clear that he considered himself to be more than merely "first among equals" within the plural executive branch. Most law enforcement agencies, such as the Department of Public Safety and the Alcoholic Beverage Control (ABC) Board, are basically under gubernatorial control because of the power of appointment previously noted.

The Governorship in Practice

When Robert Bentley was inaugurated as governor of Alabama in January 2011, he became Alabama's fifty-second man to fill this job. One woman, Lurleen Burns Wallace, served in 1967–68. She was a surrogate for her husband, George Wallace, at a time when the Alabama constitution did not allow governors to succeed themselves.

Until the 2006 election, incumbents, both Democratic and Republican, had lost three consecutive gubernatorial elections. Bob Riley broke this pattern when he defeated Lieutenant Governor Lucy Baxley for a second term by a margin of 58 percent to 42 percent. The prior inability of governors to win second terms reflected the dilemma of trying to satisfy increasing public expectations in a climate of intense public hostility to any new taxes.

The Image of the Governor

The image of Alabama became inextricably linked with its governor's (Wallace's) extremely bigoted views in the 1960s. Even in the full-blown Jim Crow era all governors did not share Wallace's racist views, however. James E. Folsom had moderate-to-liberal racial views for his times. (Folsom served as governor 1947–51 and 1955–59.) Political scientists and historians rightly credit Folsom with at least verbalizing about the need to treat African Americans more fairly and for refusing to take part in racist, demagogic politics. Sabato, whose influential book on the governorship has been mentioned earlier, identified Folsom as one of America's outstanding governors during the period 1950–75, the only Alabamian to be so recognized.[9]

A book on Alabama published in 2011 referred to "one governor resigning under threat of removal" while "another [was] led off to federal prison."[10] While both of these statements contain elements of truth, neither is factually accurate. Guy Hunt didn't resign; he was automatically removed upon his conviction for using public money for private benefit. Don Siegelman was sent to prison well after he left the governorship. On the other hand, the author—American studies scholar Allen Tullos—is totally factual in identifying former Lieutenant Governor George McMillan "as another of the potential New South governors that white Alabamians never seemed to get around to electing."[11]

Wallace defeated McMillan in 1982 when Wallace was running successfully for the fourth (and last) time. The term "New South" governor totally expired in the 1990s.

Backgrounds of Governors

In his survey of southern governors, Sabato found that in the period leading up to the publication of *Goodbye to Good-Time Charlie*, they continued to be, like their predecessors, mostly white Protestant men.[12] Governor Robert Bentley was not only a member of the Baptist church (like his predecessor Riley); he also served as a deacon. Riley's predecessor, Siegelman, was Catholic.

Alabama as a historically rural state does not show a pattern of electing big city people to the governorship. In terms of post-Wallace governors, Fob James (elected after Wallace as a Republican) grew up in a small east Alabama town (Lanett). Guy Hunt was elected from an even smaller community, Holly Pond (Cullman County). Bob Riley was a citizen of Ashland (a small town in Clay County that was also the birthplace of US Supreme Court Justice Hugo Black). The only resident of a big city to be elected governor during the previous six decades has been Siegelman, a Mobile native.

Most Alabama governors have been married family men. When Riley was succeeded by Bentley a member of the capital press corps, Dana Beyerle, pointed out that they were "somewhat alike": "Both are from small towns, have legislative backgrounds and both ran businesses. Both are Republicans. Both are . . . married and have grandchildren."[13] (Bentley's fifty-year marriage subsequently ended in divorce.)

The Business Governor

The business background of both Riley and Bentley is most notable from a comparative perspective. Over the long span of years from the beginning of statehood in 1819, most Alabama governors were attorneys. In the post-Wallace era of Alabama politics, however, only one governor, Don Siegelman, has been a lawyer. Riley ran a variety of businesses; physician Bentley established a highly successful dermatological clinic. Alabama is similar to the rest of the South in that most recent governors have been businessmen.[14] Focusing on Florida, Loren Beth and William Havard saw their state also frequently electing businessmen as their governors—men "whose major pre-occupation was keeping state government out of the way of the business community," or, better, "making state government work for it."[15]

Military Service

It used to be indispensable for a serious candidate for governor to have served in the military. That is no longer true, but military service is a political asset to make voters aware of. Bentley was accused in 2010 of running a campaign ad that to some viewers suggested that he had served in Vietnam. A close watching of the ad revealed no false claim, however, and Bentley said, "I am angry at Bradley Byrne [one of his two main opponents in the Republican primary] for bringing this up right now and criticizing my service to my country, when he never served."[16]

Legislative Experience

Even though their job will involve both cooperation and conflict with the legislative branch of state government (and we have noted that traditionally governors felt that this was their most important sphere of activity), most recent Alabama governors have not had prior state legislative experience. Bentley is the first since Wallace to have it. Showing the rarity of direct promotion from the legislature to the governorship, Bentley is the first person to accomplish this feat since Thomas Seay in 1886.

The Governor's Spouse

The spouse of the governor may have attributes that the governor does not have. Fob James sought the votes of religious conservatives but seemed not to be as comfortable talking about his faith as was his wife, Bobbie James. When James won a surprise victory over incumbent Governor Jim Folsom Jr., in 1994 she declared, "It was Jesus that gave us victory. God in his mercy heard the prayers of Christians all over."[17]

Public Expectations

Alabamians do not expect perfection out of their governors. It has been noted with respect to Bibb Graves (1927–31, 1935–39), one of Alabama's most revered governors, that "he was closely allied to the KKK and practiced patronage politics."[18] "Big Jim" Folsom had serious problems with alcohol. Even so, despite the prohibitionist sentiments of many of them, the people loved him because he brought his campaign to where they were rather than relying on the support of courthouse gangs, as many of his predecessors had done.[19]

Even though he had to leave office before the expiration of his second term, Guy Hunt was memorialized at his funeral for his "simple virtue."[20] For his championing of tax reform in the year of his first inauguration (2003), Riley was referred to by *Time* as "Alabama's most courageous politician."[21] While campaigning for governor, Dr. Bentley said: "Let me tell you—I'm a healer . . . I want to be a governor that cares about the people."[22]

The Governorship Today

Many years ago, in one-party Alabama, the gubernatorial transition would, for all practical purposes, begin just as soon as the Democratic primaries ended, since its winner would inevitably be the next governor. The Democratic nominee for governor was referred to in the newspapers as the "governor-nominate." At present, transitional activities start in earnest after the November general election, although it is now assumed that, after the Republican primaries, Alabamians know who their next governor will be.

Transition and Inauguration

During the transition period after election and before inauguration the governor-elect and volunteer staff plan the swearing-in festivities and make as many appointments as practical to ensure that gubernatorial work can begin without a sharp learning curve after the swearing in.

The most recent gubernatorial inauguration in Alabama was on January 19, 2015. In light of the state's ongoing straitened financial condition Robert Bentley's second inaugural (like his first) was a low-key event, although it did feature a parade and free public activities. A ticketed inaugural ball was held in the evening. The inauguration was financed by private donations. The first executive director of the Alabama Ethics Commission, Melvin Cooper, said inaugural donors were "paying for access and contacts and good feelings."[23] One of the most generous donors to Bentley's swearing-in events was the Alabama Power Company.

Both of Bentley's inaugural addresses stressed job creation. In the second speech he noted that unemployment in the state was lower than in the years immediately prior to his taking office for the first time. Like many of his predecessors, but much less stridently, he said in his first address that he would resist unnecessary federal involvement in state business. In the second, there was more stress on cooperation between Montgomery and Washington. Federal aid had been of crucial importance in helping the state recover from the devastating tornadoes that struck Alabama shortly after Bentley had initially assumed the governor's office in 2011. The governor takes the oath with his right hand on "the state's official Good Book (the Jeff Davis Bible)."[24]

It was at his first inaugural in 1963 that George Wallace promised "segregation . . . forever." Wallace definitely fit what Earl Black identified as the "militant segregationist" in the massive resistance era.[25] The Alabama political climate in this period did not allow the election of a "moderate segregationist" (such as Albert Brewer) and definitely not a "nonsegregationist."[26]

The Governor's Mansion

The main perquisite of office currently provided by the state for the governor and family is a mansion located on South Perry Street. A century ago governors lived in private homes or hotels. During Fob James's first term the family's choice was to reside elsewhere in Montgomery, but this was unusual. Governor Bentley said: "It is the people's house. I believe the people expect you to live in the Governor's Mansion."[27]

A Full-Time Governor

It is now expected by the people that the person who they elect to the governorship in Alabama will devote his or her full time to performing the duties of the office. This is hardly surprising, but in the Wallace era the governor didn't. "Alabama needs a full-time governor" was the message Albert Brewer used in his unsuccessful campaign against Wallace in 1970. Subordinates did most of the work required to run the state while the governor prepared for or engaged in presidential campaigns. Wallace biographer Dan Carter claimed exaggeratedly that, given his obsession with national politics (but at the end also his deteriorated physical condition), it was necessary for the state to operate on autopilot "for the entirety of his 18-year stewardship of the state."[28] Because of his lack of interest in administrative leadership, Wallace did not have turf battles of the type that Riley and King were involved in during the last full year in office for both men.

Turf Battles

The main substantive issue in the Riley-King conflict mentioned earlier in the chapter was the legality of electronic bingo games in areas authorized by local constitutional amendments to have bingo. The legitimacy of gubernatorial raids on establishments by Riley's task force was hotly contested. The fact that Riley ultimately prevailed provided a precedent that will enhance the power of his successors.

The Task Force

Riley had formed a task force in December 2008 with the mission of eliminating electronic bingo machines. His original designee as its director was forced to resign when it was revealed that he had been gambling at a Mississippi casino.

King had given the opinion in 2005 that electronic bingo was permissible in those sixteen counties that had thus far been authorized by constitutional amendment to have bingo. (There was no uniformity in the wording of the amendments.) In 2008, another King interpretation permitted the opening of the very large casino known as Country Crossing near Dothan. Riley objected to these interpretations of Alabama gambling law, and King charged Riley with provoking a "constitutional crisis" by trying to usurp authority he claimed as his own.[29] Into this situation even a usually activist federal judge (Judge Myron Thompson) declined to get involved, holding that whether slot-machine style bingo machines were legal or not was a "state-law issue."[30]

The political battle between the governor and attorney general intensified when an African American Democratic state senator representing an area with electronic bingo gambling, Bobby Singleton of Greensboro, introduced a bill that would take away the governor's power to initiate and direct criminal investigations. Passage of the measure would have effectively put an end to Riley's antigambling task force. A spokeswoman for the attorney general said he hadn't requested such legislation but liked the fact that it "reaffirm[ed] Alabama's historical system of checks and balances and separation of powers."[31] The bill Singleton authored was approved in the Senate Judiciary Committee on a 7–3 party-line vote—no Democrats opposing and no Republicans favoring. This was as far as the bill got. It was never voted on in the full Senate or House.

In another legislative attack on the formal gubernatorial powers identified at the outset of this chapter and noted in the previous chapter as well, Singleton had introduced a bill to limit the governor's constitutional power to fill vacancies in local offices. Due to a disciplined Republican minority, a local amendment proposal to make this change received forty-eight votes when it came up in the House, but this was fifteen less than the three-fifths majority required to pass it.

Attorney General King seemed to be preparing to take over the antigambling task force as a judicial decision indicated he could do. Circuit Judge

Robert Vance Jr. (who would later become the unsuccessful Democratic candidate for state chief justice in 2012) had said, "The governor lacks the authority to create his own prosecutor whenever a district attorney takes a legal position that is not to his liking."[32] Nevertheless, Riley defended his actions in "using his supreme executive power" to "overrule and nullify" King's attempt to dismiss the second commander of his task force on illegal gambling, Mobile district attorney John Tyson. Riley told King to cease from "any effort to direct or interfere" with the task force's operations.[33]

Judicial Interpretations

Ultimately, King decided against further attempts to assume command of the gambling task force. Riley had the support of the state Supreme Court and King did not. The high court ruled on May 21, 2010, that the law was on Riley's side, not King's. The court commended Riley for filling a vacuum in law enforcement in those parts of the state where illegal gambling was going on. Unless Riley had taken leadership, the court declared, "the law would continue to go unenforced in those counties during Attorney General King's tenure." Just as is the case with the president at the federal level, the Alabama Supreme Court found in the office of governor, not in that of attorney general, the primary constitutional duty "to take care that the laws be faithfully executed." Indeed, "The core power of the executive branch is the enforcement of those laws."[34]

One lower court judge, Tom Young of Macon County, was not happy about his senior colleagues' ruling, saying that they had contrived a "slippery slope" that would allow the incumbent governor and his successors "unfettered power to usurp the authority of a constitutional officer elected by the citizens."[35]

When the Supreme Court unanimously (including Democratic Chief Justice Sue Bell Cobb) reversed Judge Young's order blocking a planned Riley task force gambling raid, the former president of the state bar association, Mark White, said that the high court's ruling gave the governor "unchecked power" to take actions he deemed appropriate, even if local officials vigorously objected. "They decided that the governor is in essence the king of Alabama" and "is in total control. He has the same type of power that Saddam Hussein had in Iraq before we invaded."[36]

Showing that in addition to other attributes the governor also needs a thick skin, in the context of the electronic bingo controversy Governor Riley was the target of numerous epithets, including "terrorist," "criminal," "liar," "racist," scoundrel," "a lame duck trying to pay off debts," "a wet nurse to Mississippi casinos," and "a mean, lowdown raccoon."[37] When Alabama was

12.1. President Barack Obama and Governor Bob Riley after the Gulf oil spill. Source: Whitehouse.gov

playing for the national football championship in the Rose Bowl, Tuscaloosa businessman Stan Pate hired a plane for a flyover with the message, "Impeach Corrupt Alabama Governor Bob Riley."

Governor Riley ultimately moved on to ethics reform, as we saw in chapter 4. The new governor, Robert Bentley, discontinued the task force, and legal issues pertaining to gambling are still being litigated. Due to conflicts such as that between Riley and King, which are inevitable in a plural executive branch like Alabama's, the governor has a legal adviser as part of his or her immediate staff.

Gubernatorial Leadership

As previously noted, public expectations for the Alabama governor have greatly expanded. In the following sections we will suggest some of the current challenges of and opportunities for the governor.

Industrial Recruitment

It is now anticipated that the governor will devote a large portion of his or her time to recruiting new businesses to locate in the state, something that began in earnest in the second half of the twentieth century and continues unabated today. As he prepared to succeed Riley, Bentley promised to oversee a "seamless transition" from Riley to himself.[38] Even though they were

12.2. President Barack Obama and Governor Robert Bentley after Alabama tornados. Courtesy of the *Tuscaloosa News*

not close politically, he praised Riley for having the best business recruitment record of any governor. After about six months in office, Bentley himself was on an industry-hunting mission to France and Germany.

Natural Disasters

Bentley faced a major challenge before his first foreign trip. Item three in the list of informal gubernatorial powers noted that one of the most important current areas requiring effective gubernatorial leadership is, with massive federal assistance, helping the state to recover from natural disasters such as tornadoes, hurricanes, floods, droughts, fires, and other catastrophes. On April 27, 2011, severe tornadoes caused great losses in lives (more than 240), homes (in excess of 15,000 destroyed), and businesses (property damage of at least $4 billion). Before midnight of that disastrous day, Bentley had taken a series of steps including proclamation of a state of emergency, mobilization of the Alabama National Guard, and requesting President Barack Obama for his own declaration that would make the state eligible for the desperately needed federal aid Congress has authorized in such situations. Bentley also visited survivors everywhere the tornadoes had struck.

Bentley wanted the state to play the major role in directing relief. He said that the Federal Emergency Management Agency (FEMA) had "cause[d] a mess in a lot of states because they don't know the people and they don't know the needs." "The governor," Bentley stressed, "is in charge of a disaster in the state."[39] The governor anticipated that his performance during catastrophes such as this would strongly influence how his time in office was evaluated. After a year in office he noted: "A lot of time, governors are judged by how they respond to natural disasters—positively or negatively . . . that's where they decide on your leadership skills."[40]

Evaluating the Governors

From the day he was inaugurated for his second term in 2007, Riley was a term-limited lame duck. When he launched his antigambling crusade he was near the end of his stint as governor. He was obviously concerned about how he would be remembered for the time he served the state. The ethics reform package passed late in 2010 provided a much more positive legacy than the gambling raids.

Riley had made his final state of the state address on January 12, 2010. Like his predecessor Don Siegelman as he was about to leave office, Riley painted a rosier picture of the state's financial condition than most other observers saw.

House Democratic majority leader Ken Guin predictably said that the governor's interpretation of the state of things was "completely off base."[41] Another story related to state finances was headed: "Budget comments shock lawmakers."[42]

Despite the criticism of his last major speech, Riley was assessed mostly positively on leaving office. Historian Wayne Flynt said: "Keep in mind the bar has been pretty low, but Riley was honest and ethical and he held his cabinet and staff responsible for how they did their jobs and behaved."[43] Bob Blalock, the editorial page editor of the *Birmingham News*, said that Riley's most important contribution was in the area of education: "About the time Bob Riley became governor, it was hard to imagine anyone would ever rank our K–12 schools 25th in the nation."[44] He also noted that Riley's eight years in office were not marred by scandal. American studies scholar Tullos, who is not generally favorable toward Alabama politics, said, "Bob Riley left office as the most competent and diligent among southern Republican governors."[45]

Riley's predecessor, Don Siegelman, will always be remembered as the only governor to be sent to federal prison following conviction for what jurors believed was soliciting a bribe. A decade earlier, Governor Guy Hunt was convicted of a felony in state court but was spared from having to go to jail. Both men had accomplishments in their administrations, but history generally emphasizes the negative more than the positive.

Looking at other Alabama governors elected in the post–World War II pe-

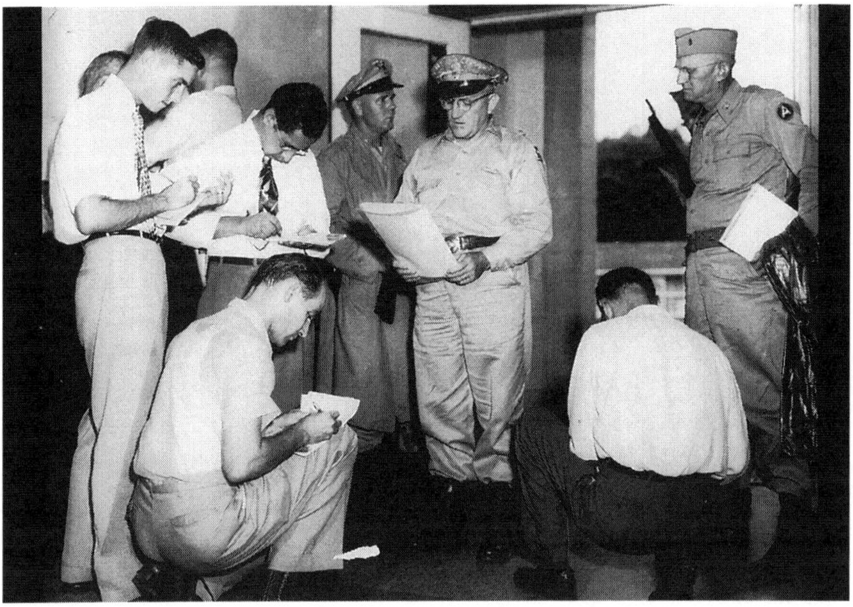

12.3. Martial law in Phenix City, Alabama. Courtesy of Steve Franklin Private collection

riod, as noted earlier Governor James Folsom (1947–51, 1955–59) is the only one to be labeled outstanding by a nationally recognized scholar (Larry Sabato). Gordon Persons (1951–55) had a very low-key personality and did not relate well to his constituency. He is remembered primarily because the assassination of the Democratic nominee for attorney general, Albert Patterson (John Patterson's father) forced him to clean up Phenix City. Governor Patterson (1959–63) was identified by one scholar (Richard Scher) as a demagogue because of the extreme racial views he expressed and demonstrated.[46]

Patterson's postgubernatorial record helped improve his legacy, however. He served for many years as an effective appeals court judge and presided over the Court of the Judiciary when it upheld the removal of Roy Moore from the chief justiceship of the Supreme Court due to his failure to follow a federal court order. An entire chapter (chapter 2) has been devoted to Patterson's gubernatorial successor, George Wallace, and his assessment and that of his surrogate, Governor Lurleen Wallace, are made there. Her successor on her death, Governor Albert Brewer, like Governor Jim Folsom Jr., had only an abbreviated term (1968–71), but is remembered positively for his interest in constitutional reform. Like Patterson, Brewer has seen a great deal of postgubernatorial service and is now regarded as Alabama's elder statesman who is ready to respond when needed, as illustrated by his current chairing of a constitutional revision commission.

Wallace's successor before his fourth and final term and Siegelman's predecessor was Fob James (1979–83, 1995–99), the only man to serve as governor both as a Democrat and as a Republican. His administration is remembered positively for the establishment of the Alabama Trust Fund but negatively because of the low esteem in which this successful businessman held state government, comparing it to a Waffle House.[47] Hunt's successor, following his ouster, was Jim Folsom Jr. (1993–95) who had only a partial term before his defeat by James. He is remembered positively because of his recruitment of the Mercedes auto manufacturing plant and his decision not to hoist the Confederate flag again after renovations to the Historic Capitol were completed.

The appellate courts are very much involved in politics, especially in how their judges get to the bench in the first place, but also in how they function on a regular basis. We saw in this chapter how the courts, especially the Supreme Court, impacted the exercise (generally in a positive way) of gubernatorial power. It is to a discussion of the Courts of Appeals and the Supreme Court that we now turn.

13
The Courts as Political Institutions

Politics very definitely enters into what meaning is given to law and how it affects specific public controversies. The courts are lobbied by groups and unaffiliated influentials just as much as are legislators and executives—even if frequently in different ways. Particularly in the past two decades, interest groups everywhere have seen how much their material livelihood depends on judicial decisions.

The Reputation of Alabama Courts

Alabama courts received notoriety in the Jim Crow era for their insensitivity toward African American defendants, most infamously in the Scottsboro Boys cases (especially *Powell v. Alabama*) of the 1930s.[1] The way the innocent young defendants (falsely accused of rape) were inhumanely treated in legal proceedings brought unfavorable international political attention to Alabama for much of the 1930s. The US Supreme Court held in *Powell* that defendants subject to the death penalty if convicted must be provided with effective counsel to assist in their defense, in state as well as in federal court. Subsequent cases extended this protection to the accused in a much wider variety of cases involving less harsh penalties.

The Alabama Supreme Court has a better relationship with the US Supreme Court than in the old Jim Crow era. One of the members of the Alabama high court once referred to "the onslaughts of federal courts" and asserted that the nation's premier court was the leading participant in the "systematic destruction of state sovereignty."[2] At present, even though the Alabama Supreme Court is very conservative, the justices usually recognize the supremacy of federal law, as was demonstrated most clearly in the Ten Commandments controversy discussed in chapter 3. That they are not so subservient to federal authority was shown when the Court told Alabama probate courts not to follow a US District Court decision calling for the issuance of marriage licenses to same-sex couples early in 2015.[3]

The State Judicial System

Previously, in chapter 6, we have identified key provisions of the judicial article of the Alabama Constitution—the only major portion of the 1901 document to be replaced by a reformed version (in 1973).

The Supreme Court

Different states have different names for their courts. In Alabama the highest court is the Supreme Court (as is true nationally). In some states (Maryland, for example) the court at the apex of the judicial system is the court of appeals.[4] Both of the New England states of Maine and Massachusetts call their highest court the supreme judicial court.

The Alabama Supreme Court is presided over by a chief justice who is also head of the judicial administrative system.

Before 1973, Alabama courts were a mélange of tribunals with inconsistent organization and jurisdiction. In that year, as just noted, the new judicial article to the constitution was approved under the leadership of Chief Justice Howell Heflin. According to former Associate Justice Janie L. Shores, Heflin's judicial reform package, the "Judicial Article," reorganized Alabama's state courts and became a model for the nation, studied by numerous other states. His court reform continues to be the only major reform of the Alabama Constitution in more than one hundred years.[5]

Heflin would have preferred to implement a merit system of choosing judges as part of his judicial reform program. However, incumbent governor George Wallace told Heflin that if "he put stuff in that judicial reform that would take away the people's right to vote on judges" he would "have to stump the state against it."[6] So partisan popular elections were retained.

The chief justice has eight colleagues who serve as associate justices. As table 13.1 shows, the Alabama Supreme Court originally consisted of five justices. Between the time of its creation in 1829 to 1969, the size of the court ranged from a low of three to a high of seven. In 1969 the latter number was raised by two, giving the Supreme Court nine justices. This is the same number as the US Supreme Court.

Occasionally, the federal judiciary will seek the assistance of their state counterparts in controversies they are wrestling with. For example, in De-

Table 13.1. Growth of the Alabama Supreme Court

Period	Number of Justices
1829–32	5
1832–51	3
1851–53	5
1853–89	3
1889–91	4
1891–1903	5
1903–69	7
1969–2014	9

Source: http://judicial.alabama.gov/docs/judicial.history.pdf.

cember 2011, the US Court of Appeals in Atlanta asked the Alabama Supreme Court to make a judgment as to whether the Alabama Education Association (AEA) was engaged in activities that influenced elections. If they answered in the affirmative, then the ban on the deduction of AEA dues from member paychecks as previously approved by the legislature was apparently appropriate.[7] Ultimately, the Alabama court advised the US Court that the AEA was indeed involved in activities the aim of which was to influence elections so dues check-off could be terminated without offense to free speech guarantees of the federal Constitution.

The Courts of Appeals

Immediately below the Supreme Court are the Court of Criminal Appeals and the Court of Civil Appeals. Each of these courts has five judges. Originally Alabama had no intermediate courts between the trial courts and the Supreme Court. Growing caseloads, however, first caused the creation of a Court of Appeals (1911) and then the two present Courts of Civil Appeals and Court of Criminal Appeals (1969).

Other Components of the Unified Judicial System

Below the appellate courts are municipal courts, district courts, and circuit courts. The circuit courts are the main trial courts. The popularly elected district attorney is an officer of the circuit court. Local governing bodies select municipal judges. District courts mostly handle relatively less serious legal problems outside city boundaries and where localities opted not to have their own municipal courts.

Table 13.2. Alabama judicial salaries compared with salaries in other states (selected) (2012) associate justice, Court of Last Resort

Location and rank	Amount
Highest (California)	$218,237
Alabama (9th)	$180,005
Mean	$152,606
Median	$146,917
Lowest (Mississippi)	$112,530

Source: National Center for State Courts, *Survey of Judicial Salaries* (2012).

The Judges

The key political actors in the Alabama judicial system are the women and men who serve as judges and preside individually or collectively over the wide variety of cases where they have jurisdiction.

Judicial Qualifications

Alabama law requires all appellate judges to be licensed Alabama lawyers for a minimum of ten years. For circuit and district judges the licensure years are five and three, respectively. Alabama is one of about thirty states that have established minimal legal experience requirements for people aspiring to be judges. The neighboring state of Mississippi sets a minimum of five years experience as a lawyer as a condition of judicial eligibility.

Compensation and Appropriations

Judges are paid generously considering the fact that Alabama is a relatively poor state. As an example, the average salary of a justice of the Alabama Supreme Court is $180,005 annually. According to a study by the National Center for State Courts, these jurists are the ninth best paid in the nation. (The chief justice makes $196,183.) All appellate court offices and court and meeting rooms are located in the Heflin-Torbert State Judicial Building on Dexter Avenue in Montgomery.

The Alabama Constitution requires that "adequate and reasonable funds be provided for the court system" (Article 6, Sec. 6.10), but this does not immunize the courts from cuts being imposed on state government during stringent financial times. In fiscal year 2011 the legislature appropriated approximately $165 million from the General Fund budget to operate the judicial system. As table 13.3 shows, General Fund appropriations declined from about $177 million in 2008 to $124 million in fiscal year 2012. Increases in

Table 13.3. Alabama judicial appropriations

Year	Total expenditures
2008	$220,811,529*
2009	228,492,055*
2010	180,715,727
2011	144,996,715
2012	124,371,162**

*These figures represent total expenditures from all fund sources.
**This figure represents the amount budgeted in the General Fund.
Source: Norris Green, director, Legislative Fiscal Office (e-mail messages of August 2012)

court costs and fees were expected to give the state judiciary a total of about $169 million to spend, however.

Judicial Decision Making

The most recent average number of days required for a justice to handle a case assigned to him or her is 199.[8] Some decisions of all three appellate courts are not accompanied by written opinions, a situation attorneys and others most interested in judicial outputs often regret (especially no-opinion affirmances).

How the Appellate Courts Operate

Unlike the US Supreme Court, the Alabama high court works through divisions, each of which consists of five justices named by the chief justice who normally is a member of each of them as well. When five justices are in agreement as to how a case assigned to them should be decided the division takes responsibility for issuing the decision on it. If a case is reported in the media as having been decided by a vote of 5–1 that means there was one dissent in the division. Whenever at least five justices do not agree on a decision, cases are referred to the court as a whole. Decisions are also made by the whole court when there is dissent on a material question as opposed to a technicality. The courts of appeals also function in divisions or panels in a manner similar to the Supreme Court.[9]

This system has its critics but is defended because it increases productivity. The members of the courts decide if they wish to hear oral arguments on cases they have accepted for review. As is true with respect to the US appellate courts, the three Alabama tribunals follow precedent in most cases and affirm decisions that have been made at lower levels.

Judicial Review and Advisory Opinions

Corresponding to federal practice, the most important function of the Supreme Court of Alabama is the exercise of judicial review, potentially declaring the actions of members of coordinate branches of government unconstitutional. For example, in June 2011 the Supreme Court held 7–2 that a recently passed state law authorizing grandparents to visit their grandchildren was unconstitutional because it conflicted with the traditional right of parents to decide on matters pertaining to their children's welfare.[10] One of the dissenters called on the legislature to pass a revised law that would be consistent with the majority decision. Other justices, among the majority, wrote concurring opinions, agreeing with the ruling but for different reasons.

Most of the Supreme Court decisions are rendered in real cases between contending parties (such as parents versus grandparents) but, unlike the US Supreme Court, the Alabama court does render advisory opinions. In most states the constitution authorizes the highest court to issue advisory opinions. In Alabama, Delaware, and Oklahoma, however, this power is conferred by legislative act. These are different from "holdings" of the court because, if the matters are ever argued before the justices, they might reach a different conclusion.[11]

The court does not issue advisory opinions that would amount to a declaration that something already done by the legislature was unconstitutional. These matters would have to be decided upon in actual cases. In March 2010 the Alabama Supreme Court was asked to issue an advisory opinion on the legality of Etowah County Commission regulations related to bingo as it was to be played in the county. It declined to do so, however, since no "justiciable controversy" existed at the time the opinion was requested.[12] Historically, the justices of the Alabama Supreme Court have issued more advisory opinions than the highest court judges in any other state. Between 1923 and 2004, the justices published 344 responses to advisory opinion requests they had received. In the fourteen-year period 1990–2004 they issued thirty-six responses, a total that was "by far the most of any advisory state" during these years.[13]

The Alabama judiciary normally does not get involved in the internal workings of the legislature. For example, the courts will not hear a claim that a quorum was not present when a particular bill was passed. As noted in chapter 11, the Alabama legislative journals present only a very summary account of what went on in the House and Senate. Votes on local bills often have occurred with locked machines on which the votes of members may be recorded who were actually not on the floor when they were taken. Also, one member may vote for one or more other members. The Supreme Court will not second-guess the accuracy of official legislative records, however.

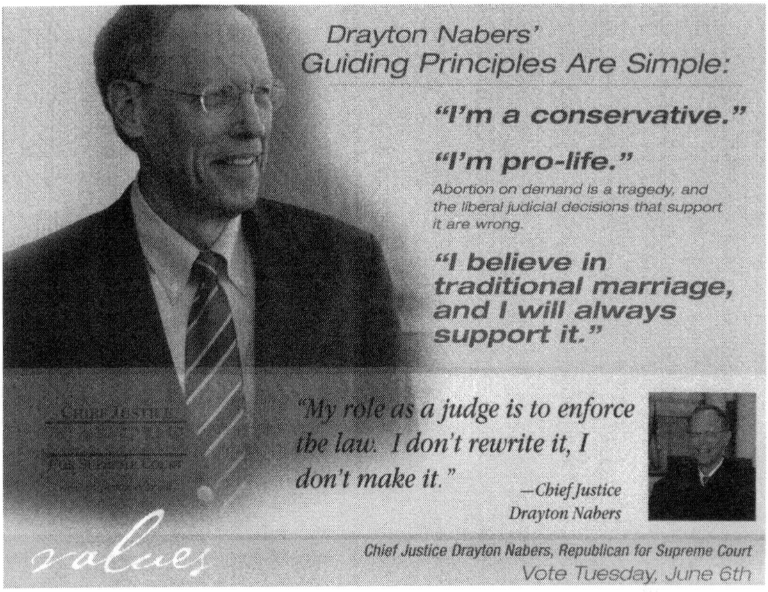

13.1. Drayton Nabers for Supreme Court flyer. From the William H. Stewart collection

Partisan Voting

With no Democrats now occupying positions on the Alabama appellate courts, it is impossible to analyze partisan voting since all justices and judges belong to the same Republican Party. Before Republican unanimity was achieved with Chief Justice Sue Bell Cobb's resignation, there was a noteworthy illustration of a partisan division. Though not a genuine case, in April 2010 the Supreme Court split 8–1 in turning back new proposals to allow members of the public to file complaints against judges for alleged unethical conduct.[14] Feeling differently than her eight Republican colleagues, Democratic Chief Justice Cobb voted to substitute a set of rules that had the endorsement of the American Bar Association. Under the rules the Republican justices voted to keep, a judge is supplied with the name of the complainant against him or her plus any evidence that may be accumulated during an investigation. The chief justice felt that such rules created dread regarding possible retaliation among people who might have a grievance against a judge. When a complaint was made against a justice a decade ago, the Judicial Inquiry Commission, to which the matter was referred, opted to drop the matter rather than comply with the rules just described.

Federal Courts in Alabama

We have previously seen how politics is also very much impacted by the trio of federal court districts into which Alabama has been divided. These are the northern, middle, and southern districts. Above the federal district courts, Alabama is located in the eleventh circuit of the US Courts of Appeals. When Alabama plaintiffs have a choice of courts in which to file cases they will likely "judge shop" and go to the federal district judge they feel will be most likely to decide cases in line with their own political and social values.

Judicial Selection

The most politically controversial matter pertaining to the Alabama courts in recent years—aside from the placement of the Ten Commandments monument—has been how judges initially get to and stay on the bench.

What the Constitution Says

The Alabama Constitution provides that "all judges shall be elected by vote of the electors within the territorial jurisdiction" (Article 6, Sec. 6.13). Judges serve six-year staggered terms. They can succeed themselves multiple times; however, an incumbent judge cannot run for another term after reaching seventy. In the 2012 Republican primary race for chief justice, only the unsuccessful incumbent, Charles Malone, would have been eligible for another term had he been selected. The other two candidates, Roy Moore (who won the nomination without a runoff and subsequently the general election) and Charles Graddick, a Mobile circuit judge (and formerly state attorney general), would both have reached seventy before their term expired so they were ineligible to run to succeed themselves.

Alabama Judicial Politics Transformed

While judicial elections may once have been described as "the sleepy backwater of electoral politics,"[15] this has not been true in Alabama for a long time. The explanation for the transformation of Alabama judicial politics lies primarily in the growth of the Republican Party and the conflict between two professional groups, plaintiffs' trial lawyers and the business interests represented by defense lawyers.

Judicial elections in the state were traditionally nonpartisan, not officially but because, until the 1990s, Alabama was still a one-party state, at least as far as court staffing was concerned. All serious candidates, no matter what their particular views were, ran in the Democratic primary and winning here was as good as getting elected. The one-party system also discouraged competition for judicial positions within Democratic primaries. Once an individual was elected as a judge he (and at that time judges were overwhelmingly male) tended to be reelected without opposition.

A common pattern at the state level was for a justice or judge to retire before the expiration of his term. The governor would then appoint a replacement who would have the advantage of running for a full term at the next election as an incumbent. A typical campaign message featured in newspaper ads was: "Keep Justice [or Judge] Smith in office!" When there were occasional contested Democratic primaries, the state and local bar associations frequently would rate candidates and, more often than not, those with the highest evaluations won the primary and took office as judges.

Historical Background

The US Constitution provided in 1787 that federal judges would be appointed by the president and confirmed by the Senate. Some states also follow this practice—New Jersey, for example.

Among the thirteen original states, eight constitutions provided that the legislatures would elect judges. This practice is still followed in Virginia and South Carolina. Alabama's circuit judges began to be popularly elected beginning in 1850, as the Jacksonian democracy movement took a continually stronger hold in the newer states. Alabama appellate judges were still elected by the legislature. Its jurists, as well as those of Kentucky, were noted at the time for verdicts that usually reflected the interests of the debtor classes.[16]

Electing judges on partisan ballots is opposed, according to Arkansas Supreme Court Justice Robert L. Brown, mostly because judicial elections "involve politics, and politics is [allegedly] fraught with corruption."[17] The method of judicial selection a state uses shows the conflict between two historic American values, judicial independence and democratic accountability. Merit selection plans emphasize independence while popular election stresses accountability. Coming down on the side of judicial independence, the thinking of the framers of the US Constitution was that judges should be insulated from the political pressures that would inevitably confront the Congress and president.

Contemporary Practice

Alabama is one of only seven states today that select supreme court judges on partisan ballots. Georgia and Mississippi use nonpartisan elections, as do twelve other states. Counting both partisan and nonpartisan states, twenty-two states allow for candidates to run against each other for supreme court seats, as Alabama does.

Surveys show that many Alabamians actually don't know much about how their judges are selected. This finding might cast doubt on their ability to assess the judicial credentials of the candidates who are asking for their votes. Nevertheless, a Harris Poll found that its Alabama respondents favored elections (although a substantial number said that they would prefer that such elections be nonpartisan).[18]

As Republicans have come increasingly to dominate Alabama courts, some Democratic lawmakers have favored making at least one or two sets of court races nonpartisan. In the news story reporting one unsuccessful measure's fate, it was noted that, "Republicans hold an 18–1 margin on the state's appeals courts and opposed the bills."[19] Before the rise of the modern Republican Party and the Democrats had all appellate judicial positions (the exact opposite of the present situation), Republicans were more likely to favor nonpartisan elections.

In 2008 four Republican Jefferson County judges switched to the Democratic Party because the increasing African American percentage of the population (and the great popularity among voters in this group of presidential candidate Barack Obama) was making Democrats' election prospects more favorable than those of Republicans. With the exodus of many whites to suburbs outside of Jefferson County, it has become more Democratic. It was one of the few counties carried by Democratic gubernatorial candidate Ron Sparks in 2010. In 2012, all countywide contested races were won by Democrats (including judgeships) while Obama was again triumphing in the presidential race.

Choosing by Merit

In merit selection of judges (also called the Missouri plan for its state of origin) a diversely appointed panel selects from a pool of judicial aspirants a small number to recommend to the governor for his or her consideration. Once appointed, the new judge serves for a limited probationary period (probably a year) after which voters are asked if they wish to keep the incumbent in office or have the original appointing process resumed. If the judge is retained, the regular judicial term is served, at which time the voters will again have the opportunity to retain or replace the judge. The judge never runs against another candidate. State bar associations, such as Alabama's, typically favor this arrangement. On its website the organized state bar featured an essay, "Which Is Right for Alabama, Partisan Elections or Merit Selection?" "What's important," according to the association, "is to what extent politics dictates who ultimately sits on the appellate bench."[20] Some sort of politics inevitably will determine who occupies judicial positions. No plan proposed can fully insulate the courts from it. Despite the assertion made by the head of the state retirement systems (David Bronner) that, "The Alabama Supreme Court must simply be above politics,"[21] this could never be accomplished.

US Court of Appeals judge and former Alabama attorney general William Pryor wrote that merit selection processes were, in fact, "no less political, often relying on lawyers, people who make their livings in courtrooms."[22] Another defender of popular election, as practiced in Alabama, professor Michael DeBow, said that, "If the choice is between election and some bar-dominated, closed-door selection plan, I'd rather have it open. . . . The election system is out in the open, where there can be a competitive airing of judicial philosophies."[23]

Actually, a variety of merit selection has been increasingly used in the selection of judges in Alabama counties designated in constitutional amendments. The first county to employ it was Jefferson (Birmingham) beginning in 1950 because legislators there didn't want Governor James Folsom to select their judges unfettered when vacancies occurred. As openings arise in judicial positions, a county judicial commission takes applications and, after evaluating them, recommends three finalists from whom the governor must choose one for the vacant judgeship. The new judge fills out the unexpired term and afterward, if he or she wants to continue in office, runs on the standard partisan ballot. The eight other counties using roughly the same procedure include most of the population centers of the state—Madison, Mobile, Baldwin, and Shelby are illustrative.

The "New Judicial Politics"

In Alabama, as in other states, relations between plaintiff and trial lawyers have been "less than cordial."[24] Plaintiff lawyers are closely associated with the Democratic Party, while business defense lawyers are, along with their employers, core constituents of the modern Republican Party.

Judicial Campaigns and Republican Victories

According to the judicial reform group Justice at Stake, which advocates merit selection, campaigns for positions on the Alabama Supreme Court have been among the most "divisive and unseemly high court campaigns ever seen in American politics."[25]

Texas, Idaho, Illinois, and West Virginia are other states where campaigns have been waged that provoked similar criticisms. In the minds of reformers such races symbolize "judicial politics run amok."[26]

As noted in chapter 8, the Alabama Republican Party initially began to compete seriously in state appellate court races in 1994 when Perry Hooper Sr., was narrowly elected chief justice. The race between Hooper and incumbent Chief Justice Sonny Hornsby was not noticeably negative. However, a subsequent race (1996) between law professor Harold See and incumbent Democratic Justice Kenneth Ingram was highly objectionable because of the notorious skunk ad run by Ingram. When See was elected over incumbent Ingram despite the extremely negative campaign against him, this was said to be "the high profile ice breaker that broke the stranglehold that the plaintiff trial lawyers had on the Alabama Supreme Court."[27] Republicans gained a majority on the high court in 1998 when they won two of the three seats up for election.

Alabama was the number one state in the nation in terms of Supreme Court campaign expenditures between 1994 and 2006.[28] In these years Alabama Supreme Court races were the objects of $54 million in campaign outlays. Texas, where $30 million was spent, ranked a distant second. A former president of the Alabama Bar Association lamented: "We're No. 1 in a category in which we should not be No. 1."[29] Although never in first place, West Virginia is another state where partisan judicial campaign spending has also been very high. One specialist in judicial campaign finance, Adam Skaggs, a senior counsel at the Brennan Center for Justice, gave Alabama "credit" for "usher[ing] in the phenomenon of arms race spending for both sides"—support for and opposition to tort reform. (The two sides were business groups and trial lawyers.)[30]

Karl Rove, who achieved his greatest fame as a political advisor to President George W. Bush, worked in Alabama judicial campaigns on the business side before he served in the White House. Rove was said to have "brought a rougher brand of politics to the races for Alabama's appellate courts."[31] The senior Montgomery capital correspondent, Phillip Rawls, observed that, "Working with . . . Rove, they [business groups] succeeded in changing the nine-member court from all Democrats going into the 1994 election to eight Republicans and one Democrat today [2010]."[32] Individuals running as "conservative Democrats" have had no success in trying to displace Republicans. Also falling on deaf ears have been Democratic judicial candidates' pleas for "greater balance" on courts where members of their party were conspicuous by their absence.[33] In a shift in strategy, plaintiff trial lawyers donated to Republicans they viewed favorably in 2010, one of whom, incumbent Tom

Parker, was successful. There were also indications that the return of former Chief Justice Roy Moore to the Supreme Court in January 2013 was supported by liberal-leaning Democrats who did not share his social and religious values. One observant attorney, Steven Noles, noted that in his previous tenure on the Supreme Court, Moore "was considerably more deferential to jury verdicts against businesses than other members of the Court. And particularly hostile to arbitration agreements."[34]

In the near term, expenditures for Alabama appellate court races will be quite modest. This was the case in 2012 when the only contested race was that between Republican Moore and Circuit Judge Robert Vance Jr., for chief justice. The Moore-Vance race was the only one in which Democrats put up a candidate. All Republican appellate judicial candidates except Moore ran unopposed. Head-to-head battles, when they occur, will be most pronounced in Republican primaries when there are open seats to be filled.

Tort Reform

The (seemingly) unduly large amounts of money that jurors were awarding plaintiffs in Alabama were attracting unfavorable national attention in business circles near the close of the twentieth century. For example, an editorial in the February 7, 1996, *Wall Street Journal* carried the headline: "Alabama Blows One." The writer argued that the state's apparent disregard of the need for tort reform was "tantamount to placing giant 'Keep Out' signs at the 'Bama borders."[35] A case involving a Birmingham physician's BMW was frequently cited as "the poster-child of outrageous verdicts."[36] In this litigation, Dr. Ira Gore got $4 million as the result of a Birmingham jury finding his BMW dealer negligent for not properly informing him that the paint on his new vehicle had been touched up before he bought it.[37] At this time Alabama was competing with other states to get Honda to build an assembly factory in the state. These efforts were jeopardized by its reputation for what critics characterized as "jackpot justice."[38]

What was most frustrating to business interests was that the legislature *had* previously passed tort reform legislation, only to see it emasculated by the then-all-Democratic Alabama Supreme Court. In one case the high court invalidated an arbitration clause in a termite protection agreement because it allegedly conflicted with the state constitution's jury trial guarantee.[39] It was in this political context that the expenditures for the Alabama Supreme Court that we have just examined began to grow exponentially. (One researcher found that in the period 1986–98 they rose by 776 percent.[40]) In 1999 Democratic governor Don Siegelman succeeded in persuading the legislature to pass new legislation to curb what business interests regarded as lawsuit abuse. These new limits were upheld by the now Republican-majority state Supreme Court.[41]

Most recently, with a Republican governor and a Republican legislature, a new set of tort reform bills was quickly passed by the lawmakers in 2011 and even more promptly signed when they reached Governor Robert Bentley's desk. The new law established $1.5 million as the maximum for any punitive damages a jury might assess (compensatory damages times three). Another aspect of the package was to restrict where lawsuits could be initiated in cases alleging wrongful death ("shopping for a favorable venue to file lawsuits").

Before this series of bills was passed a survey taken by the conservative US Chamber of Commerce had labeled Alabama trial courts, where tort cases are initially heard, as "among the least reliable in the country."[42] The 2010 Lawsuit Climate Report had Delaware as the most favorable state and West Virginia as the least. Alabama ranked forty-seventh, just ahead of Mississippi, Louisiana, and West Virginia.[43]

Now that tort reform has been mostly achieved, Alabama business groups are able to spend most of their political energies on legislative lobbying. Apparently the political activities by business interests do produce positive returns. Studies have shown a greater likelihood that litigants will prevail in court if they have previously made generous contributions to the campaigns of the judges who staff these courts.[44]

The continuing problem for business interests doesn't lie in the now strongly business-oriented Alabama appellate courts but in those trial courts that continue to be staffed by Democratic judges who are friendly to plaintiffs' interests, especially in parts of the state with large African American populations. The Republican appellate courts can be expected to reverse or lower trial court verdicts awarding actual and/or punitive damages, but this is both expensive and time consuming. In February 2011 the court tossed an $8.5 million award a jury had made to a woman who had been injured in a Ford car crash.[45]

Showing the diminution of conflict between the business and trial lawyer interests, however, was the statement by the head of the trial lawyers group who said his association was able to get the latest regulations passed in 2011 modified after "lengthy negotiations," and he was satisfied with them.[46]

Judicial Demographics

One side effect of the current total Republican dominance of Alabama appellate courts is that these courts are composed exclusively of white justices and judges. Unlike legislators, justices and appellate judges are elected statewide,

13.2. Justice Lyn Stuart for Supreme Court flyer. From the William H. Stewart collection

not from districts. Since blacks identify overwhelmingly with the Democratic Party, the odds for their being chosen for appellate court positions are slight. In the 2008 general election a black candidate for a Supreme Court seat received 854,985 votes, but his successful Republican opponent got 1.3 million. Oscar Adams was the first African American member of the Alabama Supreme Court, having been named by Governor Fob James (then a Democrat). He won election twice after that to retain his seat. Adams has the distinction of being the first of only two African American candidates who have won statewide races in Alabama. (The second was also a successful Supreme Court candidate. He, Ralph Cook, too had been appointed to replace a retiring justice, Adams.)

Another traditionally underrepresented group, women, has done very well in Alabama appellate court politics. As noted in chapter 3, three women are members of the Supreme Court and three serve on the courts of appeals. Cobb was Alabama chief justice from 2007 to 2011. In the South at large, eight of thirteen states had female chief justices. This was close to half of the national total of twenty.

Before completing this survey of the major state political arenas, we turn to an overview of the nuts and bolts of Alabama government—taking in revenue and bureaucrats spending it on a growing number of public purposes. The politics of collecting revenue and administering programs go on in a climate both of intense opposition to any new taxes and a growing desire for a wide variety of public services.

14

The Politics of Taxing and Spending

Where does the money come from that politicians fight about when decisions are made on spending it? What are bureaucrats really like? Politics is as lively here—and as contentious—as it is in any of the other arenas that we have previously looked at. Conflict is intense as interests both inside and outside of government compete to have the policies they want as the prevailing ones. We will see numerous examples of such competition in this chapter.

The Bureaucratic Image

Alabama public administration has come in for a lot of criticism. An article in *Harper's Magazine* several years ago said there were "problems with nearly every aspect of their state's bureaucracy."[1] A part of the bureaucratic reputation was developed during the George Wallace era when he regularly attacked "pointy-headed bureaucrats." He aimed his fire at those in Washington, but public servants everywhere suffered from the disdain in which he held them.

The Shape and Size of the Alabama Bureaucracy

Even though the Alabama bureaucracy has expanded exponentially over the years, the last major reorganization was in 1939, during the first year of the administration of Governor Frank Dixon (1939–43).[2] There was little emphasis on gubernatorial interest in administration in chapter 12 for good reason: Most governors have been much more concerned with other aspects of their jobs, especially influencing the legislature. Alabama has numerous departments, boards, commissions, and other agencies that have been created since Dixon's time, mostly in an unsystematic way by statute or executive order.

The largest number of state employees (4,759) in 2008 worked for the

Table 14.1. Number of FTE state government workers per 10,000 residents in southern states (2007)

State	Number of workers
Florida	489
Tennessee	528
Georgia	546
Texas	564
Virginia	574
South Carolina	577
Arkansas	585
North Carolina	600
Louisiana	605
Alabama	615
Mississippi	648

Source: Calculations made by the Tax Foundation from data found in the 2007 Census of Government Employment.

Department of Transportation. Ten state agencies had only a single employee. The average salary of a state worker as set by personnel regulations pursuant to act of the legislature was $41,799. These workers do not have the right to bargain collectively for higher salaries and improved working conditions. As we pointed out in chapter 7, Alabama nonteacher employees are, however, represented by a lobbying group, the Alabama State Employees Association. Teachers and other education employees have exercised great political clout through the AEA.

Looking at the state bureaucracy as a whole, approximately 34,000 people work in some aspect of Alabama state government other than education. In education, employees in all capacities totaled approximately 93,000 in the school year 2010–11 (including 47,573 teachers and 36,680 supporting workers). Due to revenue shortfalls experienced during the Great Recession, there has been a small decline in the number of state workers. Calculating the number of state agency employees per 10,000 inhabitants puts Alabama in second place among southern states (behind Mississippi). Data for all southern states are shown in table 14.1. The US average for all states was 546 employees per 10,000 population.

There is a large employee turnover in some areas, especially corrections. Well over half of all penal officers leave their jobs after having served no more than three years. As of September 30, 2008, the ranks of state employees were 56 percent female. The average age for a state employee was slightly under forty-five.

African Americans accounted for 41 percent of the workforce. Numerous suits in federal court were required to fully desegregate the Alabama bureaucracy, but it generally has been. According to the late federal judge Ira Dement, Alabama "State government was all too content to punt [the "Alabama punting syndrome" as it came to be called] long-festering problems to someone else rather than fix them."[3] But the problem of lack of opportunities for blacks in Alabama state government has been fixed. It was reported in 2006 that African Americans—and women as well—were "employed in much greater numbers by state government agencies than in Alabama's overall work force."[4]

Lean Government and Poor People

It is not rocket science to explain much of the disparity between Alabama and other states, as is frequently pointed out. Alabama state and local governments spend less mostly because the amounts they collect in taxes are less. Alabama is one of the nation's most "frugal" states. Its eastern and northern neighbors, Mississippi and Tennessee, are also included in this group as are other southern and border states—North Carolina, Kentucky, South Carolina, Louisiana, West Virginia, and Arkansas, plus one nonsouthern state (Montana).[5] In a 2011 ranking of the "top ten" poorest states in the United States, Alabama was ranked ninth, behind North Carolina.

The Great Recession hit Alabama especially hard. Unemployment in October 2009 was reported to be 25.1 percent in the Black Belt county of Wilcox. Wilcox ranked second highest in the country, just below Imperial County, California.[6] The fact that 24 percent of Alabama children were living in poverty in 2009 put Alabama in the top five among the states. The gap separating the most affluent and the most impoverished among Alabamians as reported the same year was the second biggest in the United States.[7]

Alabama has not had the resources or the will to provide a large number of innovations for other state "laboratories" to emulate. In the broad southern region in which Alabama is located, states such as North Carolina (despite its poverty) and Florida have been more likely to launch new programs. A ranking of all states several decades ago in terms of "leadership patterns in the diffusion of public policies" placed Alabama just behind Tennessee, Idaho, and Arkansas. Iowa was ranked slightly lower than Alabama.[8] In a more recent study, Virginia ranked highly among southern states while Alabama and Georgia in the Deep South did not.[9]

Near the beginning of the second Bob Riley term Alabama was viewed by *Governing* magazine as "a state whose agencies have advanced dramatically."[10] However, while the innovative plans professional administrators have made have been commended nationally, the funding provided to implement them has been inadequate. In an empirical study of the quality of state government published a decade ago Alabama was assigned the lowest grade given, a D, for overall performance.[11]

Bureaucratic Political Behavior Patterns

In legislative budget hearings, Alabama administrators, like their colleagues elsewhere, always request much more than the state's meager revenue collections could ever provide. They hope that somehow money will be found to adequately serve their constituents or clienteles. For example, in 2009 agency leaders testifying before legislators considering budget requests petitioned for $667 million more in appropriations from the strapped General Fund than they were currently getting. The administrators were well aware of the fact that the director of the Legislative Fiscal Office had predicted that funds available for the next fiscal year probably would drop from $2.10 billion to $1.45 billion.

The same pattern of bureaucratic political behavior was demonstrated again in interactions with the new Republican legislature. In February 2011 two state agencies asked for funding at levels that, if approved, would have consumed 70 percent of all the money expected to flow into the General Fund. The two agency representatives who chose to ignore revenue projections were those advocating for the Department of Corrections and the Medicaid Agency. These bureaucratic behavioral patterns are exactly what would have been expected. Officials in bureaucracies such as Alabama's, sociologist Theda Skocpol points out, "are loyal to their bureau's mission rather than to political parties or economic interest groups."[12] Perhaps even more important, they realize that, given Alabama's strong antitax climate, the most convincing cases must be made for existing revenues—new sources are very unlikely to be forthcoming.

Even in relatively prosperous times, Alabama government overall would fit best into the "bare bones" category. In contrast to Alabama, inhabitants of New York in 2010 received government benefits totaling $9,442. Alabamians received about half this amount, $4,919.[13] What was said of Mississippi by a recent Minnesota gubernatorial candidate could also be applied to Alabama: "Their approach is super-low taxes, super-low services and they just kind of leave people on their own."[14]

A Trio of Programs

Education is by far the most important function of Alabama state government. Figure 14.1 shows how funds were allocated by function in Alabama during the 2012 fiscal year. K–graduate school will be examined in depth

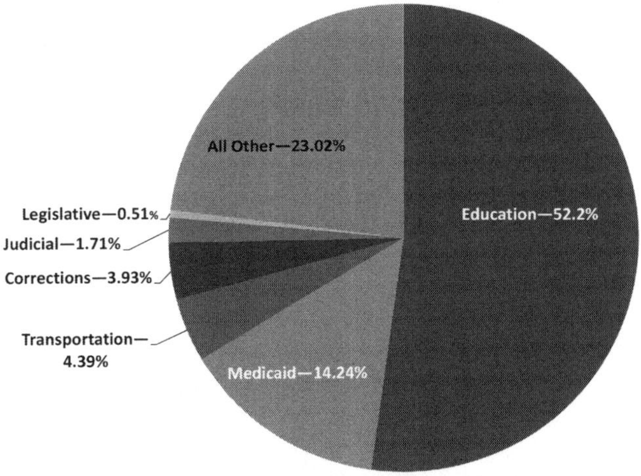

14.1. Allocation of funds by the state of Alabama, 2012. Source: Presentation to the legislature on Alabama's financial condition by Norris Green, director, Legislative Fiscal Office, February 7, 2012

later in this chapter, especially with regard to the taxes used to finance public schools. Other functional areas—and the problems they seem always to be facing—also warrant mention, however.

Corrections

Prisons have been among the most financially strapped of state institutions. The prison population in 2012 was approximately 31,000. The facilities they occupy, however, were built to house only about half that many. Prisons were operating at approximately 195 percent of designed capacity. Corrections officers at a majority of Alabama's prisons work twelve-hour shifts due to personnel shortages. Each warden is responsible for guarding a larger number of prisoners than is true in any other state.[15] In order to get more funds to meet current needs the prison system has been selling unused property to which it has title. Prison funds have not been prorated, as is the case with most government functions. (Federal courts would almost certainly intervene were this to occur.) Needs have simply outstripped normal appropriation levels.

Law Enforcement

Due to inadequate numbers of highway patrol officers (state troopers), Alabama has been identified as a "hammer state," which is to say that when motorists travel into it they know they can bear down on their vehicles' accelerators. This is because there is only a low probability that they will be ticketed

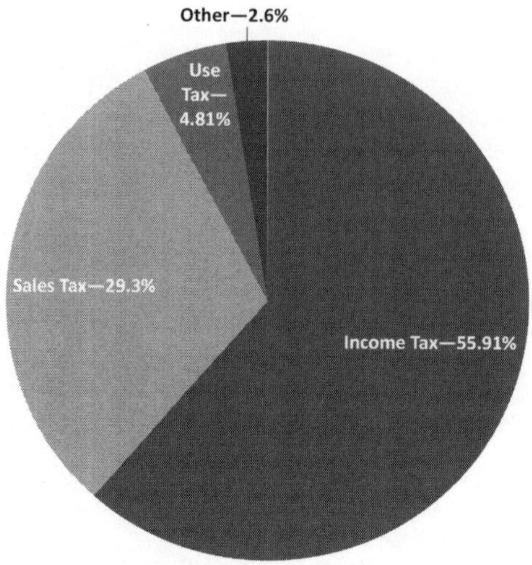

14.2. State-generated sources of revenue for the Alabama Education Trust Fund, 2011. Source: Presentation to the legislature on Alabama's financial condition by Norris Green, director, Legislative Fiscal Office, February 7, 2012

for speeding.[16] The average speed on interstate highways in Alabama has been calculated at 69.6, the fifth highest among the states.[17]

Environmental Protection

A report by the Pew Center on the States and the Rockefeller Foundation in 2011 said that Alabama was "trailing behind" as far as environmental protection was concerned.[18]

Environmental agencies fear that if they are too stringent they will discourage economic development. Thus the main environmental protection agency, Alabama Department of Environmental Management (ADEM), in May 2011 recommended classifying coal ash as nonhazardous waste. The explanation was that labeling it as hazardous would be both detrimental to the state's economy and would overload the personnel who would be required to do more permitting and perform more inspections.

Revenue Sources

Income taxes and sales taxes rank numbers one and two as sources of revenue for the Alabama treasury. This is illustrated in figure 14.2. All other tax sources besides these two are very low percentage-wise. Nontax sources, es-

Table 14.2. Condition of the Alabama General Fund (2008–12)

Year	Total Available Funds*
2008	$2,053,400,638
2009	$1,821,568,533
2010	$1,533,519,351
2011	$1,577,194,130
2012	$1,725,873,244

*Total available funds represents the beginning balance plus total receipts during the fiscal year indicated.
Source: Presentation to the legislature on Alabama's financial condition by Norris Green, director, Legislative Fiscal Office, February 6, 2013.

pecially federal aid, are much more important. In the most recent fiscal year for which authoritative data are available (2010), Alabama state government agencies spent $10,509,456,277 that had been received from agencies of the federal government.

Actual and Potential Revenue Sources

Expanded bingo and other forms of gambling, as discussed most recently in chapter 11, have been promoted as lucrative sources of new revenue that would only affect those who participated. However, the head of the state retirement system, David Bronner, dismissed these possibilities as "nickel and dime," which, he believed, would not be satisfactory responses to Alabama's financial problem, but only "divert attention away from it."[19] Closely associated with gambling, Alabama's distilled spirits monopoly contributed $190 million (not a large amount as a part of total revenues) to the General Fund in fiscal year 2010. Table 14.2 shows amounts available in the General Fund during the fiscal years 2008–12.

Tax Earmarking

Identifying and implementing priorities that could help state government better address some of the major problems confronting the people of Alabama is difficult. This is true not only due to lower than average revenue availability, but, in addition, because a very large percentage of Alabama's taxes is earmarked by existing law (sometimes in the constitution) for particular purposes. Alabama ranked number one among the states in 2008 in specifying in advance the use of incoming revenues (84 percent).[20] Michigan ranked second, with 62.6 percent of its revenues earmarked. The median for earmarking

Table 14.3. Top 10 Alabama earmarked taxes (2011)

Rank Title of Tax	Receipts	Primary Beneficiary
1. Income (individual)	$2.796B[1]	Education Trust Fund
2. Sales	1.909B	Education Trust Fund
3. Gas/motor fuels	386M	Roads and Bridges
4. Utility Gross Receipts	982M	Mental Health Fund
5. Property	359M	Public School Fund
6. Medicaid provider	303M	Medicaid[2]
7. Income (corporate)	291M	Education Trust Fund
8. Insurance company	273M	General Fund[2]
9. Use	265M	Mental Health Fund
10. Utility license	150M	General Fund

[1]These figures represent rounded billions and millions of dollars.
[2]Medicaid is the primary beneficiary of General Fund receipts; Corrections ranks second.
Source: Presentation to the legislature on Alabama's financial condition by Norris Green, director, Legislative Fiscal Office, February 7, 2012.

for all the states was only 19.2 percent. Paul Hubbert, former executive secretary of the Alabama Education Association, believed that "Alabamians like[d] having their tax dollars restricted . . . because they [didn't] trust legislators."[21]

The Tax Burden

Looking only at taxes levied by the state, Alabama is a relatively high tax jurisdiction. Ranking the states at the end of the twenty-first century's first decade, Alabama was found to be midrange in a listing based on total state tax collections.[22]

When the burden of all taxes was computed, however, Alabama was found to have a lower than average tax load. In the 2007 fiscal year, for example, Alabama individuals and businesses paid a smaller amount in taxes than was the case anywhere else. Alabama's per-person tax average of $2,909 ranked fiftieth in the nation.[23] The combined federal, state, and local tax burden in Alabama placed the state at number thirty-six in a ranking of states by the conservative Tax Foundation.[24] In 2009 Alabama state and local governments were found by the Census Bureau to have collected $2,793 in taxes per capita.[25] The national median at the time was $3,799. It was calculated that had Alabama governments collected at the national figure, they would have had $4.81 billion in extra money to spend on public services. In 2010 governments at all levels in Alabama collected about a thousand dollars less per capita in taxes than the national median.[26] Alabama Supreme Court associate justice Tom Parker ran a successful reelection campaign message that

Table 14.4. Tax load: Alabama gets less in state and local taxes per person than most states

Average state and local taxes collected per person:	
1. Alaska	$7,268
2. New York	$6,898
3. Wyoming	$6,205
4. Connecticut	$6,044
5. New Jersey	$5,944
50-state median	**$4,011**
46. South Carolina	$3,134
47. South Dakota	$3,009
48. Tennessee	$3,005
49. Mississippi	$2,989
50. Alabama	**$2,909**

Average state and local taxes collected person as a percentage of personal income:	
1. Alaska	18.01%
2. New York	14.56%
3. Wyoming	14.36%
4. Hawaii	13.10%
5. Vermont	12.85%
50-state median	**10.65%**
46. Texas	9.25%
47. Tennessee	9.03%
48. Alabama	**8.89%**
49. South Dakota	8.87%
50. New Hampshire	8.71%

Note: Tax collections are for the 2007 fiscal year, which for most states ended June 30, 2007, and for Alabama ended September 30, 2007. Twenty-five states had higher totals or percentages than the median and twenty-five had lower. Sources: US Census Bureau reports on FY 2007 tax collections; Census Bureau population estimates for July 1, 2007; Census Bureau and US Bureau of Economic Analysis reports on average personal income in 2007.

year boasting that "Alabama taxes are the lowest in the nation."[27] The implication was that, were he to be reelected, he would do what he could to keep them that way.

Taxes

Now we will look at some of the most important Alabama taxes past and present, beginning with the traditional source of revenue for American state and local governments—the ad valorem or property tax.

Table 14.5. Combined state and local taxes paid per resident: Selected states (2010)

State	Amount
1. Alaska	$8,884
2. New York	7,030
National Average	4,112
42. Georgia	3,108
45. Mississippi	3,023
47. Tennessee	2,875
48. South Carolina	2,845
49. Alabama	**2,779**
50. Idaho	2,769

Source: *Birmingham News*, September 30, 2012, 14A. The newspaper made use of US Bureau of the Census reports using state populations as tabulated in the 2010 census and combined state and local tax collections in fiscal year 2010.

Property Tax

In Alabama, as elsewhere, historically the most important tax source for state and local governments was the property tax. Plaintiffs in the most recent property tax case, *Lynch v. Alabama*, tried unsuccessfully to convince a federal district judge (Lynwood Smith) to void state constitutional provisions relating to property taxes. They contended that the tax laws violated the US Constitution and were motivated by the desire of their architects specifically to limit the amount of money spent to educate African Americans in Alabama.

However, Judge Smith, following precedents set by the US Supreme Court and Courts of Appeals, declined to order the removal of property tax laws from the state constitution—as the *Lynch* plaintiffs desired. His decision came on October 21, 2011, and was accompanied by an 854-page opinion. The preceding trial had featured testimony from thirty-six witnesses and in excess of seven hundred exhibits introduced to support or deny the plaintiffs' claims. Despite his sympathy with *Lynch*'s arguments, Smith wrote: "Like it or not, [US] Supreme Court precedent compels a conclusion that the property tax scheme embedded in Alabama's 1901 Constitution and subsequent amendments does not offend the 14th Amendment's Equal Protection Clause."[28] Smith took the opportunity, however, "to criticize state powerbrokers [who] show[ed] little interest in a quality education system since the children of their most powerful constituents 'are generally enrolled in exclusive suburban schools, with large local tax bases, or in private schools.'"[29] (The internal quotes are the words of Judge Smith; the others are those of the writer, Brian Lawson.)

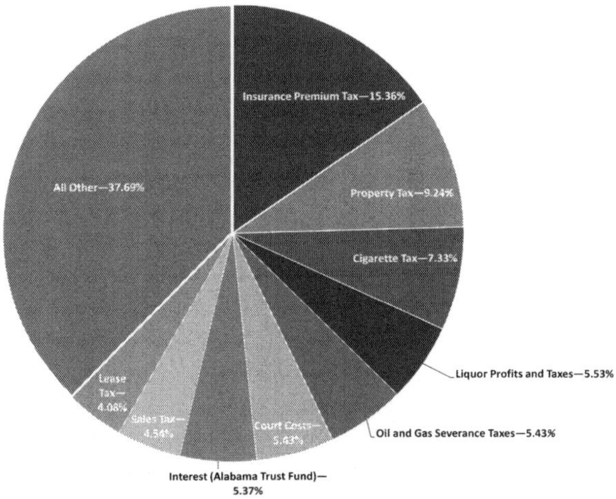

14.3. Sources of General Fund receipts, 2011. Source: Presentation to the legislature on Alabama's financial condition by Norris Green, director, Legislative Fiscal Office, February 7, 2012

"The argument over adequate taxes was lost in 2003," a *Birmingham News* editorial writer contended.[30] That was when voters decisively (68 percent–32 percent) rejected Governor Bob Riley's plan to raise $1.7 billion in new revenue through a series of progressive tax hikes and tax cuts. In the minds of many Alabamians, "tax reform" has come to be synonymous with "tax increase," and the debate about increasing them does indeed seem to have shut down almost as soon as it started a decade ago. Figure 14.2 shows state-generated revenue sources for the Education Trust Fund in the 2011 fiscal year.

Property taxes represented such a small portion of these funds that revenues so generated are classified in the "other" category. Figure 14.3 shows the much less lucrative sources of revenue for the General Fund in the same fiscal year.

For many years there was a problem with widely varying property tax assessments in different parts of the state. In the late 1960s assessment ratios for the sixty-seven counties varied from 6.7 percent of an item of property's fair market value in a Black Belt county (Hale) to a high of 26.8 percent in the state's most populous county (Jefferson). In the *Weissinger* case[31] the state was ordered to correct this situation, and a series of constitutional amendments followed, amendments that were most responsive to the interests of large rural landowners (both residents and nonresidents).

A Public Affairs Research Council of Alabama (PARCA) study in 2007 found the Alabama state and local property tax burden to be "next to lowest" in the nation.[32] It accounted for slightly in excess of 1 percent of the average Alabamian's tax load. In percentage terms the Alabama state property tax has been calculated to be 0.0065 percent on real and personal property.[33]

State property taxes yielded just 9.7 percent of fiscal year state tax receipts in 2010. For the fiscal year 2012 it was estimated that property taxes would bring in approximately $141.5 million out of a total of $1.821 billion in tax revenue.

All property tax collections per capita amounted to $455 in 2010, which in a per capita listing of states would have Alabama at fifty.[34]

ALFA Insurance/Alabama Farmers Federation, a powerful interest group mentioned in several places in this book, regularly opposes all proposed property tax increases at the state or local level. They had a big role in establishing the present constitutional arrangements attacked in the *Lynch* case and want to keep them like they are.

Seventy-one percent of Alabama's open space is timberland. Owners of this land pay just 2 percent of the property taxes levied by Alabama, or not quite $1 per acre. Ten percent of the timberland's market value provides the basis for property tax assessment under the property cap (lid) amendment (373, Section 217 in the Recompiled Constitution of Alabama). Defenders of this system say that Alabama's low current use property taxes give the state an advantage over other southern states in attracting natural-resources-related industries. Low property taxes and other modest corporate taxes generally (as well as incentives and abatements) are used in sales pitches for other types of businesses as well.

Sales Tax

The sales tax was the first major new tax source the legislature adopted in the twentieth century, coming during the Great Depression in 1935. At the same time the legislature established the Minimum Program Fund to provide a rudimentary floor for local school funding.

In addition to property taxes bringing in about a fourth of the revenue yielded by a much more balanced tax system than Alabama has, sales taxes are recommended for about a third. (For the fiscal year 2012 it was estimated that Alabama's state sales and use tax would yield $72,193,000 of the total estimated tax collections of $1,820,923,687. This would be about 39 percent—not far off the recommended percentage.)

In terms of the costliest function of state government, public education, a little over a fourth of the annual appropriation typically comes from sales taxes and somewhat over half from income taxes. Most of the rest comes from federal aid and local taxes. In fiscal year 2010 Alabama received the huge sum of $1,214,169,304 in federal education aid. Of this amount, $405,833,434 (33.42 percent) was to help Alabama—other states got large sums as well—cope with state revenue shortfalls due to the Great Recession. Only a very minimal amount of state funds for education comes from state property taxes. Citizens have clearly shown that they will not approve new taxes on themselves by ratifying constitutional amendments that would raise state property taxes. Thus the hands of legislators are essentially tied as far as coming up with substantial new sources of tax revenue—for schools or any other state function—is concerned. All potentially lucrative sources of new tax revenue must be approved by the voters except sales taxes, and these have already been "maxed out" by local taxes increasing the amount citizens pay at the cash register to as much as eleven cents on the dollar.

The combined amount of sales taxes levied by state and local governments in Alabama gave the state a ranking of number six in a 2007 study assessing use of this tax.[35] Sales taxes apply to virtually all purchases, including groceries bought for home consumption. Alabama and its western neighbor, Mississippi, are the only states that don't refrain from taxing groceries or offer food purchase rebates for low-income taxpayers.

Critics identify the levy on retail sales as the "classic regressive tax [that] had long been supported by the Big Mules as the only way to ensure that blacks and other poor Alabamians paid their 'fair share' of the tax burden."[36] Many educators were uncomfortable about placing such heavy reliance on regressive sales taxes to fund public schools at the time they were originally adopted in the mid-1930s, but they realized the futility of asking the business and agricultural sectors to pay higher property taxes.

Income Tax

When the income tax was adopted by Amendment 61 to the Alabama constitution in 1947, its proceeds were designated for teacher salaries. A ranking of the states made in 2009 based on income tax burdens had Alabama fourth from the bottom.[37] In 2006 the base point at which income would be liable for taxation by Alabama was raised from $4,600 to $12,600. A dozen other states besides Alabama also acted near this time to moderate the tax burden on poor people. Even after this change, however, Alabama was still requiring impoverished families to shoulder an income tax burden nine times greater than that of equally distressed Mississippians.[38]

Nearly a century ago, the Russell Sage Foundation discovered that, "The financial difficulties of [Alabama were] being met, not by distributing the

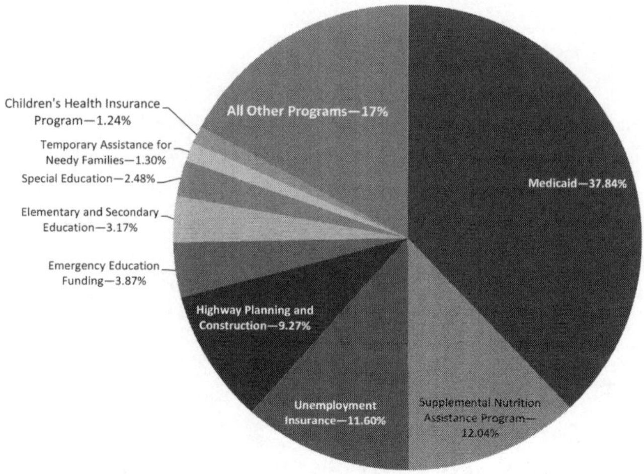

14.4. Major programs for federal assistance for Alabama, fiscal year 2010. Source: Alabama Department of Examiners of Public Accounts, September 7, 2012

burden equitably, but by throwing the burden upon . . . those least able to bear it."[39]

More recently southern politics scholars Bass and De Vries said: "Few states can match the regressive nature of the Alabama tax structure."[40]

Also criticizing the extent of tax regressivity in Alabama, the liberally oriented Citizens for Tax Justice, in a study it released in the mid-1990s, put Alabama in its "Terrible 10" because of the higher percentages of their incomes poor families were forced to pay in taxes.[41] The bottom 20 percent of wage earners paid about 10 percent of the money they made to satisfy state and local tax obligations while the most affluent 1 percent paid about 4 percent.

Federal Aid

The most important nontax revenue source for Alabama by far is federal aid. During the last three fiscal years for which data are available the amounts were $6,875,153,734 (2008), $8,224,307,396 (2009), and $10,509,456,277 (2010). The last figure is 34.58 percent greater than the first. As noted earlier, Washington came to the aid of financially strapped subnational governments during the Great Recession in ways that were identified as "one-time money." The future of what is popularly referred to as "Obamacare" could

Table 14.6. Federal agencies dispensing the largest amounts of aid to Alabama state programs (Fiscal Year 2010)

Agency	Amount
Department of Health and Human Services	$4,808.041,632
Department of Agriculture	$1,726,946,357
Department of Labor	$1,294,721,988
Department of Education	$1,214,169,304
Department of Transportation	$1,003,265,335
Department of Housing and Urban Development	$98,275,149
Department of Homeland Security	$72,206,572
Department of Defense	$68,248,135
Social Security Administration	$50,772,812
Department of Energy	$42,750,689
Department of Justice	$38,156,622
Environmental Protection Agency	$26,256,388
Department of the Interior	$24,630,256
Department of Veterans Affairs	$13,503,969
Department of Commerce	$13,356,278
All other agencies	$141,154,791
Total federal awards	$10,509,456,277

Source: Alabama Department of Examiners of Public Accounts (report filed September 7, 2012).

mean the resumption (at least temporarily) of significant annual federal assistance increases, however.

A "Moocher" State

In 2010, Alabama received $1.66 for every tax dollar it paid into the US Treasury.[42] In contrast, seventeen states paid in more than they received back less than they paid in. This group included New Jersey (0.61 for each 1.00), California (0.78), Texas (0.94), and Florida (0.97). States in addition to Alabama that were getting back more than they paid in included Georgia (1.01), Tennessee (1.26), Louisiana (1.78), Mississippi (2.02), and New Mexico (2.03). New Jersey fared worst among the states (0.61) and New Mexico got the best return on its federal investment (2.03). A *USA Today* analysis found that, looking at the nation as a whole, federal money was being directed from richer states, especially those in the Northeast and West, to poorer ones, particularly Southern states.[43] Unlike the calculations made in the preceding paragraph, the figures used in this set include federal payments made directly to individual recipients, not just their governments. Further, they are based on taxes paid, whereas the others were based on congressional appropriations regardless of tax remittances by state residents.

Pork Politics

Alabama Republicans in the US Congress, especially senior senator Richard Shelby, are highly skilled in bringing back as much pork as possible to their home state. Senator Shelby has been notably skillful in earmarking spending for particular Alabama projects. He is condemned by out-of-state critics (or credited by many within the state) for larding federal spending bills with many items designated specifically for Alabama. It was estimated that through his political clout Shelby had gotten $1 billion for Alabama that it would not otherwise have received. Earmarks per resident in 2009 were $55.52, putting Alabama at sixteenth in a ranking of states.[44] Even though the Senate was majority Democratic at that time, Shelby had significant political influence as a high-ranking Republican on the Appropriations Committee.

Disaster Assistance

The catastrophic storms that hit Alabama in April 2011, most severely on April 27, were identified by the disaster recovery coordinator for the Federal Emergency Management Agency (FEMA) as "the worst disaster Alabama has ever had, and for FEMA, it will rank in the top 10."[45] Forty-two of sixty-seven counties, representing about two-thirds of the state's population, were declared disaster areas and thus eligible for massive amounts of federal disaster relief assistance. FEMA expected to spend $1 billion in the state before its work was done. (This would be about a tenth of the amount spent in fiscal year 2010 for all purposes by state government.) President Barack Obama made a personal visit soon after the April 27 disaster to console suffering Alabamians and promise massive amounts of federal help.

"Thanks, But No Thanks"

After the Katrina hurricane in August 2005 and the BP oil spill in April 2010, Alabama had also wanted all of the federal money it could get—and more. Federal aid is not always welcomed, however. There are occasional exceptions. For example, in February 2009, Governor Riley rejected more than $65 million from a federal economic stimulus package that would have liberalized unemployment benefits. The reason for his decision was that it would have caused businesses, which are politically powerful in Alabama, to have to pay $17 million more in taxes after the federal program expired a few years hence. (In fiscal year 2010, the US Department of Labor channeled $1,294,721,988 to Alabama state government, mostly for unemployment benefits.)

In recent years Medicaid has covered about 20 percent of Alabama's population, and total outlays have accounted for about 30 percent of General Fund expenditures. Federal funds have matched state funds on a roughly two-one basis. In fiscal 2010 the Medicaid cluster of federal programs netted Alabama state government $3,977,243,543. Table 14.6 identifies federal agencies allocating sums in at least the tens of millions of dollars to their Alabama functional counterparts in fiscal year 2010. Figure 14.2 employs a pie chart to show the major state-administered programs that benefited most from federal aid in this year.

There is a definite disconnect between Republicans representing Alabama in Washington and the Republican gubernatorial administration back home. In mid-2010, for example, failure of a jobs bill in the Senate meant $200 million less for the Alabama Medicaid budget. Both of Alabama's Republican senators supplied votes to defeat this bill. Under the Patient Protection and Affordable Care Act (Obamacare) program it was estimated that there would be more than 200,000 additional participants in the Medicaid program in Alabama, with Washington initially covering about 96 percent of the projected new expenditures. Approximately 442,000 additional Alabamians would be medically insured by 2019 outside of Medicaid. At the present time, all members of the congressional delegation would still favor repeal of the Obama health care program except for the one African American Democrat, Representative Terri Sewell. Such a repeal became a political impossibility with the reelection of President Obama and the continuation of a Democratic US Senate in November 2012, however.

While 4 percent more in additional state funds does not seem like much (and would be a worthwhile investment in the health of impoverished Alabamians), based on the 2010 federal Medicaid allocation it would require at least $160 million in additional state funds—an amount that would be politically difficult (to put it mildly) to find in existing state revenue sources. State political leaders, reflecting public opinion, strongly oppose any new taxes.

Proration

As long ago as the early 1940s, public administration experts were pointing to "the essentially negative nature of Alabama's budget," oriented as heavily as it was (and still is) toward ensuring that there is no deficit spending.[46] When revenue receipts do not total as much as had been expected (or hoped for) at the time budgets were enacted into law, the governor must order proration—across the board cuts—unless specific programs or agencies have previously been exempted (prisons previously being noted as one of these). The nonproratable public employee salaries and benefits account for the overwhelming percentage of public budgets. On average, proration has been declared every three years since 1979. Because of a rainy-day account established by a 2008 constitutional amendment (803), the state is able to tap into its savings account, the Alabama Trust Fund, both to cushion the blow of proration and to address anticipated revenue shortfalls in the General Fund budget. (Withdrawals from the trust fund over a four-year period were most recently authorized in September 2012. No specific plan for repayment was specified in the constitutional amendment the voters approved.)

In its 2011 regular session the Alabama Republican legislature enacted a "15-year rolling average" budget method that is supposed to prevent education proration in future fiscal years. It builds budgets by multiplying the budget for the current fiscal year by the average increase or decrease experienced during the previous fifteen years. In some respects the problems perennially experienced with education funding are a legacy from the Jim Crow era when a state hardly affluent enough to operate one school system tried (unsuccessfully) to operate two.

The State of Public Education

Education funding historically has been strongly centralized in Alabama and has become even more so with the passing of time. At the turn of the twentieth century, Alabama was alone among southern states in not allowing local taxation for public schools. The 1901 constitution permitted local levies for schools but made them very difficult to enact.

Local Education Support

Because of the historic constitutional hostility just mentioned, Alabama was unable to develop a strong tradition of local support for K–12 schools. As we saw in chapter 11, Alabama is not a state in which localities (especially counties) have much home rule, so this is another important factor that has contributed to state centralization. Municipalities do have considerable power to tax, however, and they have used it liberally, especially to levy high sales taxes. Local sales tax revenue goes mostly for nonschool purposes, however—leaving the state with the primary responsibility to fund city and county schools.

Table 14.7. Condition of the Alabama Education Trust Fund (2008–12)

Year	Total available funds*
2008	$6,694,675,698
2009	$5,679,120,475
2010	$5,217,470,126
2011	$5,349,436,943
2012	$5,608,603,889

* Total available funds represents the beginning balance plus total receipts during the fiscal year indicated.
Source: Presentation to the legislature on Alabama's financial condition by Norris Green, director, Legislative Fiscal Office, February 7, 2012.

Dividing the Pie

In recent years, about 70 percent of public school K–12 funds have been appropriated by the state, mostly from state income and sales tax collections. This percentage varies among different areas of the state. One impoverished school district looked to the state to provide 80 percent of its school money. Given that Alabamians at large will not vote higher taxes on themselves for schools (or any other purpose), there is no politically viable source of revenue to use to equalize school funding among the state's 172 districts. Within these districts in mid-2010 there were 1,547 public schools. There were also 420 private schools and an unknown number of home-schooled students.

The politics of race unquestionably intensifies the opposition of Alabamians to paying higher taxes, especially for schools. For the first time since public schools were established in the South, whites became a minority in 2009. In Alabama specifically, minority students (mostly African Americans but also Latinos and Asian Americans) made up 41.4 percent of school enrollees. Nonwhite students were expected to achieve majority status by 2017, however.

Natural revenue growth has meant a 180 percent increase in the amount of money available to schools in the past three decades.[47] As table 14.5 shows, however, decline and stagnation rather than growth have been the chief characteristics of the Education Trust Fund in very recent years. In an apparent contradiction, surveys regularly show that a majority of Alabamians believe that additional money should be allocated to them—while the voters just as regularly vote against taxes that would do this. A story in the AEA house organ, the *Alabama School Journal*, contended that, based on their surveys, "Public schools are the number one priority of Alabama voters."[48] The

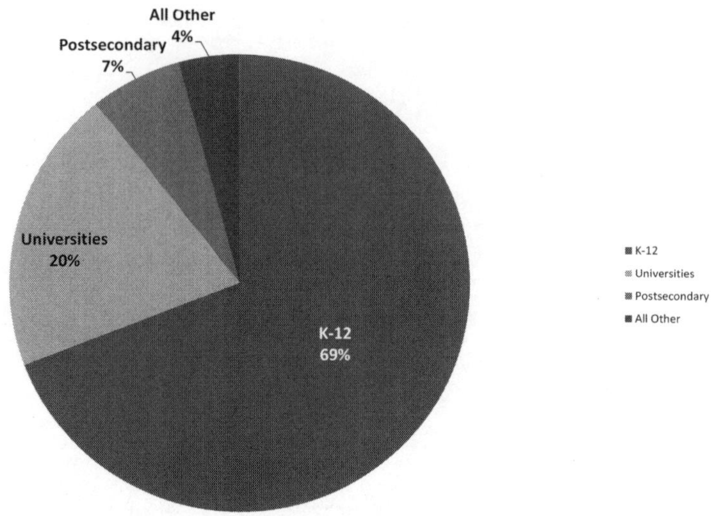

14.5. Allocations from the Alabama Education Trust Fund in percentages, 2012. Source: Alabama Department of Examiners of Public Accounts, September 7, 2012

only way to reconcile these data is to conclude that Alabamians want better-funded schools but believe someone else should provide them.

The split of money between K–12 schools and higher education has been a politically contentious issue for many years. Traditionally, it was about two-thirds for K–12 and one-third for higher ed. Recently it has been more like 73–27. Figure 14.5 shows the allocations of money from the Alabama Education Trust Fund for the 2012 fiscal year. The amount of money that can go to higher education has been greatly diffused for half a century by the extensive network of community colleges created during the George Wallace era and discussed in chapter 2.

We have now completed our examination of Alabama politics from a contemporary perspective by looking at how politics operates in both governmental and nongovernmental arenas. We have also identified the key participants in the political process—as well as those who are largely silent. At this point it is appropriate to summarize some of the key attributes of Alabama politics as gleaned from the chapters leading up to the conclusion.

15
Conclusion

People participating in politics has been our main concern on practically every page of this book. We found that for most the involvement was not on a continuous basis. Politics is not central to most people's lives. That much should be evident by this point in the book. Even though the index following the "Notes" and "Select Bibliography" is reasonably lengthy, it still represents only a minuscule percentage of the Alabama population. (Many more names could be added and this statement would still be true.)

People and Politics

Voting is the way that most people take part in politics—if they do. Thanks to the removal of barriers to the ballot box that in the Jim Crow era worked mostly to prevent African American Alabamians from voting, people generally who are eighteen and over have an easily exercisable right to choose their favorites at election time. What is "costly" is not getting one's name on the voter rolls but getting sufficient information to be able to exercise this fundamental right in a satisfying way. Even with the information explosion that has occurred in recent years, usable political information is still hard to obtain. District lines (one of the subjects of chapter 10) for state legislative and other substate candidates have become so convoluted that it is hard even to know what district one lives in.

Actual voting percentages in elections in Alabama are about like they are elsewhere in the nation—somewhat over half of the voting-age population typically votes in presidential elections. (In the 2012 election this percentage was calculated to be 57.03 percent.) Candidates for state offices in Alabama—also like candidates elsewhere—will compete for attention from a generally inattentive electorate. Alabama is a state where many of the citizens historically have felt disconnected from government and where the general expectation is that trying to take part in or influence what goes on in government is not everyone's responsibility. This mindset perpetuates public cynicism and distrust toward government. Despite disconnectedness between citizens and their leaders, these leaders remain sensitive to shifts in opinion and will try to make decisions that they feel will either be popular with voters or that they can make as palatable as possible. (This was seen especially in chapter 11 dealing with the legislature.)

Due to the extensive centralization that is vital to understanding how Alabama government functions, people at the grassroots do not have a lot of experience in trying to solve problems on their own. The state constitution does not grant localities much in the way of home rule, so the habit was formed years ago of turning to Montgomery with all kinds of matters that could probably be handled more effectively in Atmore, Attalla, or in Autauga County. In November 2012 voters locally (in nineteen cases) or statewide (in three) approved new, strictly local (and from a statewide perspective trivial) amendments to the bloated state constitution that the legislature had previously passed for their consideration. We saw in chapter 11 that Alabama was currently one of only a very few states in which much of the legislative agenda involves passing local bills.

For people who are not totally disconnected, about the only thing that they feel they can do is to protest changes they don't like by speaking out against them and—on Election Day—showing their preference for candidates who are least likely to try to bring about unwanted change. Resentment of federal judges did not die with the passing of George Wallace in the late 1990s. That was demonstrated in 2012 when first Republican primary voters renominated and then the electorate statewide chose Roy Moore to be chief justice of the Alabama Supreme Court, a position from which he had been removed in 2003 because of his refusal to obey federal Judge Myron Thompson's order that he remove the Ten Commandments monument from the Alabama judicial building. In 2015 Moore took the unusual step of advising county probate judges not to issue marriage licenses to same-sex couples despite federal judge Callie V. S. Granade's ruling that the state constitution's attempted ban on such unions was invalid. (His colleagues subsequently backed Chief Justice Moore's stance on this issue.) Besides voting on Election Day citizen protest mostly involves complaining about actions of state government they become aware of and don't like—such as legislative pay raises that they felt were not justified. (In November 2012 voters ratified a constitutional amendment that would prevent legislators from raising their own pay in the future.)

The Wallace Legacy

The Wallace influence, the subject of chapter 2, will continue to decline as the time he has been away lengthens. Whereas Wallace was very nationally oriented, most Alabama politicians today are very state-centered. Those Alabama politicians who are currently most nationally focused predictably are its members of Congress. Most contemporary Alabama politicians don't aspire to national prominence. While condemning federal deficit spending in the abstract, most of Alabama's representatives in Washington will try to ensure that the $1.66 in benefits that Alabama currently gets for every dollar it pays in taxes does not decline but maybe increases.

We saw in chapter 14 that Alabama state government received about $10.5 billion in federal assistance in fiscal year 2010.

In former times in Alabama, as recently as the George Wallace heyday, politics was a major source of entertainment for the white population that was allowed to participate. As we saw especially in chapter 9, "hokey" activities that the parents and grandparents of present generations of Alabamians found to be very amusing, their descendants would probably regard as terribly corny. The eras when Alabama politics as practiced was regarded in large part as a form of entertainment were mostly when Alabama was a rural society. Even though Alabama has for decades been classified as a mostly urban entity, its politics are still what one would expect where many families retain a strong attachment to their rural roots (but without the entertainment value).

Social and Religious Values

Even though Alabama continues to be referred to as an integral part of the Bible Belt—and for good reason due to high levels of church attendance and survey responses that indicate the importance of religion in many peoples' daily lives (as shown in chapter 3)—it is not immune to secularizing trends felt elsewhere in the nation. Religious leaders do not have the influence over the populace generally or even over their own parishioners as they did in times past. When the Siegelman lottery proposal (discussed in chapter 4) went down in defeat in 1999, it was demonstrated that opponents had wisely chosen to capitalize on the preexisting public distrust of government rather their own belief in the immorality of gambling.

The religious right is active on a continuous basis in Montgomery. Sponsors can readily be found for bills that would seek to restrict the impact of *Roe v. Wade* (the US Supreme Court's decision legitimizing abortions) as well as measures that would seek to reduce church-state separation. Gradually, however, religion is losing its foundation for political coalitions, but like other changes in Alabama, this one has also come slowly. Liberalization of laws related to alcoholic beverages is another big change previously tardy in happening but nevertheless showing dramatically (and at an accelerating rate) the decline of influence of conservative Protestant ministers.

African Americans in Contemporary Alabama Politics

The biggest change to occur in Alabama politics in recent decades, as we saw in chapter 5, is undoubtedly the emergence of African Americans as a potent political force. The second biggest (and very closely related to the first) is the emergence of the Republican Party as the dominant party. This was our subject in chapter 8. At the same time that blacks have become the dominant group in the Alabama Democratic Party, from which they were excluded in the Jim Crow era, whites were abandoning the Democratic fold in even greater numbers. This meant that while blacks could expect to get seats in the legislature based on their numbers in the total population, thanks to amendments to the Voting Rights Act of 1965, they would no longer have formal leadership positions—unless a few could possibly be persuaded to become Republicans instead of Democrats (something that is not currently happening). Due to legislative expertise acquired over years of service in the State House some especially skilled black legislators will undoubtedly be able to exercise influence without holding chairmanships of committees or other leadership positions. Also, because of the rule of legislative courtesy (that applies most of the time) they will continue to have a lot of influence over what goes on in the localities from which they were elected.

The Decline of the Democratic Party

The Alabama Democratic Party's presently poor condition, as assessed in chapter 8, reflects both unwise decisions of the party in decades past, but also national trends over which the state party had absolutely no control. The Democratic Party has become much more responsive nationally to liberally oriented groups (for example, gay Americans) that remain politically powerless in the state of Alabama at large. Also, the election and reelection of the first African American as president, Barack Obama, drove a further wedge between more Alabama whites and the national Democratic Party. As we saw in chapter 8, it is estimated that slightly less than one in ten white Alabamians voted for Obama when he ran the first time in 2008. In 2012, the white Obama vote rose by a few percentage points. On both occasions an even more overwhelming percentage of blacks were supporting his candidacy. We also pointed out in chapter 8 that the Alabamians who do retain their Democratic loyalties, even though they are a decided minority, nevertheless feel for the most part as deeply about social and economic issues as their Democratic counterparts elsewhere. They are not "Alabama" Democrats but simply Democrats. (This is true despite the fact that the party substituted "Alabama Democrats" for the traditional donkey on the 2012 general election ballot.) The Alabama Democratic Party under its present leadership does not campaign for the return of wayward sheep to the fold, and the necessity of appearing to endorse positions taken by a few entrenched black Democratic leaders could only encourage more whites to become ex-Democrats. When Joe Reed refers to white men as "bubba" this is almost as demeaning as whites in the Jim Crow era referring to African American adult males as "boy."

Interest Groups

The number of interest groups available to be involved in the making of public decisions (as we saw in chapter 7) has increased at the same time as a highly disciplined Republican Party was showing its muscle in the legislature. These two phenomena do not mesh well. One or the other will have to yield. It is most likely that Republican Party discipline will weaken and that decisions in Montgomery will reemerge as the product of interest group negotiations. We identified in chapter 7 the resources that, if particular groups have them, will make some much more influential than others. Those interest group representatives who have the most in common with official decision makers will always be most successful. Also, lobbyists who are in Montgomery continuously will have the greatest success. No single lobbyist in the future will have the influence that the late AEA executive secretary Paul Hubbert had during his many years at the center of Alabama politics, however.

Corruption

Alabama government has attempted periodically (and usually unsuccessfully) to cleanse itself of alleged corruption (as we saw in chapter 4). As in so many other areas, the state has had to depend heavily on the federal government to do this. Besides having the help of federal authorities, the maturing of the political parties in Alabama also has been of assistance because, as we saw in chapter 4, one party always has an incentive to catch the other in wrongdoing.

For this to work, however, the Republican majority will have to be kept within sufficient limits so that there are enough properly positioned Democrats to perform the catching function. The ethics reform passed in 2010 as the swan song of the Bob Riley administration, also discussed in chapter 4, did not change the behavior or the cast of characters in Montgomery (a subject to be explored in more depth later) nor the A-list of the most important lobbying groups. Campaigns, especially Republican, even if not for judgeships, will become even more expensive in the future, and most Alabamians either can't afford to donate or don't want to. Money to fund them will have to come from somewhere and these are likely to be the same sources as in the past—those most dependent on the decisions of government as far as the profitability of their businesses is concerned. "Bribery through campaign donations" will remain a fact of Alabama political life.

One of the most commonly used acronyms in this book was "PAC" (political action committee). PACs will continue to be the primary means by which the costly Alabama political campaigns are financed. That the 2010 attempted ban on PAC-to-PAC transfers will succeed in its objective of making campaign finance transparent is very doubtful. The record of campaign finance reform efforts in Washington as well as in other states does not give one reason to have a lot of optimism in this regard. Using experiences in other settings as a guide, ways will usually be found to get around the ban.

The Cast of Characters

Many years ago, when Alabama was mostly a rural state, there were not a lot of opportunities for talented people to make full use of their abilities outside of politics. In the much more economically developed Alabama of today there are many more such opportunities, and the most gifted young men and women are finding other venues besides politics in which to maximize their potential. People who are Democrats philosophically and who are not as pragmatic as George Wallace will probably have to watch from the sidelines, however, whether they wanted to formally enter the political arena or not. This is because their prospects for winning the favor of a statewide conservative Republican-oriented electorate would be poor.

As shown in chapter 1, the people deemed to be "most influential" in Alabama are not, for the most part, elected officials. They had rather exercise power while remaining in the private sector—an arrangement much easier on both them and their families than all of the struggles frequently involved in getting elected to office (as we saw mostly in chapter 9). Once elected, advantages will overwhelmingly accrue to incumbents, but one has to be elected first! Both parties, but especially the Republican since its candidates have the best prospects for success, will continue (or begin in the case of the lagging Democrats) to function as parties should—recruiting the best available candidates and then equipping them, especially with the technological resources needed to wage winning campaigns.

The candidates will also have help from the party in raising the big bucks needed to wage their campaigns.

Modern Campaigns and Candidates

As we observed earlier, candidates have dropped those campaign techniques that wouldn't work today and adopted others that they feel would better connect their electioneering efforts to a mostly unconcerned electorate. Many of these involve creative ads on TV or the use of social networks, as we saw in chapter 9. Despite their best efforts, most campaign methods would still be regarded as dull—except for the occasional TV ad that "goes viral." These most entertaining aspects of current campaigns do not necessarily translate into the greatest number of votes, however. The typical Alabama politician today is a conservative businessman. These people will have much more voter appeal than those who their opponents have been successful in labeling as "liberals." The flamboyancy of previous generations of Alabama politicians is something that is only read about or seen in videos. It is not experienced today. The current Alabama political environment is conservative even if this doesn't appear rational to critics who wish the majority of its people would both think and act differently. In time, with increasing educational levels and different demographics, this will change—but such change will occur quite slowly. If the issue on the ballot is a proposed constitutional amendment—and in chapter 6 we found Alabama to have well over eight hundred of these—the typical Alabama voter will say a resounding "no" if it involves any kind of a tax increase. This will be true even if evidence (that on its face is credible) is presented to show that the increased revenue to be derived from the money coming in from the tax measure will result in better governmental services—or even that a majority of taxpayers will actually be paying less than before. As noted in chapter 2 dealing with the Wallace legacy, this opposition to *any* new taxes (and politicians signing no new taxes pledges) is a relatively new phenomenon. It definitely did not start with the four-term governor. He was a tax-and-spend liberal compared to many of today's Montgomery politicians who really are fiscal conservatives.

The Constitution

Most Alabamians do not deem constitutional reform to be a serious issue. Some within the Republican supermajority seem to feel, however, that business values would be best served by cleaning up the constitution by discarding outmoded and/or unconstitutional verbiage so, as we saw in chapter 6, a little-publicized review of most articles of the constitution is currently in progress. Provisions of the constitution dealing with taxation were specifically excluded from the review. Two of the twenty-nine amendments adopted in November 2012 replaced the original constitutional articles dealing with banking and private corporations. With these additions and those approved in 2014, the total number of amendments stood at 893.

Alabama is not unique in being uninterested in constitutional reform. Such reform has generally occurred in the American states in waves, and such a wave has not arisen in more than four decades. Like Alabama, other states also have more immediate problems to deal with than the seemingly abstract issue of constitutional improvement. Advocates of constitutional reform have never been able to convince a large enough number of Alabama voters that the "bad" current constitution has made the quality of their lives poorer than if the state had a constitution deemed to be good by reformist standards.

The fact that Alabama can operate as well as it does—which is often not *very* well—shows how irrelevant the quality of a state's constitution may be to its general state of health. If the constitution seems to present a barrier to doing what state leaders wish, it is much simpler to work around it or to propose yet another amendment than to attempt any kind of comprehensive reform.

Too many interests are served by the constitution in its present condition for any new constitution to be substituted for it until much more time has elapsed, and a crisis the nature of which cannot be anticipated will have to occur. Most constitutional reform that has taken place in Alabama in the past half century has been the result of federal court decisions voiding portions of the original 1901 racist constitution or subsequent amendments to it. Since the federal judiciary is currently not as activist as it was during the Second Reconstruction, federally ordered reforms, generally no longer needed based on racial fairness concerns, are much rarer.

Even African Americans have lost interest in ridding the 1901 constitution of its racist language, particularly if it is viewed as only a symbolic gesture. In November 2012 an effort to remove language related to segregated schools was defeated. The leading black political organizations—and the AEA—opposed the move because it didn't restore the right to an education at public expense that had been removed from the constitution in the mid-1950s. With regard to nonracial provisions, black powerbrokers in Montgomery, like their white counterparts, enjoy the control the present constitution gives them over local affairs and will not make broad grants of home rule.

Immigration (although not a state constitutional issue) is a good example of an area that would benefit from federal intervention—most immediately a definitive court decision that the entire Alabama immigration law of 2011 is in conflict with the US Constitution. Even more desirable would be an act of Congress to reform national immigration policy. Since political polarization has been as bad at the national level as it is in Alabama—if not worse—the likelihood of such occurring is problematic. Given Republicans' need for more Hispanic votes if they are to be nationally competitive, however, some congressional legislation related to immigration reform is at least foreseeable.

The Legislature

Chapters 11–14 dealt with Alabama state government institutions—the legislative, executive, and judicial branches—plus the bureaucracy that is mostly, but not entirely, located in the executive branch. The Alabama political system and its governmental mechanisms, especially the legislative branch, are in stages of transition, as Republican-dominated government becomes the norm. All branches of Alabama state government now reflect the dominance of conservative values, as does its congressional delegation in Washington. This doesn't mean that Alabama government was previously liberal—certainly not by national standards. It was basically pragmatic, nonideological. Now a party belief system infuses Alabama government in a way that it hasn't since white supremacist beliefs were consistently followed throughout state government (with a few exceptions as during the James E. Folsom terms) in the Jim Crow era.

The Decline of Legislative Power

The legislature, as looked at in chapter 11, is not the central institution of Alabama state government that it was in former times. This change has occurred as a result of developments identified in chapter 12 dealing with the governor.

The legislature's power position has not been helped by the fact that the constitution still limits when it meets and for how long—plus the agenda it may consider when senators and representatives assemble at the State House. In the twenty-first century, only the governor can provide the continuity of leadership that state government—and the people of Alabama—require.

Legislative Representativeness

The legislature has been properly apportioned for many years. Senate and House districts are within only a few percentage points of exact mathematical equality. Also, due to amendments to the Voting Rights Act of 1965 noted earlier that passed during the Second Reconstruction, African Americans, who compose about a fourth of the Alabama population, are assured that they will be represented by about this percentage of the legislators. Women, who were not the beneficiaries of such federal favor, remain seriously underrepresented. We saw in chapter 11 that Alabama is in the bottom group of states based on its percentage of female legislators.

The political impact of the African American minority-majority districts has not turned out to be what many of those who campaigned for their creation had hoped for, however. While they do assure that African American voters can elect black candidates if they wish to do so, they do nothing to encourage building coalitions between black and white voters since black-majority districts frequently include many more blacks than are necessary to give an African American a good chance of being elected. And it is in the black-majority parts of the state, especially in the impoverished Black Belt, that such partnerships are most needed. The districts are also hurtful to the interests of white Alabamians who have remained loyal to the Democratic Party. As blacks are packed into "their" own districts, the other districts are likely to have larger numbers of Republicans.

In legislative reapportionments prior to the 2010 census, blacks and Republicans were the primary beneficiaries, even though this was not the intention of the Democratic-majority legislature that did the districting. As we saw in chapter 11, the majority of Democrats in the legislature currently are black, but, combining with the small number of their white fellow Democrats, they still are a decided minority.

A positive aspect of the majority-minority districts, however, is that they ensure that even an overwhelmingly Republican Alabama will never be as one-party dominant as it was in the Jim Crow Democratic days. Due to their full political emancipation black Democrats will continue to dominate local offices in black-majority counties as well as legislative delegations in the Black Belt and black-majority urban communities. In urban Jefferson County (Birmingham) blacks and white Democrats recently have formed winning coalitions.

Given the exceptionally strong loyalty of blacks to the Democratic Party and the fact that this loyalty will not diminish markedly any time soon, it is possible to imagine a situation where an African American Republican who had been appointed by the governor to fill a vacancy in a statewide office, possibly an appellate judicial position, subsequently wins election to a full term despite the fact that she or he did not receive a majority of black votes cast. Also, some especially talented men and women (white and black) who bear the Democratic brand will continue to be able to sometimes win election in white-majority counties, even while the prospects for the election of these same people to statewide office would remain poor.

We need to keep in mind that Alabamians' conversion to Republicanism is still a relatively recent phenomenon and should not be interpreted to mean that they fully subscribe to every belief that may be associated with the Republican Party. (Party identification percentages on occasion showed higher numbers of Republican adherents when Republicans did not dominate state government to the extent they do now—occupancy of all statewide elective offices.) The masses of Alabamians who are not regularly in receipt of Republican loyalty-building messages, would not experience cognitive dissonance by voting for the occasional Democrat who they found especially appealing.

Legislative Partisanship

In the first legislative sessions dominated by a Republican majority, the party functioned in a very disciplined way. The Alabama legislature seemed at that time to be shedding its previous reputation for inefficiency, even if the legislation that was being rather quickly passed was not to everyone's liking.

Legislative outputs won't be forthcoming that will be cheered by elements of the Alabama attentive public perceived as liberal (such as some of the less influential associations mentioned in chapter 7 dealing with interest groups). Those that were most vocal in their opposition to HB 56, the immigration law of 2011, are illustrative of the forces that will almost invariably be disappointed with the results of political struggles in contemporary Alabama. None of the current crop of statewide officials—in any of the three branches of government—owes their election to these elements of the Alabama population, so they won't be sensitive to their political demands. (Governor Bentley probably owed his first election to AEA but he was not very responsive to their interests after taking office.)

The lockstep behavior demonstrated by the legislature in its initial Republican sessions won't continue indefinitely. Already in 2012, there were increasing signs of Republican division. A decade from now it is quite possible that party tie will come to mean as little as it did during most of the long period of Democratic domination. Even at this point the division within the dominant Republican Party between two sets of conservatives—economic versus socioreligious—is a serious schism, as it is nationally. Some future Republicans may be classified as "moderate" or "progressive," especially by newspaper/Net editorial writers. None, however, will let themselves be stigmatized with the label of "liberal." The Republican Party within the legislature, strongly influenced by the socioreligiously oriented conservatives, probably will wish to pursue an agenda dominated by issues such as immigration, abortion, and perhaps religion in public life.

The Legislative Agenda

And because social issues will generally be easier to legislate on, the legislature may devote a disproportionate amount of its time to debates the end products of which will make little difference as far as the lives of most people are concerned. Ironically, there is sometimes less difference between the parties on the most important issues—the primary example being the Education Trust Fund and General Fund budgets. Given the overwhelming earmarking of revenues, the constitutional requirement that the budgets be balanced, and the fact that significant tax increases are unlikely, there is little the parties can do except to approve the budgets, disagreeing only on items that amount to a small percentage of total spending, and this primarily to make a partisan statement of some kind.

The dominant leaders of the Republican Alabama legislature will prefer to pursue an agenda that is substantially different, both from that of the most recent Democratic predecessor of 2010 and that desired by other Republican identifiers. Rather than focus on gambling as Democrats did or, for example, abortion as the socioreligious group might prefer, the Republican leadership will emphasize the application of business values to Alabama government across the board. The legislature represents "management," and it will try multiple approaches to reducing labor costs. In the present political environment a majority of Alabama voters have become convinced that something that would be perceived as unfavorable to business—such as higher taxes or more regulation—is not good. It would hurt the state in its competition with other states for job-creating enterprises. The state may ultimately turn to the expansion and taxation of gambling as other conservative Republican states, notably Mississippi, have done, but this is at least several years off. In 2015 regular and special legislative sessions there were significant divisions between Republicans who were willing to approve at least a few of the higher taxes recommended by Governor Bentley (a legislative majority) and those who were not—despite the predicted adverse impacts on what opinion leaders outside the legislature agreed were vital state services.

Legislative Expertise

Whatever subjects it tackles, the legislature continues to lack the intellectual resources to produce a satisfactory legislative product. The 2011 immigration law (HB 56) illustrates this deficiency. It was written for the most part by an out-of-state resident and not studied thoroughly before it was passed. Probably rather quickly the legislature's popularity under Republican control will be shown to be not any greater than it was when Democrats were in the majority. (This long-continuing lack of popularity did not result in the loss of Democratic control until 2010.) Dependence on interest groups and other external sources for information will continue to increase because the legislature has not been able to create research infrastructure such as Congress and more advanced state legislatures possess. The resources that the legislature does have, especially the Legislative Fiscal Office, are adequate but insufficient. The Alabama legislature, as powerful as it is, remains a part-time operation and is not rigorously studying state problems on a continuing basis such as occurs with Congress.

In terms of race-related legislation, the Alabama legislature has taken about all of the symbolic actions it can take in apologizing for the wrongs of the Jim Crow era. Long voided racist language remains in the constitution, however, and undoubtedly getting rid of it will be among the recommendations when the currently operating constitutional commission makes its final report.

The Governor

As we saw in chapter 12, Alabama's most recent governors have been generally conservative in orientation, not just ideologically but also in personal style. The most important political figure to emerge since Wallace, outside of the judiciary's Roy Moore, has been Governor Bob Riley (2003–11). If he had not been limited to two consecutive terms he would probably have been able to continue in office. He showed a Wallace-like ability to rebound from political loss (most notably in the case of his tax increase/tax reform plan in 2003) and to leave office almost as popular as in his honeymoon period, although the gambling raids that took up a lot of his time and energy during his last full year in office were widely criticized.

Centrality of the Governorship

The governor was looked at mostly in chapter 12, but the governor is so central to the functioning of Alabama state government that the office was mentioned in some context almost every few pages. No leader has emerged on the state scene in recent years who has had anywhere near the charisma or staying power of George Wallace. All governors after Wallace have been very different from him. This has been true regardless of the political party affiliation of the governor or the governor's professed political ideology.

The Job of the Governor

The governor of Alabama is basically the CEO of an inadequately funded and very complex bureaucratic organization that constantly has to cope with one crisis after another. These crises may have been a long time in the making or they may be sudden occurrences such as tornadoes, floods, and oil spills.

Problems facing Alabama, especially those of a financial nature, will continue to be dealt with on a piecemeal, case-by-case basis, with the governor taking the most visible role.

They fit the analogy of boiling pots on a stove. They are shifted around from eye to eye just as each state problem will be dealt with in turn as it is deemed to be most serious. The problems are too difficult to actually be solved in the present political environment; they can only be managed. The governor has the primary responsibility for keeping crises from getting out of hand. He or she will also continue to be the industry recruiter-in-chief to bring in jobs and payrolls so that the need to provide new revenue through significantly increased taxation can be further delayed. The governor will not be able to dictate to the legislature, but he or she may be able to persuade legislative leaders that the Republican Party's best electoral interest lies in taking a particular course of action, whether related to economic development or some other area. On other occasions the persuasive arts may be exercised from the State House (where the legislature sits) rather than the Historic Capitol (where the governor's office remains).

The Judiciary

It is worth remembering that, as we saw in chapter 13, the only *major* article of the constitution to be replaced—the judicial article—has been more impacted by the Republican takeover of the appellate courts beginning in the 1990s than it was by the adoption of the new judicial article in 1973. The chief architect of the 1973 reform, Chief Justice Howell Heflin, had wanted to do away with partisan election of judges, but Governor Wallace vowed to "stump the state" against it if merit selection were a part of the new judicial article.

The judicial branch of Alabama state government today functions primarily to reinforce conservative economic, political, and social values. Partisan elections, which were noted in chapter 13 as often being the most expensive in the nation in the recent past, will ensure that this continues to be true. The Alabama appellate judiciary, unlike the highest courts in some other states, will not increase the number of positive rights enjoyed by Alabama citizens. Campaign costs, however, will decrease dramatically as Democratic zeal to contest Republicans for judicial posts virtually disappears (as it did in 2012). The competition between plaintiffs' trial lawyers and corporate interests has also declined markedly in recent years and, when the most recent set of Republican-sponsored tort laws was passed in 2011, a representative of the trial lawyer faction who participated in pre-passage negotiations said he was satisfied with the finished product.

Trial lawyer interests continue to hold sway particularly in those areas with black population majorities, and they will frequently win favorable verdicts from sympathetic juries. However, the corporate-oriented Alabama appellate judiciary can be depended on to overturn jury awards deemed to be excessive. In terms of the racial representativeness of the courts, blacks will continue to elect judges in areas where they constitute a population majority as well as in some areas where they don't. Where blacks have been appointed to the bench by a Democratic governor (the last such naming having been possible in 2003), there is sometimes a tacit agreement among members of the local bar that the black (Democratic) judge will not be challenged by a white Republican candidate.

Although Republican governors would undoubtedly be delighted to be able to appoint blacks to the appellate judiciary (in the case of vacancies), these nominees would have to promise to run at the next election as Republicans. So far there have been no takers. We saw in chapter 5 that blacks in Alabama are not monolithic politically—as evidenced by the activities of both the Alabama Democratic Conference and the Alabama New South Coalition. However, the loyalty of practically all blacks to the Democratic Party is too strong to induce politically gifted African Americans to offer themselves as Republican candidates for statewide office, even judicial positions.

Blacks will continue to occupy high federal administrative and judicial positions in the state. Democratic presidents will regularly appoint a generous number of them to federal judgeships, both because of their qualifications and because of the loyalty of blacks to the Democratic Party in the years since their modern political emancipation.

The Bureaucracy

As far as blacks in state leadership positions is concerned, the best opportunities are in administration where Republican governors often name African Americans to prestigious positions, the most notable being the appointment of Marquita Davis as state finance director by Governor Robert Bentley. She was both the first woman and the first African American to hold this premier cabinet post (2011–13). The barriers to the advancement of blacks in less visible administrative positions have long since been removed (with the aid of federal courts no longer needed), so blacks are actually represented in state administration (as we saw in chapter 14) at present in greater numbers than their percentages in the total population. Administrative excellence is not possible in the "bare-bones" government environment in which it has to function regardless of the ethnicity of bureaucrats, however.

Education is easily the costliest function the Alabama state government performs, and there will be improvements in the future with the application of increasing professional expertise from K–12 through graduate school. These will be made without the infusion of massive amounts of new state money. Labor, as represented by the AEA under its post-Hubbert leadership, and management, as represented by the Republican legislature and by the Republican governor, regularly stake out their positions. AEA will generally be on the losing side when it comes to the conditions under which teachers perform their jobs, and the legislature will not be eager to help them. The fact that the percentage of white students enrolled in public schools will continue to decline to the point where it no longer represents a majority of enrollees—as it has in Mississippi, for example—will not encourage more financial support for public education nor will the establishment of recently authorized charter schools.

Final Thoughts

Maybe someday things will change dramatically from what we have described here. But not right away. Problems will continue to be dealt with seriatim—one at a time and modest improvements will be made. There will be no systematic, sustained effort to address problems (or even universal agreement on what the problems are). The advantage will always be with solutions that can be identified as conservative and as in line with Alabama's traditional way of doing things. The situation will get worse—possibly a lot worse—before it gets better. In the long term demographic changes will so change Alabama politics that it will be dramatically different than what we have analyzed here. But that is in the long term.

Recently the number of people moving in and out of the state has been about equal, and this fact works against dramatic political change. So in the short term, Alabama will inch step by step into the future following well-worn paths that have not always served it well.

Notes

Chapter 1

1. See http://scienceblogs.com/mikethemadbiologist/2006/09/why_does_the south_dakota_legi.php.

2. E. Culpepper Clark, *The Schoolhouse Door: Segregation's Last Stand at the University of Alabama* (Tuscaloosa: University of Alabama Press, 1995), xi.

3. See www.irregularnews.com/states/alabama.html. Accessed October 4, 2015.

4. Harold W. Stanley, "Presidential Elections and the South," in *Writing Southern History*, ed. Robert P. Steed and Laurence W. Moreland (Lexington: University Press of Kentucky, 2006), 233.

5. Harper Lee, *To Kill a Mockingbird* (Philadelphia: J. B. Lippincott, 1960).

6. Wayne Greenhaw, "Why the 50th anniversary of 'To Kill a Mockingbird' Matters to Us," *Press-Register* (Mobile), April 25, 2010. http://blog.al.com/press-register-commentary/2010/04/insight_why_the_50th_anniversary_of_to_kill_a_mockingbird_matters_to_us.html.

7. Ashley Boyd, "Contestants Praise Portrayal of Courage in 'Mockingbird,'" *Tuscaloosa News*, January 30, 2010, 3B.

8. E. J. Dionne, *Why Americans Hate Politics* (New York: Simon and Schuster, 2004), 119.

9. "Alabama's Most Influential," *Tuscaloosa News*, January 23, 2009, 1A.

10. Virginia Van der Veer Hamilton, "Lister Hill, Hugo Black, and the Albatross of Race," *Alabama Law Review* 36 (1984): 845–60.

11. Reported in Kathleen Parker, "You Can Kiss My Cheesy Grits, Please," *Tuscaloosa News*, March 14, 2012, 3B.

12. Glenn Feldman, "Race, Sex, Class, and the Status Quo Society: Developing Racial, Political, and Religious Attitudes in 1940s Alabama," *History* 91 (2006): 360–85.

13. David Meeks, "Poll: Obama's a Muslim to Many GOP Voters in Alabama, Mississippi," *Los Angeles Times*, March 12, 2012. http://articles.latimes.com/2012/mar/12/news/la-pn-poll-obamas-a-muslim-to-many-gop-voters-in-alabama-mississippi-20120312.

14. Greg Richter, "Outside Looking In," *Birmingham News*, December 13, 2009, 2A, and "Senator's Challenge 'Ignorant,' Shelby Says," *Birmingham News*, December 15, 2009, 1B.

15. Bob Ingle and Sandy McClure, *The Soprano State: New Jersey's Culture of Corruption* (New York: Macmillan, 2009).

16. "Illinois No. 2 Sees Need to 'Fumigate' Politics," *Tuscaloosa News*, January 8, 2009, 3A.

17. William Thornton, "Riley Hails 'Historic' Ethics Bills in Speech," *Birmingham News*, December 17, 2010, 4A.

18. Dana Beyerle, "Alabama Politics a Hotbed of Religion: State Politicians Have a History of Invoking Religious Themes," *Tuscaloosa News*, August 31, 2009, 1B.

19. Shaun Wilson, "A Little Bit of Alabama: On Australia's Low Tax Consensus," *Australian Review of Public Affairs*, May 30, 2005. ww.australianreview.net/digest/2005/05/wilson.html.

20. Richard K. Scher, *Politics in the New South: Republicanism, Race, and Leadership in the Twentieth Century* (Armonk, NY: M. E. Sharpe 1997), 343, see also 397.

21. Ibid., 336.

22. See Glen Browder, *The South's New Racial Politics: Inside the Race Game of Southern History* (Montgomery, AL: NewSouth Books, 2009).

23. Jack Bass and Walter De Vries, *The Transformation of Southern Politics: Social Change and Political Consequence since 1945* (New York: Basic Books, 1976), 81.

24. Ibid.

25. Wayne Flynt, in *Alabama: The History of a Deep South State*, by William Warren Rogers, Leah Rawls Atkins, Robert D. Ward, and Wayne Flynt (Tuscaloosa: University of Alabama Press, 2010), 566.

26. Brian Lawson, "Battle over Alabama Immigration Law Heads to Court Wednesday," *Huntsville Times*, August 23, 2011. http://blog.al.com/breaking/2011/08/battle_over_alabama_immigratio.html.

Chapter 2

1. See Jack Bass and Walter De Vries, *The Transformation of Southern Politics: Social Change and Political Consequence since 1945* (New York: Basic Books, 1976), 81.

2. Brian Lawson, "Property Tax Trial Puts Racial, Political History on Display," *Birmingham News*, April 24, 2011, 7A.

3. Don Noble, "Author Sad about State's Condition," *Tuscaloosa News*, June 12, 2011, 4E. The language is that of Nobles reviewing Allen Tullos, *Alabama Getaway: The Political Imaginary and the Heart of Dixie* (Athens: University of Georgia Press, 2011).

4. Tullos, *Alabama Getaway*, 241.

5. Chapter 4 of Bass and De Vries, *Transformation of Southern Politics*, is titled "Alabama: The Wallace Freeze," 57–86.

6. Dan T. Carter, *The Politics of Rage: George Wallace, the Origins of the New Conservatism, and the Transformation of American Politics* (Baton Rouge: Louisiana State University Press, 1996), 9.

7. Richard K. Scher, *Politics in the New South: Republicanism, Race, and Leadership in the Twentieth Century*, 2nd ed. (Armonk, NY: M. E. Sharpe, 1997), 68.

8. Stephan Lesher, *George Wallace: American Populist* (Cambridge, MA: Da Capo Press, 1995), xi.

9. Richard Pearson, "Ex-Gov. George C. Wallace Dies at 79," *Washington Post*, September 14, 1998. http://www.washingtonpost.com/archive/politics/1998/09/14/ex-gov-george-c-wallace-dies-at-79/813dc676-3c32-4973-867e-24ebfcf44715/.

10. Bass and De Vries, *Transformation of Southern Politics*, 63.

11. "1965: Selma Voting Rights Demonstration," in *Disasters, Accidents, and Crises in*

American History: A Reference Guide to the Nation's Most Catastrophic Events, by Ballard C. Campbell (New York: Infobase, 2008), 1965.

12. Maggie Riechers, "Racism to Redemption: The Path of George Wallace." www.neh.gov/news/humanities/2000–03/wallace.html.

13. Timothy S. Huebner, Review of Carter, *The Politics of Rage, Florida Historical Quarterly* 75 (1996): 97–98.

14. Scher, *Politics in the New South,* 316.

15. Numan V. Bartley and Hugh D. Graham, *Southern Politics and the Second Reconstruction* (Baltimore: Johns Hopkins University Press, 1976), 118.

16. V. O. Key Jr., *Southern Politics in State and Nation* (New York: Alfred A. Knopf, 1949), 36.

17. Scher, *Politics in the New South,* 321.

18. Quoted in Jeff Frederick, *Stand Up for Alabama: Governor George Wallace* (Tuscaloosa: University of Alabama Press, 2007), 285.

19. Scher, *Politics in the New South.*

20. Quoted in Carter, *Politics of Rage,* 381.

21. Steven M. Farina, Review of Larry W. Yackle, *Reform and Regret: The Story of Federal Judicial Involvement in the Alabama Prison System* (New York: Oxford University Press, 1989), in *Michigan Law Review* 88 (1990): 1885.

22. Robert F. Rich and William D. White, *Health Policy, Federalism, and the American States* (Washington, DC: Urban Institute, 1996), 174.

23. Quoted in John Lewis, "Reflections on Judge Frank M. Johnson, Jr.," *Yale Law Journal* 99 (2000): 1253.

24. Stephen G. Katsinas, "George C. Wallace and the Founding of Alabama's Public Two-Year Colleges," *Journal of Higher Education* 65 (1994): 448.

25. Bass and De Vries, *Transformation of Southern Politics,* 73.

26. The biographer writes: "Yet Wallace's attempt to revise Alabama's tax structure failed." See "George C. Wallace" in the *Encyclopedia of Alabama.*

27. Brian Lawson, "Property Tax System Stays as Is, Judge Says: Rebukes State of Education," *Birmingham News,* October 22, 2011, 2A.

28. W. Bartley Hildreth, "The Politics of a Windfall: Allocating Special Offshore Oil and Gas Receipts in Four Southern States Facing Fiscal Retrenchment," *International Journal of Public Administration* 11 (1988): 581–600.

29. Melvin G. Cooper, "The Alabama Ethics Act—Milestone or Millstone," *Cumberland-Samford Law Review* 5 (1974): 187.

30. Bass and De Vries, *Transformation of Southern Politics,* 74.

31. Ibid., 67.

Chapter 3

1. During the period November 9–10, 2010, the Capital Survey Research Center of the Alabama Education Association conducted a survey that disclosed these findings.

2. Maria Recio, "Poll: Miss. Leads in Prayer, Belief in God," *Tuscaloosa News,* December 26, 2009, 3D.

3. See https://en.wikipedia.org/wiki/Christian_right.

4. Alexander Lamis, ed., *Southern Politics in the 1990s* (Baton Rouge: Louisiana State University Press, 1999), 382.

5. John C. Green, Lyman A. Kellstedt, Corwin E. Smidt, and James L. Guth, "The

Soul of the South: Religion and the New Electoral Order," in *The New Politics of the Old South: An Introduction to Southern Politics*, ed. Charles S. Bullock III and Mark J. Rozell (Lanham, MD: Rowman and Littlefield, 1998), 235.

6. Reported in Dana Beyerle, "Alabama Politics a Hotbed of Religion: State Politicians Have History of Invoking Religious Themes," *Tuscaloosa News*, August 31, 2009, 1B.

7. Bob Johnson, "New Gov.'s Words Don' Upset Many: Most Say Bentley's 'Christian' Comments Could Have Been Nicer," *Tuscaloosa News*, January 23, 2011, 1B.

8. Associated Press, "Rick Santorum Wins Alabama Republican Primary," *Birmingham News*, March 13, 2012. http://blog.al.com/spotnews/2012/03/ap_calls_alabama_republican_pr.html.

9. Beyerle, "Alabama Politics a Hotbed of Religion."

10. Glassroth v. Moore, 229 F. Supp. 2d 1290 (m.D. Ala. 2002, aff'd 335 F.3d 1282 (11th Cir.), cert. Denied sub nom. Moore v. Glassroth, 540 U.S. 1000 (2003).

11. See www.conservativeusa.org/JusticeRoyMoore2.htm.

12. Searcy et al. v. Strange (-F. Supp. 3Dd—(Jan. 23, 2015) (WL).

13. Ex parte State ex rel. Alabama Institute (—So. 3d ___ (2015). http://judicial.alabama.gov/doc/sc/SC RL 030315.pdf.

14. Linda Beck Fenwick, *Should the Children Pray?* (Waco, TX: Baylor University Press, 1989), 130.

15. George Altman, "GOP Candidates Favor School Prayer: Most Believe in Creationism, Literal Bible," *Birmingham News*, November 16, 2009, 1B.

16. 472 U.S. 38.

17. The Alabama Secular Humanism Decision is formally Chandler v. James, 180 F. 3d 1254 (11th Cir. 1999).

18. Wayne Grayson, "Evolutionary Studies Emerge on UA Campus," *Tuscaloosa News*, April 9, 2011, 5A.

19. Christopher Clausen, "America's Design for Tolerance," *Wilson Quarterly* 31 (2007): 28.

20. Ibid., 26.

21. Carrie Chapman Catt and Nettie Rogers Shulter, *Woman Suffrage and Politics: The Inner Story of the Suffrage Movement* (Buffalo, NY: W. S. Hein, 2004), 12.

22. Asjylyn Loder, "Fund-Raising Stymies Women Candidates," October 25, 2002. http://womensenews.org/story/campaign-trail/021025/southern-women-racing-congress-face-tough-odds.

23. White v. Crook, N.D. Ala., 251 F. Supp. 401.

24. "No Pride in This National Ranking," *Birmingham News*, September 24, 2011, 8A.

25. Figure cited in Greg Garrison, "Face of Faith Changing in Once-Monolithic Alabama," *Birmingham News*, November 23, 2008, 6A.

26. Jamie Winders, "Bringing Back the (B)order: Post 9/11 Politics of Immigration, Borders, and Belonging in the Contemporary US South," *Antipode* 39 (2007): 920–21.

27. Kim Chandler, "House OKs Tough Immigration Bill," *Birmingham News*, April 6, 2011, 1A.

28. Phillip Rawls, "Ala. Senator: 'Empty Clip' Remark Just a Metaphor," *Tuscaloosa News*, February 9, 2011, 2B.

29. Ibid.

30. Bob Johnson, "Immigration Law, Budgets Approved: Advocacy Groups Vow to Protest; Bentley Confident Law Will Stand," *Tuscaloosa News*, June 10, 2011, 1A.

31. Phillip Rawls, "Battle over New Law Recalls Civil Rights Past," *Tuscaloosa News*, October 30, 2011, 1A.

32. Ibid.

33. Mary Orndorff, "Obama Rips Immigration Law: Congress Members to Protest Nov. 21," *Birmingham News*, November 12, 2011, 1A.

34. Bob Johnson, "Justice Dept. Challenges Alabama Immigration Law," *Tuscaloosa News*, August 2, 2011, 3A.

35. Steve Flowers, column, July 29, 2009. See http://steveflowers.us.

36. V. O. Key Jr., *Southern Politics in State and Nation* (New York: Alfred A. Knopf, 1950), 233.

37. Hanes Walton Jr. and James E. Taylor, "Blacks and the Southern Prohibition Movement," *Phylon* 32 (1971): 247–59.

38. See, for example, "Dr. J. R. Hobbs to Speak Here for Dry Rally: Alabama Anti-Saloon League President Will Address Meeting Monday," *Tuscaloosa News*, January 11, 1933.

39. Paul L. Murphy, "The Early Social and Political Philosophy of Hugo Black: Liquor as a Test Case," *Alabama Law Review* 36 (1984–85): 871.

40. "Wets Win in 4 Ala. Communities, Lose in 2," *Tuscaloosa News*, November 8, 2012, 3B.

41. Michael Tomberline, "Gov. Bentley Plans to Sign Beer Bill into Law," *Birmingham News*, June 9, 2011, 1D.

42. Richard K. Scher, *Politics in the New South: Republicanism, Race, and Leadership in the Twentieth Century*, 2nd ed. (Armonk, NY: M. E. Sharpe, 1997), 323.

43. 410 U.S. 113 (1973).

44. See www.naral.org.

45. See Carol Sanger, "Regulating Teenage Abortion in the United States: Politics and Policy," *International Journal of Law, Policy, and the Family* 18 (2004): 315.

46. Dana Beyerle, "Governor Hopefuls Tout a Gulf Coast Convention Center," *Tuscaloosa News*, August 18, 2010, 2B.

47. Molly Davis, "Conservatives Push Bills That Challenge Roe v. Wade Ruling," *Tuscaloosa News*, June 5, 2011, 1A.

48. Mack v. Carmack, So. 3d, 2011 WL 3963006 (Ala. 2011).

49. Lamis, *Southern Politics in the 1990s*, 401–2.

50. Coker v. Georgia, 433 U.S. 584.

51. Bob Johnson, "24 Inmates Executed under Riley," *Tuscaloosa News*, December 28, 2010, 3B.

52. Furman v. Georgia, 408 U.S. 238 (1972).

53. "Anti-Death Penalty Bills Keep Talks Alive," *Gadsden Times*, May 3, 2004. http://www.gadsdentimes.com/article/20040503/NEWS/405030322.

54. Esther Brown (letter to the editor), "Decline in Use Shows Time to End Executions" *Birmingham News*, December 23, 2010, 6A. Brown is Alabama executive director, Project Hope to Abolish the Death Penalty.

55. Baze v. Rees, 553 U.S. 35 (2008) gave US Supreme Court approval to the method of injecting three drugs as used by Kentucky.

56. "A Lively Call for Suspending Executions," *Birmingham News*, June 29, 2010, 4A.

57. 513 U.S. 504 (1995).

58. Marienne Thomas-Ogle, "Australian AG Wants No Death Penalty," *Birmingham News*, February 10, 2010, 1B.

Chapter 4

1. See, for example, Wayne Sandholtz and William Koetzle, "Accounting for Corruption," *International Studies Quarterly* 44 (2000): 31.

2. Peter Rodriguez, Klaus Uhlenbruck, and Lorraine Eden, "Government Corruption and the Entry Strategies of Multinationals," *Academy of Management* 30 (2005): 83–96.

3. Charles J. Dean, "McGregor Wiretap Played for Grand Jury—Lawmaker: Didn't Sound Inappropriate," *Birmingham News*, May 7, 2010, 5A.

4. Jay Reeves, "Gilley Describes the Underside of Alabama Politics," *Tuscaloosa News*, June 23, 2011, 11A.

5. Ben Windham, "Shorty Price's Sharp Wit Sorely Needed in Politics Today," *Tuscaloosa News*, August 2, 2009, 1B, 11B.

6. Carl Grafton and Anne Permaloff, *Big Mules and Branchheads: James E. Folsom and Political Power in Alabama* (Athens: University of Georgia Press, 2008), 170.

7. Harvey H. Jackson, *Inside Alabama: A Personal History of My State* (Tuscaloosa: University of Alabama Press, 2004), 121.

8. Henry Clay Warmoth, *War, Politics, and Reconstruction: Stormy Days in Louisiana* (Columbia: University of South Carolina Press, 1930), xii.

9. Patricia Sullivan, ed., *Freedom Writer: Virginia Foster Durr, Letters from the Civil Rights Years* (Athens: University of Georgia Press, 2008), 86–87.

10. Nicholas Apergis, Oguzhan S. Dincer, and James E. Payne, "The Relationship between Corruption and Income Inequality in US States: Evidence from a Panel Cointegration and Error Correction Model," *Public Choice* 145 (2010): 128.

11. Kim Chandler, "Ethics: State Trails Many," *Birmingham News*, November 21, 2010, 9A.

12. John Fritze, "North Dakota Tops Analysis of Corruption," *USA Today*, December 10, 2008. http://usatoday30.usatoday.com/news/nation/2008-12-10-corruptstates_N.htm.

13. "Alàbama May Be No. 1—in Corruption," *Press-Register* (Mobile), May 5, 2010. http://blog.al.com/press-register-commentary/2010/05/editorial_alabama_may_be_no_1_—_in_corruption.html.

14. Pamela Tyler, *Silk Stockings and Ballot Boxes: Women and Politics in New Orleans, 1920–1963* (Athens: University of Georgia Press, 2009), 10.

15. Eddie Curran, "Will Wrong about Siegelman," *Birmingham News*, February 28, 2012, 5A. "In 2002," Curran recalls, "over a four-month period, the *Press-Register* published 10 stories proving that Siegelman's lottery foundation had, after publicly dissolving itself, engaged in a secret rebirth." It was to this foundation that, Curran believes he showed, Scrushy was coerced into contributing a half-million dollars because of previous political disloyalty.

16. Robin DeMonia, "Battling Corruption in Birmingham," *Birmingham News*, December 7, 2008, 2C.

17. Robin DeMonia, "So Long, Two-Year College Probe," *Birmingham News*, November 14, 2010, 2F.

18. The most comprehensive study of the community college scandals is Donald L. Kelly, "Unethical Leadership in Higher Education and the Precarious Journey to Recovery: A Case Study of the Alabama Community College System," a dissertation written at the University of Alabama, 2009.

19. James R. Simmons, "Altruistic Corruption: The Downsian Bureaucrats Revisited," *Administrative Theory and Praxis* 21 (1999): 265.

20. Quoted in Gerald R. Webster and Rebecca Webster, "Taxing Issues: Geography, Politics, and the 2003 Tax Referendum in Alabama," *Southeastern Geographer* 44 (2004): 196.

21. "Voters Should Know the Facts about Bingo Bill," *Tuscaloosa News*, February 14, 2010. http://www.tuscaloosanews.com/article/20100214/NEWS/100219808?Title=Voters-should-know-the-facts-about-bingo-bill.

22. Supreme Court decision: Barber v. Cornerstone Community Outreach, Inc., 42 So. 3d 65 (Ala. 2009).

23. "Bad Business All the Way Around," *Birmingham News*, February 2, 2010, 4A.

24. Charles J. Dean, "Poll: 72% Back Taxing Gambling: Riley Skeptical of Questions, Data," *Birmingham News*, February 6, 2010, 1A.

25. "Poll Finds Broad Support for Gambling in Alabama," *Press-Register* (Mobile), January 19, 2009. http://www.clantonadvertiser.com/2009/01/19/poll-finds-broad-support-for-gambling-in-alabama/.

26. Phillip Rawls, "Gambling Tax Lacks Needed Support," *Tuscaloosa News*, February 1, 2009, 1B.

27. Kim Chandler, "300-Room Hotel at VictoryLand Debuts to Boost Casino Attraction," *Birmingham News*, November 1, 2009. http://blog.al.com/businessnews/2009/11/300-room_hotel_at_victoryland.html.

28. Charles J. Dean, "Riley, King Trade Barbs on Raid: AG Warns Action Could Invite Lawsuits," *Birmingham News*, January 30, 2010, 6A.

29. "The End Game," *Birmingham News*, October 20, 2010, 8A.

30. Shannon McCaffrey, "Scandalized Georgia Adopts New Ethics Laws: No Cap on Lobbyist Gifts," *Birmingham News*, December 26, 2010, 19A.

31. The governor was the "lame duck." All legislators, who take office just as soon as election returns are certified, had begun new four-year terms only a few weeks earlier.

32. "Ethics Laws Open New Era in State Politics," *Tuscaloosa News*, December 20, 2010, 7D.

33. Phillip Rawls, "New Law to End Feasts for Legislators," *Tuscaloosa News*, December 19, 2010, 1B.

34. James L. Sumner Jr., "Alabama's New Day in Ethics," *Birmingham News*, January 19, 2011, 7A.

35. See legal scholars Steven J. Saltzburg and Edward J. Imwinkeiried, "Keeping the Reformist Spirit Alive in Evidence Law," *University of Pennsylvania Law Review* 149 (2000–2001): 1277.

36. David Brooks, "Government Can't Solve Everything," *Tuscaloosa News*, November 18, 2011, 6D.

Chapter 5

1. The Alabama Constitution of 1901: Official Proceedings, July 18, 1900, 2389.

2. J. Morgan Kousser and James M. McPherson, eds., *Region, Race, and Reconstruction: Essays in Honor of C. Vann Woodward* (New York: Oxford University Press, 1982), xxv.

3. Robert Dean Pope, "Of the Man at the Center: Biographies of Southern Politicians in the Age of Segregation," in ibid., 89–112.

4. William Warren Rogers and others, *Alabama: The History of a Deep South State* (Tuscaloosa: University of Alabama Press, 2010), 244.

5. Wayne Flynt, *Alabama in the Twentieth Century* (Tuscaloosa: University of Alabama Press, 2004), 77.

6. See Cleve Webb, ed., *Massive Resistance: Southern Opposition to the Second Reconstruction* (New York: Oxford University Press, 2005).

7. See www.avoiceonline.org/voting/history.html.

8. Mary Orndorff, "Shelby Voting Rights Case Goes to D.C. Judge Friday," *Birmingham News*, September 9, 2010, 1A.

9. 570 U.S. ___ (2013).

10. Mary Orndorff, "DOJ to Exempt Pinson: First City in Alabama Released from Voting Rules," *Birmingham News*, March 17, 2012, 1B, 2B.

11. Susan A. MacManus, "V. O. Key's *Southern Politics*: Demographic Changes Will Transform the Region; In-migration and Generational Shifts Speed Up the Process," in *Unlocking V. O. Key, Jr.: Southern Politics for the Twenty-First Century*, ed. Angie Maxwell and Todd G. Shields (Fayetteville: University of Arkansas Press, 2011), 198.

12. Harold Meyerson, "Rallying the Democratic Base," *Birmingham News*, September 30, 2010, 9A.

13. Charles J. Dean, "Alabama Now Ready for Black Governor, 53% Say in Survey," *Birmingham News*, August 7, 2008. http://www.democraticunderground.com/discuss/duboard.php?az=view_all&address=225x2213.

14. Gwen Ifill, *The Breakthrough: Politics and Race in the Age of Obama* (New York: Anchor Books, 2009), 172, quoting Charles J. Dean, "Obama Victory Enhances Davis," *Birmingham News*, February 8, 2008.

15. Ibid., 105.

16. Adam Nossiter, "For South, a Waning Hold on National Politics," *New York Times*, November 10, 2008. http://www.nytimes.com/2008/11/11/us/politics/11south.html?pagewanted=all&_r=0.

17. This formula was derived from Earl Black and Merle Black, *Politics and Society in the South* (Cambridge, MA: Harvard University Press, 1987), 140–41.

18. Staci B. Brooks, "What Does Obama's Victory Mean for Black Candidates in Alabama?" *Birmingham News*, November 5, 2008. http://blog.al.com/spotnews/2008/11/what_does_obamas_victory_mean.html.

19. Ibid.

20. *The 2010 Statistical Abstract*. See www.census.gov/compendia/statab.

21. See Hasan Kwame Jeffries, *Bloody Lowndes: Civil Rights and Black Power in Alabama's Black Belt* (New York: New York University Press, 2009).

22. Quoted in Errin Haines, "Mismanagement Claimed at SCLC," *Birmingham News*, December 23, 2009, 3A.

23. See, for example, V. O. Key Jr., *Southern Politics in State and Nation* (New York: Alfred A. Knopf, 1949), 628, 631.

24. Jack Bass and Walter De Vries, *The Transformation of Southern Politics: Social Change and Political Consequence since 1945* (New York: Basic Books, 1976), 77.

25. Richard K. Scher, *Politics in the New South: Republicanism, Race, and Leadership in the Twentieth Century*, 2nd ed. (Armonk, NY: M. E. Sharpe, 1997), 153.

26. Cynthia Tucker, "Dethrone the Kingmaker: Reed Has No Right to Play Race Card in Davis' Gubernatorial Run," *Birmingham News*, December 17, 2009, 11A.

27. Phillip Rawls, "Black Leader: Davis Can't Win Election," *Tuscaloosa News,* May 13, 2010, 1A.

28. "40 Years since Supreme Court Allowed Interracial Marriage," *Baltimore Sun,* June 13, 2007. Also: www.archives.can.com/2000.

29. Jeff Hansen, "State among Leaders in Black-White Marriages: Trend Reflects Shift in Attitudes," *Birmingham News,* February 17, 2012, 1A, 7A.

30. 388 U.S. 1.

31. Faye Gaillard, with Jennifer Lindsay and Jane DeNeefe, *Alabama's Civil Rights Trail* (Tuscaloosa: University of Alabama Press, 2010).

32. Crystal Bonvillian, "State Earns 'A' for Schools Teaching Civil Rights History," *Birmingham News,* September 29, 2011, 1A.

33. Rick Bragg, "30 Years Later, Wallace Apologizes to Marchers," *Baltimore Sun,* March 11, 1995. http://articles.baltimoresun.com/1995-03-11/news/1995070104_1_marchers-montgomery-wallace.

34. Norris v. Alabama, 294 U.S. 587 (1935). More is said about the *Norris* case in chapter 13.

35. David Brewer, "Scottsboro Boys Museum Planned," *Birmingham News,* December 20, 2009, 16A.

36. David Kuyk (letter to the editor), "Conjures Up Images of Hate," *Birmingham News,* April 24, 2010, 6A.

Chapter 6

1. Carl Dimick (letter to the editor), "We're No. 1 in the World," *Birmingham News,* January 19, 2010. http://blog.al.com/birmingham-news-commentary/2010/01/your_views_alabama_were_no_1_i.html.

2. Albert L. Sturm, "The Development of American State Constitutions," *Publius* 12 (1982): 57–98. See Sturm's table on 58.

3. From Albert P. Brewer, "Constitutional Revision in Alabama: History and Methodology," *Alabama Law Review* 48 (1997): 583.

4. J. Mills Thornton III, *Politics and Power in a Slave Society: Alabama, 1800–1860* (Baton Rouge: Louisiana State University Press, 1981), 12.

5. William D. Barnard, *Dixiecrats and Democrats: Alabama Politics, 1942–1950* (Tuscaloosa: University of Alabama Press, 1984), 9.

6. Julie Novkov, *Racial Union: Law, Intimacy, and the White State in Alabama, 1865–1954* (Ann Arbor: University of Michigan Press, 2008), 7.

7. Wayne Flynt, "Alabama's Shame: The Historical Origins of the 1901 Constitution," *Alabama Law Review* 53 (2001): 74.

8. Nigel Bowles, *The Government and Politics of the United States* (New York: Palgrave Macmillan, 1993), 5.

9. James Quayle Dealey, *Our State Constitutions* (Philadelphia: American Academy of Political and Social Science, 1907), 13.

10. Charles Austin Beard, *American Government and Politics* (New York: Macmillan, 1910), 706.

11. John Forrest Dillon, *Commentaries on the Law of Municipal Corporations,* vol. 4 (Charleston, SC: Bibliobazaar, 2010), 2508.

12. Will Parker, "Still Afraid of Negro Domination? Why County Home Rule Limi-

tations in the Alabama Constitution of 1901 are Unconstitutional," *Alabama Law Review* 57 (2005): 547, 549–51.

13. "Legislature's Reach Extends Too Far," *Montgomery Advertiser*, March 7, 2010.

14. Smith v. Allwright, 321 U.S. 649 (1944).

15. This is the conclusion one reaches after reading numerous studies of state constitutions, also including David Sollars, "Institutional Rules and State Legislator Compensation: Success for the Reform Movement?" *Legislative Studies Quarterly* 19 (1994): 507–20.

16. "State's Constitution Dated, Lengthy," *Montgomery Advertiser*, June 3, 2010.

17. Christopher W. Hammons, "Was James Madison Wrong? Rethinking the American Preference for Short, Framework-Oriented Constitutions," *American Political Science Review* 93 (1999): 837.

18. George Will, "Calif., Nation Share Budget Woes," *Tuscaloosa News*, May 22, 2011, 5D.

19. Jeffrey C. Tuomala, "In Defense of Chief Justice Roy S. Moore" (2003). Liberty University, Faculty Publications and Presentations, Paper 35. http://digitalcommons.liberty.edu/cgi/viewcontent.cgi?article=1034&context=lusol_fac_pubs.

20. Bryan K. Fair, "Equality for All—The Case for a New Declaration of Rights in the Alabama Constitution," *Cumberland Law Review* 33 (2002–3): 339–85.

21. Richard J. Tobin, "Some Observations on the Use of State Constitutions to Protect the Environment," *Boston College Environmental Affairs Law Review* 3 (1974): 473.

22. See Michele Arington, "English-Only Laws and Direct Legislation: The Battle in the States over Language Minority Rights," *Journal of Law & Politics* 7 (1990): 325.

23. Robert Force, "State Bills of Rights: A Case of Neglect and the Need for a Renaissance," *Valparaiso University Law Review* 3 (1969): 125–82.

24. See Joyce A. McCray Pearson, "The Federal and State Bills of Rights: A Historical Look at the Relationship between America's Documents of Individual Freedom," *Howard Law Journal* 36 (1993): 72.

25. Susan Thompson Spence, "The Usurpation of Legislative Power by the Alabama Judiciary: From Legislative Apportionment to School Reform," *Alabama Law Review* 50 (1998): 941.

26. 369 U.S. 186.

27. Reynolds v. Sims, 377 U.S. 533 (1964).

28. Malcolm Cook McMillan, *Constitutional Development in Alabama, 1798–1901: A Study in Politics, the Negro, and Sectionalism* (Chapel Hill: University of North Carolina Press, 1955), 195.

29. Quoted in ibid., 198.

30. Loving v. Virginia, 388 U.S. 1 (1967).

31. Lane W. Lancaster, "Alabama State Reorganization," *National Municipal Review* 34 (1945): 69–73.

32. Mirjan R. Damaska, *The Faces of Justice and State Authority* (New Haven, CT: Yale University Press, 1986), 189.

33. Robert J. Norrell, "Law in a White Man's Democracy: A History of the Alabama State Judiciary," *Cumberland Law Review* 32 (November): 137, paraphrasing Governor John Winston.

34. Associated Press, "Massachusetts Court Rules Ban on Gay Marriage Is Unconstitutional," November 18, 2003, http://www.boston.com/news/local/massachusetts/articles/2003/11/18/sjc_gay_marriage_legal_in_mass/.

35. Opinion of the Justices, 81 So. 2nd 678.

36. State v. Manley, 441 So. 2nd 864 (1983).

37. Ex parte King, 50 So. 3d 1056 (Ala. 2010).

38. "A Constitutional Conundrum," *Birmingham News*, April 29, 2010, 6A.

39. Thomas Spencer, "Davis, Sparks Clash over Rewriting Constitution," *Birmingham News*, April 29, 2010, 2B.

40. Phillip Rawls, "Davis, Sparks Lay Out Plans for Constitution," *Tuscaloosa News*, April 28, 2010, pp. 1A, 7A.

Chapter 7

1. Robert C. Lowery, "Explaining the Variation in Organized Civil Society across States and Time," *Journal of Politics* 67 (2005): 577.

2. Center for Public Integrity, "Ratio of Lobbyists to Legislators 2006," December 29, 2007. www.iwatchnews.org.

3. James Q. Wilson, *American Government: Brief Version* (Farmington Hills, MI: Cengage Learning, 2011), 344–45.

4. "Alabama Education Association Drastically Cuts Funds to Republicans," *Birmingham Blues* (blog), September 8, 2006.

5. *Webster's Unabridged Dictionary*.

6. V. O. Key Jr., *Politics, Parties, and Pressure Groups* (New York: Thomas Y. Crowell, 1942).

7. Paul Brace, "The Political Economy of Collective Action: The Case of the American States," *Polity* 20 (1988): 654.

8. See Phillip Rawls, "Legal Spat Killed Texting Ban," *Tuscaloosa News*, April 27, 2010, 3B.

9. V. O. Key Jr., *Southern Politics in State and Nation* (New York: Alfred A. Knopf, 1949), 55.

10. William J. Canary and Ralph Stacy, "Policies Need to Help Free Enterprise System," *Birmingham News*, December 4, 2009, 9A.

11. See Eugenia F. Toma, Indrias Berhane, and Corinna Curl, "Political Action Committee Contributions to Education," *Public Choice* 128 (2006): 465–84.

12. Physicians also use "lobby days" as the following article indicates: "Alabama Chapter Hosts Lobby Day," *Bulletin of the American College of Surgeons* 96 (2010): 54.

13. "Oil Money Makes Messy Politics: Exxonmobil Political Contributions and Lobbying Handouts," *ExxposeExxon in the News* (2005). http://www.exxposeexxon.com/newsroom/valdezsupremect.html.

14. See Don Eddins, *Head of the Class in Alabama Politics: A History of the Alabama Education Association* (Montgomery, AL: The Association, 1997).

15. Debra Viadero, "Head of Alabama Teachers' Union Tests Power in Governor's Race," *Education Week*, May 21, 1990. http://www.edweek.org/ew/articles/1990/03/21/09310022.h09.html.

16. Robert J. Norrell, "Labor at the Ballot Box: Alabama Politics from the New Deal to the Dixiecrat Movement," *Journal of Southern History* 57 (1991): 201–34.

17. Roy L. Williams, "Alabama Union Rate Leads in the Southeast," *Birmingham News*, February 5, 2012.

18. Edmund R. Beckwirth, "Alabama Law and Jurisprudence," *Alabama Lawyers Journal* 14 (1925–26): 18.

19. See Harris S. Cohen, "On Professional Power and Conflict of Interest," *Journal of Health Politics, Policy, and Law* 5 (1980): 291.

20. US Chamber of Commerce, "U.S. Chamber Joins Gov. Riley and Alabama Business Leaders in Dialogue to Jumpstart Jobs and Growth," December 4, 2009. http://www.highbeam.com/doc/1G1-215933780.html.

21. Charles J. Dean, "Alabama Retail Association Backs Byrne for Governor," *Birmingham News*, January 6, 2009, 2B.

22. See www.alabamabankers.org.

23. Kenneth J. Meier, "The Political Economy of Consumer Protection: An Examination of State Legislation," *Western Political Quarterly* 40 (1987): 350.

24. See http://www.counterterrorismtraining.gov/victim/index.html.

25. See www.alavoices.org.

26. "Regional and State-Based Organizations." See National Organizers Alliance website, www.noacentral.org.

27. See John A. Hird, "Policy Analysis for What: The Effectiveness of Nonpartisan Policy Research Organizations," *Policy Studies Journal* 33 (2005): 83–105.

28. "Alfa Official Warns State GOP on Insurance Efforts," *Birmingham News*, June 13, 2009, 3B.

29. Cynthia Opheim, "Explaining the Differences in State Lobby Regulation," *Western Political Quarterly* 44 (1991): 405–21.

Chapter 8

1. See http://eideambrose.blogspot.com/2013/06/political-parties-and-political.html.

2. See dictionary.reference.com.

3. See, for example, *Times Daily* (Florence), "At War! The Two Republican Factions in Alabama—A Sample of Old-Time Radical Enmity," September 3, 1892.

4. Jack Bass and Walter De Vries, *The Transformation of Southern Politics: Social Change and Political Consequence since 1945* (New York: Basic Books, 1976), 23.

5. Bob Johnson, "Armistead to Lead Alabama GOP," *Tuscaloosa News*, February 20, 2011, 2B.

6. J. Mills Thornton III, *Politics and Power in a Slave Society: Alabama, 1800–1860* (Baton Rouge: Louisiana State University Press, 1981). See, for example, 7ff., 15.

7. Malcolm Cook McMillan, *Constitutional Development in Alabama, 1798–1901: A Study in Politics, the Negro, and Sectionalism* (Chapel Hill: University of North Carolina Press, 1955), 260–61.

8. Margaret K. Latimer, "No-Party Politics at the End of the Wallace Era," *Publius* 9 (1979): 215.

9. V. O. Key Jr., *Southern Politics in State and Nation* (New York: Alfred A. Knopf, 1949), 280.

10. Bass and De Vries, *Transformation of Southern Politics*, 33.

11. Bernard Cosman, *Five States for Goldwater: Continuity and Change in Southern Presidential Voting Patterns* (Tuscaloosa: University of Alabama Press, 1966), 45.

12. Norman L. Parks, "Tennessee Politics since Kefauver and Reece: A Generalist's View," *Journal of Politics* 28 (1966): 151.

13. Harold W. Stanley, "Presidential Elections and the South," in *Writing Southern Politics*, ed. Robert P. Steed and Laurence W. Moreland (Lexington: University Press of Kentucky, 2006), 222.

14. Cosman, *Five States for Goldwater*.

15. Bass and De Vries, *Transformation of Southern Politics*, 28.

16. Earl Black and Merle Black, *The Rise of Southern Republicans* (Cambridge, MA: Belknap Press of Harvard University Press, 2002), 206, quoted in Stanley, "Presidential Elections and the South," 230.

17. Richard K. Scher, *Politics in the New South: Republicanism, Race, and Leadership in the Twentieth Century*, 2nd ed. (Armonk, NY: M. E. Sharpe, 1997), 156.

18. Harold W. Stanley, "Alabama: Republicans Win the Heart of Dixie," in *The New Politics of the Old South: An Introduction to Southern Politics*, ed. Charles S. Bullock III and Mark J. Rozell (Lanham, MD: Rowman and Littlefield, 1998), 77.

19. Alexander P. Lamis, ed., *Southern Politics in the 1990s* (Baton Rouge: Louisiana State University Press, 1999), 390.

20. Jeffrey M. Jones, "State of the States: Political Party Affiliation," *Gallup*, January 28, 2009. http://www.gallup.com/poll/114016/state-states-political-party-affiliation .aspx. Alabama was the top southern Republican state, two notches above South Carolina, which ranked ninth.

21. Quoted in Eugene Robinson, "Mississippi Gov. Haley Barbour Cannot Rewrite U.S. History," *Tuscaloosa News*, September 7, 2010, 7A.

22. Noah Millman, "Framing the Alabama Democratic Primary Results," *The American Scene*, June 3, 2010. See www.theamericanscene.com.

23. Facebook: Left in Alabama. These comments are no longer available online.

24. These data were furnished by Phillip Rawls, reporter, the Associated Press, in an e-mail message dated November 8, 2012.

25. Dana Beyerle and Jason Morton, "Sparks, Bentley Deliver Final Campaign Messages to Voters," *Tuscaloosa News*, November 2, 2010. http://www.tuscaloosanews.com /article/20101102/news/101109944.

26. This statement was made by Grisham in an interview with Bill Moyers on January 25, 2008. See www.pbs.org/moyers/journal/.

27. Numan V. Bartley and Hugh D. Graham, *Southern Politics and the Second Reconstruction* (Baltimore: Johns Hopkins University Press, 1976), 186.

28. Ibid., 195.

29. Kay Ivey press release, September 15, 2010.

30. Tom Gordon, "Connors to Step Down as State GOP Leader," *Birmingham News*, November 12, 2004, 8C.

31. Kim Chandler, "Democrat Chairman Says Beason Should Resign over Comments: State GOP Deals with Fallout," *Birmingham News*, June 17, 2011, 3B.

32. Charles J. Dean, "Other Choice Sought in Race: Issues with Candidates Take On a New Urgency," *Birmingham News*, March 18, 2012, 13A, 16A.

33. Charles J. Dean, "Moore Talks about God, Government in Speech," *Birmingham News*, March 22, 2012, 5A.

34. "10 Great Places to Retire for Democrats and Republicans," November 1, 2008. See http://money.usnews.com/money/personal-finance/.

35. David White, "Democrat State House Dominance Nears End," *Birmingham News*, November 4, 2010, 4A.

36. Charles J. Dean and Kim Chandler, "Big Win for Bentley," *Birmingham News*, November 3, 2010, 1A.

37. "Crimson Tide," *Weekly Standard*, November 13, 2010.

38. Noted in Susan A. MacManus, "V. O. Key Jr.'s *Southern Politics*: Demographic

Changes Will Transform the Region; In-migration and Generational Shifts Will Speed Up the Process," in *Unlocking V. O. Key Jr.: "Southern Politics" for the Twenty-First Century*, ed. Angie Maxwell and Todd G. Shields (Fayetteville: University of Arkansas Press, 2011), 198.

39. Ibid., 200.

40. Key, *Southern Politics in State and Nation*, 277.

41. Phillip Rawls, "Ex-State Supreme Court Justice to Lead Democrats," *Birmingham News*, January 30, 3011, 1B, 2B.

42. West Alabama "Reagan Republicans" is how the group identifies itself on its Facebook page.

43. Phillip Rawls, "GOP Leaders Aim to Root Out Fakes: Group Targets Disguised Democrats," *Birmingham News*, March 4, 2011, 2B.

44. Ben Evans, "Rep. Artur Davis Forms Rival Committee on Appointees," *Tuscaloosa News*, December 10, 2008, 3B.

45. Charles J. Dean, "Days May Be Numbered for Alabama's Democrats," *Birmingham News*, November 14, 2010, 6A.

46. Natalie Davis, "After the Fall: Alabama's Democratic Party on Life Support; Change Needed for Comeback," *Birmingham News*, November 21, 2004, 7D.

47. Rawls, "Ex-State Supreme Court Justice to Lead Democrats."

48. Phillip Rawls, "Ron Sparks Looks Back at Loss, toward Future," *Tuscaloosa News*, November 26, 2010, 2B.

49. Dana Beyerle, "Sexton Candidacy Emblematic of GOP Plan," *Tuscaloosa News*, June 22, 2011, 1B.

50. Ibid.

51. George Talbot, "Democratic Party Chair Says Election a Big Win," *Birmingham News*, November 9, 2012, 13A.

Chapter 9

1. Richard K. Scher, *Politics in the New South: Republicanism, Race, and Leadership in the Twentieth Century*, 2nd ed. (Armonk, NY: M. E. Sharpe, 1997), 318.

2. Numan V. Bartley and Hugh D. Graham, *Southern Politics and the Second Reconstruction* (Baltimore: Johns Hopkins University Press, 1976), 38.

3. Pope, "Of the Man at the Center," quoting W. J. Cash, *The Mind of the South* (New York: Alfred A. Knopf, 1941), 247.

4. Scher, *Politics in the New South*, 310.

5. Ibid., 322.

6. Ibid., 323.

7. Richard K. Scher, *The Modern Political Campaign: Mudslinging, Bombast, and the Vitality of American Politics* (Armonk, NY: M. E. Sharpe, 1997), 4.

8. John Fleming, "The Political Scene: Color Is Life, and Politics," *Anniston Star*, October 26, 2008.

9. This statement was attributed to Auburn political scientist Paul Johnson during the 2000 presidential campaign. http://www.auburn.edu/administration/univrel/news/archive/11_00news/11_00ele ction.html.

10. V. O. Key Jr., *Southern Politics in State and Nation* (New York: Alfred A. Knopf, 1949), 402.

11. Ibid., 404.

12. Dana Beyerle, "Graddick Expects Chief Justice Race to Be Decided in Primary: Malone Qualifies to Run," *Gadsden Times*, November 17, 2011. http://www.gadsdentimes.com/article/20111117/NEWS/111119805.

13. David White, "Folsom Will Seek Re-Election, Skip Race for Governorship," *Birmingham News*, April 2, 2009, 1B.

14. Tim Lockette, "Population Experts: Immigrants Needed in Ala.," *Tuscaloosa News*, March 11, 2012, 3B.

15. Wayne Flynt, *Poor but Proud: Alabama's Poor Whites* (Tuscaloosa: University of Alabama Press, 2002), 6.

16. Charles J. Dean and David White, "Bentley Wins GOP Nomination: Little-Known Bentley Defied the Political Experts," *Birmingham News*, July 14, 2010, 6A.

17. Facebook message from Jeremy Sherer, January 11, 2010.

18. Larry Sabato, *Goodbye to Good-Time Charlie: The American Governor Transformed* (Lexington, MA: Lexington Books, 1978), 157.

19. See www.opensecrets.org/races/geog.php?cycle=2012&id=AL02.

20. Kim Chandler, "Jury Mostly Female as Trial Set to Begin," *Birmingham News*, June 10, 2011, 3B.

21. "Democratic Input for King," *Inside Alabama Politics*, April 30, 2010, 4.

22. Flowers column, January 7, 2009. See http://steveflowers.us.

23. Robin DeMonia, "The Ultimate in Political Gift-Giving," *Birmingham News*, December 12, 2010, 2F.

24. Kim Chandler and Brendan Kirby, "McGregor Taped: He Supports His Friends—Beason Believed Gambling Interests Would Buy Vote," *Birmingham News*, June 14, 2011, 2A.

25. Key, *Southern Politics in State and Nation*, 403.

26. Terri R. Day, "Nasty as They Wanna Be Politics: Clean Campaigns and the First Amendment," *Ohio Northern University Law Review* 35 (2009): 651.

27. Thomas Spencer, "Stacks of PAC Filings Don't Tell All: Campaign Donors Can Stay Unknown," *Birmingham News*, March 21, 2010, 1A, 10A, 11A.

28. Thomas Spencer, "Huge Sums Aside, Don't Call Him a Fundraiser," *Birmingham News*, March 21, 2010, 11A.

29. "An Expensive Gamble," *Birmingham News*, November 4, 2010, 6A.

30. See www.museum.tv/debateweb/html/equalizer/print/tvguide_jfkforce.htm.

31. Rebecca Mitchell (letter to the editor), "Character Means Nothing without Issues," *Tuscaloosa News*, May 23, 2010, 7D.

32. "McCain-Palin Ticket Featured in Alabama Republican's Ad," *CNN News*, September 10, 2008. http://politicalticker.blogs.cnn.com/2008/09/10/mccain-palin-ticket-featured-in-alabama-republicans-ad/.

33. Ben Smith, "The Amazing Campaign Ads of Alabama," *Politico*, May 16, 2010. http://www.politico.com/blogs/ben-smith/2010/05/the-amazing-campaign-ads-of-alabama-027028.

34. Drew Westen, "Politicians Use Attack Ads, Despite Voters' Complaints, Because They Work," *Tuscaloosa News*, February 27, 2012, 9A.

35. Joey Kennedy, "If We Don't Want Negative Campaign Ads, We Have to Punish the Candidates Who Allow Them," *Birmingham News*, May 17, 2010. http://blog.al.com/jkennedy/2010/05/joey_kennedy_if_we_dont_want_n.html.

36. Montague Kern, *30-Second Politics: Political Advertising in the Eighties* (New York: Praeger, 1989), 4.

37. "Peterson Phenomena," *Inside Alabama Politics*, May 21, 2010, 3.

38. Gail Collins, "Candidates Lean On Outrageous Ads," *Tuscaloosa News*, June 1, 2010, 4A.

39. Tim Lockette and John Fleming, "Tweet Home, Alabama: Can the Internet Be a Game-Changer in the Politics of a Relatively Un-Wired State?" *Anniston Star*, May 30, 2010.

40. Patrick R. Cotter and Tom Gordon, "Alabama: The GOP Rises in the Heart of Dixie," in *Southern Politics in the 1990s*, ed. Alexander P. Lamis (Baton Rouge: Louisiana State University Press, 1999), 242–43.

41. Matt Osborne, "Fear, Loathing, and Faith-Based Politics," *Crooks and Liars* (blog), October 31, 2010.

42. Mary Orndorff, "Davis Closes Door on State Politics," *Birmingham News*, October 3, 2010, 1A, 4A.

43. Key, *Southern Politics in State and Nation*, 402.

44. Tiffany Ray, "26% of Voters Go to Polls Despite Weather," *Birmingham News*, December 9, 2009, 6A.

45. Associated Press, "Candidates Close In on Primary Elections," *Birmingham News*, May 31, 2010.

Chapter 10

1. See especially Baker v. Carr, 369 U.S. 186 (1962); Wesberry v. Sanders, 376 U.S. 1 (1964); and Reynolds v. Sims, 377 U.S. 533 (1964).

2. Tommy Stevenson, "4th Congressional District Is Unprecedented," *Tuscaloosa News*, June 19, 2011. http://www.tuscaloosanews.com/article/20110619/NEWS/110629998. The individual referred to is former US representative Ronnie Flippo.

3. William Warren Rogers and others, *Alabama: The History of a Deep South State* (Tuscaloosa: University of Alabama Press, 1994), 249.

4. Finding cited in Jack Bass and Walter De Vries, *The Transformation of Southern Politics: Social Change and Political Consequence since 1945* (New York: Basic Books, 1976), 47.

5. Barbara J. Fields, "Ideology and Race in American History," in *Region, Race, and Reconstruction: Essays in Honor of C. Vann Woodward*, ed. J. Morgan Kousser and James W. McPherson (New York: Oxford University Press, 1982), 158.

6. Richard K. Scher, *Politics in the New South: Republicanism, Race, and Leadership in the Twentieth Century*, 2nd ed. (Armonk, NY: M. E. Sharpe, 1997), about 169.

7. Matthew D. Itkin, "Felon Disenfranchisement and the Systemic Racism of the Criminal Justice System," *Journal of Race, Gender, and Ethnicity* 4 (2009): 73.

8. Kim Chandler, "Felon Voting Bill Ensnares Riley: Governor Would Defy GOP If He Signed It," *Birmingham News*, June 22, 2003.

9. Shaila Dewan, "In Alabama, a Fight to Regain Voting Rights Some Felons Never Lost," *New York Times*, March 2, 2008. http://www.nytimes.com/2008/03/02/us/02felons.html?pagewanted=all&_r=0.

10. John Clifford Green, Mark J. Rozell, and Clyde Wilcox, eds., *Prayers in the Precincts: The Christian Right in the 1998 Elections* (Washington, DC: Georgetown University Press, 2000), 155.

11. Jeffrey M. Jones, "Ideology: Three Deep South States Are the Most Conservative," *Gallup*, February 3, 2010. http://www.gallup.com/poll/125480/ideology-three-deep-south-states-conservative.aspx.

12. See especially Smith v. Allwright, 321 U.S. 649 (1944).

13. Numan V. Bartley and Hugh D. Graham, *Southern Politics and the Second Reconstruction* (Baltimore: Johns Hopkins University Press, 1976), 111.

14. Donald S. Strong, *Registration of Voters in Alabama* (Tuscaloosa: Bureau of Public Administration, University of Alabama, 1956), 57–58 and 75, cited in ibid., 40.

15. Bass and De Vries, *Transformation of Southern Politics*, 47.

16. Bartley and Graham, *Southern Politics and the Second Reconstruction*, 188.

17. Ibid., 134.

18. Ibid., 198.

19. Associated Press, "Voter Turnout 'Very Positive,'" *Birmingham News*, March 15, 2012, 4B.

20. Adam Nossiter, "For South, a Waning Hold on National Politics," *New York Times*, November 11, 2008. http://www.nytimes.com/2008/11/11/us/politics/11south.html?pagewanted=all.

21. David Broder, "U.S. Politics Could Face Major Shift," *Birmingham News*, June 15, 2010, 7A.

22. Harold W. Stanley, "Alabama: Republicans Win the Heart of Dixie," in *The New Politics of the South*, ed. Charles S. Bullock III and Mark J. Rozell (Lanham, MD: Rowman and Littlefield, 1998), 80.

23. Robert DeWitt, "GOP's Boman Upsets Incumbent Thigpen," *Tuscaloosa News*, November 3, 2010, 5B.

24. Bob Johnson, "Segall Challenges Incumbent Rogers," *Tuscaloosa News*, October 30, 2008. https://news.google.com/newspapers?nid=1817&dat=20081030&id=xZYnAAAAIBAJ&sjid=Mr0EAAAAIBAJ&pg=6664,6492859&hl=en.

25. Andy Brownfield, "PSC President Seems Headed for Runoff," *Tuscaloosa News*, March 14, 2012, 5B.

26. Robert DeWitt, "Sumter Sees Rise in Voting Absentee, *Tuscaloosa News*, October 29, 2010, 1A.

27. Erin Stock, "'Voter Fatigue' Will Factor into Turnout," *Birmingham News*, December 6, 2009, 8A.

28. "Study: Women, Baby Boomers Are Big Voters," *Tuscaloosa News*, September 8, 2009, 1B.

Chapter 11

1. J. Thomas Askew, Review of William Vernon Holloway and Charles W. Smith, *Government and Politics in Alabama* (University, AL: University Supply Store, 1941), in *Journal of Politics* 3 (1941): 381, 382.

2. V. O. Key Jr., *Southern Politics in State and Nation* (New York: Alfred A. Knopf, 1949).

3. Branwell DuBose Kapeluck, Robert P. Steed and Laurence W. Moreland, "Southern Governors and Legislatures," in *Writing Southern Politics: Contemporary Interpretations and Future Directions*, ed. Robert P. Steed and Laurence W. Moreland (Lexington: University Press of Kentucky, 2006), 269.

4. Ibid., 270.

5. William J. D. Boyd, "New Study Ranks State Legislatures: Citizens Conference Cites Procedures, Operations," *National Civic Review*, March 1971, 155.

6. Bob Blalock, "Why Does Freeing Hops, Other Bills, Take So Long?" *Birmingham News*, June 7, 2009, 2F.

7. "Alabama Senators Slug It out in Legislature," *Taipei Times*, June 10, 2007. http://www.taipeitimes.com/News/world/archives/2007/06/10/2003364624.

8. See www.ncsl.org/legislatures-elections/.

9. Victor L. Lin, "The Possible Consequences and Effects of Moderately Restrictive Term Limits on the California State Legislature," Senior Honors Thesis, Department of Political Science, University of California, San Diego, March 28, 2011.

10. Nancy Martorano Miller, "Paths, Events, and Strategic Choices: The Evolution of American State Legislatures," paper presented at the American Political Science Association 2009 Toronto Meeting, 38.

11. Noted in Mark Crawford, "Don't Forget Legislature's Pay Raise," *Birmingham News*, May 23, 2010, 3F.

12. For an analysis of the office of lieutenant governor as it operated many years ago, see Warren Rex Isom, "The Office of Lieutenant Governor in the States," *American Political Science Review* 32 (1938): 921–26.

13. See Donald S. Lutz and Richard W. Murray, "Coalition Formation in the Texas Legislature: Issues, Payoffs, and Winning Coalition Size," *Western Political Quarterly* 28 (1975): 296–315.

14. Phillip Rawls, "Tornadoes Define Bentley's First Year: Governor Talks about the Trials of April 27," *Tuscaloosa News*, January 16, 2012, 3B.

15. David White, "Senate Taking Snail's Pace: Road Bill Debate Called Typical," *Birmingham News*, February 1, 2010, 1A, 5A.

16. Dana Beyerle, "Session Has Light Year in Terms of Passing Bills," *Tuscaloosa News*, May 20, 2012, 6D.

17. Nancy Burns, Laura Evans, Gerald Gamm, and Corrine McConnaughy, "Urban Politics in the State Arena," *Studies in American Political Development* 23 (2009): 1–22.

18. Ibid., 1–2.

19. Larry Sabato, *Goodbye to Good-Time Charlie: The American Governor Transformed* (Lexington, MA: Lexington Books, 1978), 82.

20. Phillip Rawls, "Alabama Ethics Talk Leads to Zero Action: Year after Year, Bills Pop Up, Are Debated, Then Forgotten," *Tuscaloosa News*, April 26, 2010, 3B.

21. Rex Thomas, "Black Belters Primed for Do-or-Die Battle," *Decatur Daily*, April 16, 1961, A-11.

22. Bob Johnson, "House Panel to Consider Electronic Bingo Bill," *Tuscaloosa News*, January 21, 2010, 1B.

23. "PACT Bailout Vote Delayed," *Birmingham News*, January 14, 2010, 2B.

24. Quin Hillyer, "Not Our Cup of Tea," *American Spectator*, February 15, 2010. http://spectator.org/articles/40092/not-our-cup-tea.

25. Michael Tomberlin, "Bentley Criss-Crosses State, Focuses on Meeting Voters," *Birmingham News*, May 17, 2010, 3A.

26. Bob Lowry, "Sen. Paul Sanford Shocked at 'Dysfunctional' Alabama Senate," *Huntsville Times*, May 10, 2010. http://blog.al.com/breaking/2010/05/sanford_shocked_at_dysfunction.html.

27. Ibid.

28. Phillip Rawls, "Beason Says He Worked with FBI for a Year: Mask Predicts Grand Jury Will Issue Indictments," *Tuscaloosa News*, May 6, 2010, 2A.

29. Dana Beyerle, "Panel's 6–0 Vote Passes Bingo Bill: Amended Bill Had Been Withdrawn," *Tuscaloosa News*, February 12, 2009, 1B.

30. Kim Chandler, "Bill to Kill Retirement Plan Clears Committee," *Birmingham News*, March 10, 2011, 4A.

31. Reported in Gerald W. Johnson, "The Value of Democracy: What Does It Mean in Alabama?" *Anniston Star*, March 4, 2012.

32. Lowry, "Sen. Paul Sanford Shocked at 'Dysfunctional' Alabama Senate."

33. Robert Harmel, "Minority Partisanship in One-Party Predominant Legislatures: A Five-State Study," *Journal of Politics* 48 (1986): 729–40, cited in Kapeluck, Steed, and Moreland, "Southern Governors and Legislatures," 277.

34. Robin DeMonia, "A New Day in Alabama, or Maybe Not," *Birmingham News*, February 27, 2011, 2F.

35. Tommy Stevenson, "Robert Bentley Is a Leader—Not a Follower—in His Party," *Tuscaloosa News*, July 18, 2010, 6D.

36. Blalock, "Why Does Freeing Hops, Other Bills, Take So Long?"

37. "Alabama Voters Feel Voiceless in Legislature, According to Poll" (Political Skinny blog), *Press-Register* (Mobile), March 28, 2011.

38. Bob Lowry, "Alabama Chief Justice, Senators Warn of Federal Court Takeover of Overcrowded State Prison System," *Birmingham News*, June 21, 2011. http://blog.al.com/breaking/2011/06/alabama_chief_justice_senators.html.

39. "State Budgets Appear Responsible," *Montgomery Advertiser*, April 27, 2010. http://www.montgomeryadvertiser.com/article/20100427/OPINION01/4270302/1006/rss06.

40. Joel A. Thompson, "State Legislative Reform: Another Look, One More Time, Again," *Polity* 19 (1986): 32.

Chapter 12

1. See Larry Sabato, *Goodbye to Good-Time Charlie: The American Governor Transformed, 1950–1975* (Lexington, MA: Lexington Books, 1978), 9.

2. Ibid., cited in Branwell DuBose Kapeluck, Robert P. Steed, and Laurence W. Moreland, "Southern Governors and Legislatures," in *Writing Southern Politics*, ed. Robert P. Steed and Laurence W. Moreland (Lexington: University Press of Kentucky, 2006), 282.

3. Jack Bass and Walter De Vries, *The Transformation of Southern Politics: Social Change and Political Consequence since 1945* (New York: Basic Books, 1976), 75.

4. Joseph A. Schlesinger, "The Politics of the Executive," in *Politics in the American States*, ed. Herbert Jacob and Kenneth Vines, 2nd ed. (Boston: Little, Brown, 1971), 229, cited in Richard K. Scher, *Politics in the New South: Republicanism, Race, and Leadership in the Twentieth Century*, 2nd ed. (Armonk, NY: M. E. Sharpe, 1997), 278.

5. Coleman B. Ransone Jr., *The Office of Governor in the South* (Tuscaloosa: Bureau of Public Administration, University of Alabama, 1951), cited in Kapeluck, Steed, and Moreland, "Southern Governors and Legislatures," 273.

6. Sabato, *Goodbye to Good-Time Charlie*, 83.

7. David White, "Troy King Blasts Alabama Gov. Bob Riley for Endorsement of His Opponent," *Birmingham News*, May 28, 2010. http://blog.al.com/spotnews/2010/05/campaign_2010_troy_king_blasts.html.

8. Michael DeBow, "The State Tobacco Litigation and the Separation of Powers in State Governments: Repairing the Damage," *Seton Hall Law Review* 31 (2001): 575.

9. Ibid., 52.

10. Allen Tullos, *Alabama Getaway: The Political Imaginary and the Heart of Dixie* (Athens: University of Georgia Press, 2011), 10.

11. Ibid., 119.

12. Sabato, *Goodbye to Good-Time Charlie*.

13. Dana Beyerle, "Bentley's Past Helped Pave Path to Office," *Tuscaloosa News*, December 26, 2010, 1A.

14. Scher, *Politics in the New South*, 310.

15. William C. Havard and Loren P. Beth, *The Politics of Mis-Representation: Rural-Urban Conflict in the Florida Legislature* (Baton Rouge: Louisiana State University Press, 1972), cited in Scher, *Politics in the New South*, 309.

16. Tommy Stevenson and Dana Beyerle, "Bentley Blasts Byrne Campaign," *Tuscaloosa News*, July 1, 2010, 1A.

17. Michael Lienesch, *Redeeming America: Piety and Politics in the New Christian Right* (Chapel Hill: University of North Carolina Press, 1993), 2.

18. "David Bibb Graves," *Encyclopedia of Alabama*.

19. See www.archives.state.al.us/govs_list/g_folsom.html.

20. Tom Gordon, "Hunt Praised at Memorial for Simple Virtue," *Birmingham News*, February 5, 2009, 2B.

21. Mitch Frank, "Alabama's Most Courageous Politician," *Time*, August 15, 2003. http://content.time.com/time/nation/article/0,8599,476249,00.html.

22. Wayne Grayson, "The Doctor Is In: Bentley, Supporters Revel in Hard-Fought Victory," *Tuscaloosa News*, July 14, 2010, 4A.

23. Phillip Rawls, "Donors Raised $1.6 Million for Bentley's Inauguration: Foundation to Donate Leftover $300,000 to State General Fund," *Tuscaloosa News*, February 27, 2011, 5B.

24. Tullos, *Alabama Getaway*, 146.

25. Earl Black, "Southern Governors and Political Change: Campaign Stances on Racial Segregation and Economic Development, 1950–69," *Journal of Politics* 33 (1971): 703–34, cited in Kapeluck, Steed, and Moreland, "Southern Governors and Legislatures," 278.

26. Ibid.

27. David White, "Bentley Ready to Take Oath of Office," *Birmingham News*, January 17, 2011, 8A.

28. Dan T. Carter, *The Politics of Rage: George Wallace, the Origins of the New Conservatism, and the Transformation of American Politics* (Baton Rouge: Louisiana State University Press, 2000), 464.

29. Phillip Rawls, "AG Says Governor Causing Constitutional Crisis on Bingo Issue," *Tuscaloosa News*, April 10, 2010, 2B.

30. Phillip Rawls, "Judge Refuses to Block Raid: Legality of Slot-Style Bingo Machines Deemed 'State-Law Issue,'" *Tuscaloosa News*, February 2, 2010, 1A.

31. Kim Chandler and Charles J. Dean, "Halls Seek Way to Reopen: Lawyers Work While Casinos Shuttered," *Birmingham News*, February 7, 2010, 11A.

32. Patricia C. McCarter, "Riley, King Share Continued Bingo Battle Talk with Huntsville Civic Groups," *Huntsville Times*, March 17, 2010. http://blog.al.com/breaking/2010/03/post_236.html.

33. Rawls, "AG Says Governor Causing Constitutional Crisis on Bingo Issue."

34. Riley v. Cornerstone Community Outreach, Inc., 57 So. 3d 704 (Ala. 2010).

35. Bob Johnson, "Judge Delays Task Force Bingo Raid: VictoryLand Machines Cannot Be Seized until Court's Ruling Is Final," *Tuscaloosa News*, August 6, 2010, 1B.

36. Bob Johnson, "State Justices Give OK for VictoryLand Raid," *Tuscaloosa News*, July 31, 2010, 4A.

37. Jon Archibald, "Uncivil War: Greene County Wants to Secede," *Birmingham News*, July 2, 2010, 4B.

38. Stan Diel, "Bentley Mortgaged House, Took Savings to Fund His Run," *Birmingham News*, August 12, 2010, 2B.

39. Phillip Rawls, "Bentley Takes Lead in Post-Tornado Recovery," *Birmingham News*, June 20, 2011, 4B.

40. Phillip Rawls, "Tornadoes Define Bentley's First Year: Governor Talks about the Trials of April 27," *Tuscaloosa News*, January 16, 2012, 3B.

41. Kim Chandler, "Charter Schools, Ethics on Riley's To-Do List: Challenges Legislators to Push His Agenda in Final Year in Office," *Birmingham News*, January 13, 2010, 1A, 8A.

42. Dana Beyerle, "Budget Comments Shock Lawmakers," *Tuscaloosa News*, January 13, 2010, 1A.

43. Kim Chandler and Charles J. Dean, "Riley Leaves with No Regrets," *Birmingham News*, January 9, 2011, 11A.

44. Bob Blalock, "Riley Legacy: Education Governor," *Birmingham News*, January 26, 2011, 2F.

45. Tullos, *Alabama Getaway*, 178.

46. Scher, *Politics in the New South*, 318.

47. Ricky Thomason, "If Public Notices Reflected Reality," *Huntsville Times*, February 22, 2010. http://blog.al.com/times-views/2010/02/columnist_ricky_thomason_if_pu.html.

Chapter 13

1. 287 U.S. 45 (1932).

2. Bradley C. Canon, "Reactions of State Supreme Courts to a US Supreme Court Civil Liberties Decision," *Law and Society Review* 8 (1973): 110. This statement was attributed to Chief Justice J. Ed Livingston.

3. Ex parte State ex rel. Alabama Policy Institute, __ So. 3d ___ (2015).

4. See, for example, the Maryland Court of Appeals, www.courts.state.md.us/coappeals/.

5. Janie L. Shores, William Mike House, and Paul Simon, "Tributes to Senator Howell Heflin," *Alabama Law Review* 48 (1997): 438–39.

6. Bob Martin, "Should We Change the Way Judges Are Chosen?" *Hartselle Enquirer*, September 18, 2010, A-4.

7. Bob Johnson, "Federal Court Seeks Help in AEA Dues Suit: Payroll Deduction Part of Issue," *Birmingham News*, December 24, 2011, 1C, 2C.

8. Eric Velasco, "High Court Shows Range in Productivity," *Birmingham News*, October 11, 2010, 2A.

9. Alabama Rules of Appellate Procedure, Rule 16.

10. Ex parte E.R.G., 73 So. 3d 634 (Ala. 2011).

11. Jonathan D. Persky, "Ghosts That Slay: A Contemporary Look at State Advisory Opinions," *Connecticut Law Review* 37 (2004): 1159.

12. Etowah Baptist Ass'n v. Entrekin, 45 So. 2d 1266 (Ala. 2010).

13. Persky, "Ghosts That Slay."

14. This was not a "'decision' of the Court, but rather a ruling on proposed rule changes for the Judicial Inquiry Commission." This ruling may be located at http://judicial.alabama.gov/rules/rules.cfm under "Rules of Procedure of the Judicial Inquiry Commission." I am indebted to professor Michael DeBow for this information.

15. See www.progressivestates.org/state/yourstate/al.

16. Stuart H. Perry, "Politics and Judicial Administration," *Annals of the American Academy of Political and Social Science* 169 (1933): 77.

17. Robert L. Brown, "From Whence Cometh Our State Appellate Judges? Popular Election versus the Missouri Plan," *University of Arkansas at Little Rock Law Journal* 20 (1997): 317. Justice Brown is repeating a view he doesn't share.

18. Chris Rizo, "Poll: Voters Want State Judges to Run in Non-Partisan Elections," Legal Newsline.com, October 22, 2008.

19. "Nonpartisan Judge Elections Scuttled," *Birmingham News*, April 8, 2010, 3B.

20. See www.alabar.org/members/Which_is_Right_for_Alabama.pdf.

21. "Dr. Bronner Speaks Out on Exxon Case," *Jere Beasley Report*, October 27, 2006. http://www.jerebeasleyreport.com/2006/10/dr-bronner-speaks-out-on-exxon-case/.

22. Erin Stock, "ABA President, Judge Spar over Judicial Elections," *Birmingham News*, February 20, 2009.

23. Eric Velasco, "National Poll Says Voters Want Special Interests out of Judicial Races," *Birmingham News*, September 11, 2010, 8A.

24. Cosby Woodruff, "Survey Gives State's Low Courts Low Marks," *Montgomery Advertiser*, March 24, 2010. http://www.montgomeryadvertiser.com/article/20100324/BUSINESS/3240369/1003/.

25. Quoted in Rizo, "Poll: Voters Want State Judges to Run in Non-Partisan Elections."

26. Alexander Tabarrok and Eric Helland, "Partisan Judicial Elections and Home Court Advantage," *Corporate Legal Times*, March 2002. http://www.independent.org/newsroom/article.asp?id=225.

27. Steve Flowers, weekly column, February 27, 2008. See http://steveflowers.us/.

28. Stated in "So Much Money, so Little Justice," *Birmingham News*, November 14, 2008, 8A.

29. Quoted in Velasco, "National Poll Says Voters Want Special Interests out of Judicial Races,"

30. Phillip Rawls, "Alabama at the Top in Supreme Court Campaign Costs," *Tuscaloosa News*, August 16, 2010, 4B.

31. See http://journals.democraticunderground.com/madfloridian/.

32. Rawls, "Alabama at the Top in Supreme Court Costs."

33. Eric Velasco, "High Court Shows Range in Productivity," *Birmingham News*, October 11, 2010, 2A.

34. Facebook message from Steven Noles, March 20, 2012.

35. *Wall Street Journal*, February 7, 1996.

36. Joshua Green, "Karl Rove in a Corner," *The Atlantic*, November 2004. http://www.theatlantic.com/magazine/archive/2004/11/karl-rove-in-a-corner/303537/.

37. BMW of North America, Inc. v. Gore, 517 U.S. 559 (1996).

38. Kevin Sack, "Alabama Businesses and Trial Lawyers Fight to Deadlock on Jury Awards," *New York Times*, February 3, 1996. http://www.nytimes.com/1996/02/03/us/alabama-businesses-and-trial-lawyers-fight-to-deadlock-on-jury-awards.html.

39. Dobson v. Allied-Bruce Terminix Companies, Inc. This decision was reversed by the US Supreme Court in Allied-Bruce Terminix Companies, Inc. v. Dobson, 513 U.S. 265 (1995).

40. Adam Champagne, "Tort Reform and Judicial Selection," *Loyola of Los Angeles Law Review* 38 (2004–5): 1484, citing Phil Hadberger, "Juries under Siege," *St. Mary's Law Journal* 30 (1998): 1, 4–5.

41. "The punitive damages provision at Ala. Code § 6-11-21 . . . survived a very weak 'due process' challenge in *Boles v. Parris*, 952 So. 2d 364 (Ala. 2006)." Message of Professor Michael DeBow, February 27, 2012.

42. Woodruff, "Survey Gives State's Courts Low Marks."

43. US Chamber of Commerce, Ranking the States: Lawsuit Climate 1010. See www.uschamber.com.

44. Joanne M. Shepherd, "The Influence of Retention Politics on Judges' Voting," *Journal of Legal Studies* 38 (2009): 171.

45. Ex parte Ford Motor Co., 47 So. 3d 234 (Ala. 2010).

46. Bob Johnson, "Lawmakers Pass Bills to Limit Lawsuit Abuse in State," *Tuscaloosa News*, May 28, 2011, 3B.

Chapter 14

1. Scott Horton, "Crazy in Alabama: The Imminent Threat Posed by Teachers," *Harper's Magazine*, March 2008. http://harpers.org/blog/2008/03/crazy-in-alabama/.

2. Roscoe C. Martin, "Alabama's Administrative Reorganization of 1939," *Journal of Politics* 2 (1940): 436–47.

3. Bob Blalock, "Will Judge Make State Remedy Sins of the Past?" *Birmingham News*, February 20, 2011. http://blog.al.com/bblalock/2011/02/bob_blalock_will_judge_make_st.html. (Blalock was paraphrasing Judge Dement.)

4. Phillip Rawls, "White Men Continuing to Dominate State Boards: Today's Percentages Almost Same as in 2003," *Tuscaloosa News*, July 7, 2009, 1B, 3B.

5. Meg Handley, "The 10 Poorest States in the Union," *U.S. News Money*, September 23, 2011. See http://money.usnews.com.

6. Lydia Seabol Avant, "24% of Alabama Kids Living in Poverty," *Tuscaloosa News*, July 29, 2009, 1A.

7. Linda Tilly, "Flawed Tax Systems Keep Us Last in Many Rankings," *Birmingham News*, November 29, 2009, 1F.

8. James M. Lutz, "Regional Leadership Patterns in the Diffusion of Public Policies," *American Politics Quarterly* 65 (1987): 393.

9. Sarah M. Morehouse and Malcolm E. Jewel, "States as Laboratories: A Reprise," *Annual Reviews in Political Science* 7 (2004), 177–203. See the discussion, "States as Laboratories of Social Experimentation," 197ff.

10. See www.governing.com/gpp/2008/al.htm.

11. Steven Knack, "Social Capital and the Quality of Government: Evidence from the States," *American Journal of Political Science* 46 (2002): 775.

12. See Theda Skocpol, "Strategies of Analysis in Current Research," in *Bringing the State Back In*, ed. Peter B. Evans, Dietrich Rueschemeyer, and Theda Skocpol (New York: Cambridge University Press, 1985), 3–37.

13. Dennis Cauchon, "New Yorkers Lead Pack in Government Benefits: Comes to $9,442 Per Person, Per Year, on Average," *USA Today*, April 26, 2011, 2A.

14. Emily Wagner Pettus, "Minnesota Democrat Criticizes Mississippi in Campaign," *Tuscaloosa News*, June 8, 2010, 6B.

15. "Conditions in State's Prisons about to Worsen," *Birmingham News*, September 29, 2008, 10A.

16. Phillip Rawls, "Riley Announces Crackdown on Speeding in Alabama," *Tusca-*

loosa News, August 27, 2004. https://news.google.com/newspapers?nid=1817&dat=20040827&id=b84dAAAAIBAJ&sjid=w6cEAAAAIBAJ&pg=3719,3243474&hl=en.

17. Ginny McDonald, "Hammer's Down in Yellowhammer State: Average Speed on Alabama Interstates is 69.6 Study Says," *Birmingham News*, March 18, 2010, 1A.

18. Jeremy Gray, "State 'Trailing' on Transportation Data," *Birmingham News*, May 12, 2011, 2B.

19. Russell Hubbard, "Bronner Warns of Crash," *Birmingham News*, February 25, 2010, 7B.

20. David White, "Laws Keep Tax Use Restricted: Earmarks Make It Hard to Shift Taxes to Needed Areas," *Birmingham News*, December 1, 2008, 8A.

21. Ibid.

22. Dana Beyerle, "Alabama Taxes Still the Lowest in the Nation," *Tuscaloosa News*, January 2, 2010, 1A.

23. Ibid.

24. Associated Press, "Ala. Collected Lowest Taxes of Any State," *Tuscaloosa News*, November 14, 2011, 1B.

25. David White, "Alabama's Tax Load Is U.S.'s Second Least," *Birmingham News*, August 9, 2010. http://blog.al.com/businessnews/2010/08/alabama_tax_load_is_uss_second.html.

26. Ibid.

27. The New Politics of Judicial Elections: 2006, 10. See http://brennan.3cdn.net.

28. Brian Lawson, "Property Tax System Stays as Is, Judge Says: Rebukes State of Education," *Birmingham News*, October 22, 2011, 2A.

29. Ibid.

30. "Back of the Pack," *Birmingham News*, August 12, 2010, 6A.

31. Weissinger v. Boswell, 330 F. Supp. 615 (M.D. Ala. 1971).

32. Beyerle, "Alabama Taxes Still the Lowest in the Nation," 1A.

33. Kevin Hagen, "What Taxes Will You Pay If You Retire in Alabama? Low Cost of Living in the Yellowhammer State," *Yahoo! Voices*, November 10, 2008. See http://voices.yahoo.com.

34. Steve Campbell, "Artur Davis and Ron Sparks Spar over Grocery Tax," *Huntsville Times*, April 20, 2010. http://blog.al.com/breaking/2010/04/artur_davis_and_ron_sparks_spa.html. The reporter's source for these data was the Tax Foundation.

35. Beyerle, "Alabama Taxes Still the Lowest in the Nation," 1A.

36. Anne Permaloff and Carl Grafton, *Political Power in Alabama: The More Things Change . . .* (Athens: University of Georgia Press, 1995), 174–75.

37. Beyerle, "Alabama Taxes Still the Lowest in the Nation," 1A.

38. "Redistributing," *Birmingham News*, November 3, 2008, 6A.

39. Ibid., quoting from the Russell Sage Foundation.

40. Jack Bass and Walter De Vries, *The Transformation of Southern Politics: Social Change and Political Consequence since 1945* (New York: Basic Books, 1976), 73.

41. Cited in Phillip Rawls, "Study: Poor in Ala. Pay Highest Income Taxes," *Tuscaloosa News*, November 5, 2009, 3B.

42. "United States Federal Tax Dollars" (2010). See http://visualeconomics.creditloan.com.

43. Cauchon, "New Yorkers Lead Pack in Government Benefits: Comes to $9,442 Per Person, Per Year, on Average."

44. "No Real Pork Chop," *Birmingham News*, March 30, 2010, 8A.

45. Robin DeMonia, "Storms to Cost FEMA $1 Billion," *Birmingham News*, June 23, 2011, 1A.

46. Lane W. Lancaster, Review of *Alabama's Balancing Budget* by Paul E. Alyea (Tuscaloosa: Bureau of Public Administration, University of Alabama, 1942), in *Journal of Politics* 4 (1942): 417.

47. See www.freerepublic.co, August 29, 2003.

48. "Capital Poll: Public Attitudes toward Alabama Public Schools," *Alabama School Journal*, December 1, 2008, 3.

Select Bibliography

Newspapers

Anniston Star, May 30, 2010.
Associated Press (2008–12).
Atlanta Journal Constitution, January 5, 2003.
Baltimore Sun, March 11, 1995, June 13, 2007.
Birmingham News (ongoing).
Decatur Daily, April 14, 20, 1961; September 13, 2005.
Gadsden Times, May 3, 2004.
Hartselle Enquirer, September 18, 2010.
Huntsville Times, March 17, April 4, May 2, 2010; June 23, 2011.
Los Angeles Times, March 12, 2012.
Montgomery Advertiser, March 7, March 8, March 24, April 27, June 3, 2010.
New York Times, November 30, 1909; February 3, 1996; March 2, November 11, December 13, 2008; November 30, 2009.
Press-Register (Mobile), January 19, 2009; May-November, 2010.
Taipei Times, June 10, 2007.
Times Daily (Florence), September 3, 1892; January 17, 1931; March 7, 2010.
Tribune Newspapers, December 1, 2009.
Tuscaloosa News, January 11, 1933; ongoing.
USA Today, June 1, December 10, 2008; April 26, 2011.
Wall Street Journal, February 7, 1996.
Washington Post, September 14, 1998.

Books

Alabama Constitution of 1901: Official Proceedings (1902).

Alyea, Paul E. *Alabama's Balancing Budget*. Tuscaloosa: Bureau of Public Administration, University of Alabama, 1942.

Barnard, William D. *Dixiecrats and Democrats: Alabama Politics, 1942–1950*. Tuscaloosa: University of Alabama Press, 1984.

Bartley, Numan V., and Hugh D. Graham. *Southern Politics and the Second Reconstruction*. Baltimore: Johns Hopkins University Press, 1976.

Bass, Jack, and Walter De Vries. *The Transformation of Southern Politics: Social Change and Political Consequence since 1945*. New York: Basic Books, 1976.

Beard, Charles Austin. *American Government and Politics*. New York: Macmillan, 1910.

Bell, Jonathan. *The Liberal State on Trial: The Cold War and American Politics in the Truman Years*. New York: Columbia University Press, 2004.

Black, Earl. *Southern Governors and Civil Rights: Racial Segregation as a Campaign Issue in the Second Reconstruction*. Cambridge, MA: Harvard University Press, 1976.

———, and Merle Black. *The Rise of Southern Republicans*. Cambridge, MA: Belknap Press of Harvard University Press, 2003.

Bowles, Nigel. *The Government and Politics of the United States*. New York: Palgrave Macmillan, 1993.

Browder, Glen. *The South's New Racial Politics: Inside the Race Game of Southern History*. Montgomery, AL: NewSouth Books, 2009.

Bullock, Charles S., III, and Mark J. Rozell, eds. *The New Politics of the Old South: An Introduction to Southern Politics*. Lanham, MD: Rowman and Littlefield, 2007.

Campbell, Ballard C. *Disasters, Accidents, and Crises in American History: A Reference Guide to the Nation's Most Catastrophic Events*. New York: Infobase, 2008.

Carlson, Jody. *George C. Wallace and the Politics of Powerlessness: The Wallace Campaigns for the Presidency, 1964–1976*. Piscataway, NJ: Transaction, 1981.

Carter, Dan T. *The Politics of Rage: George Wallace, the Origins of the New Conservatism and the Transformation of American Politics*. Baton Rouge: Louisiana State University Press, 1996.

Cash, W. J. *The Mind of the South*. New York: Alfred A. Knopf, 1941.

Catt, Carrie Chapman, and Nettie Rogers Shulter. *Woman Suffrage and Politics: The Inner Story of the Suffrage Movement*. Buffalo, NY: W. S. Hein, 2004.

Clark, E. Culpepper. *The Schoolhouse Door: Segregation's Last Stand at the University of Alabama*. Tuscaloosa: University of Alabama Press, 1995.

Cotter, Patrick R. "Alabama: From One Party to Competition, and Maybe Back Again." In Bullock and Rozell, *New Politics of the Old South*, 73–92.

Curran, Eddie. *The Governor of Goat Hill*. New York: iUniverse, 2009.

Damaska, Mirjan R. *The Faces of Justice and State Authority*. New Haven, CT: Yale University Press, 1986.

Dealey, James Quayle. *Our State Constitutions*. Philadelphia: American Academy of Political and Social Science, 1907.

Dillon, John Forrest. *Commentaries on the Law of Municipal Corporations*. Vol. 4. Charleston, SC: Bibliobazaar, 2010.

Dionne, E. J. *Why Americans Hate Politics*. New York: Simon and Schuster, 2004.

Eddins, Don. *AEA: Head of the Class in Alabama Politics*. Montgomery: Alabama Education Association, 1997.

Evans, Peter B., Dietrich Rueschemeyer, and Theda Skocpol, eds. *Bringing the State Back In*. New York: Cambridge University Press, 1985.

Feldman, Glenn. *From Demagogue to Dixiecrat: Horace Wilkinson and the Politics of Race*. Lanham, MD: University Press of America, 1995.

———. *Reading Southern History: Essays on Interpreters and Interpretations*. Tuscaloosa: University of Alabama Press, 2001.

Fenwick, Linda Beck. *Should the Children Pray?* Waco, TX: Baylor University Press, 1989.

Flynt, Wayne. *Alabama in the Twentieth Century*. Tuscaloosa: University of Alabama Press, 2004.

———, ed. *Encyclopedia of Alabama*. www.encyclopediaofalabama.com.

———. *Poor but Proud: Alabama's Poor Whites*. Tuscaloosa: University of Alabama Press, 2002.

Frady, Marshall. *Wallace: The Classic Portrait of Alabama Governor George Wallace*. New York: Random House, 2009.

Frederick, Jeff. *Stand Up for Alabama: Governor George Wallace*. Tuscaloosa: University of Alabama Press, 2007.

Gaillard, Faye, with Jennifer Lindsay and Jane DeNeefe. *Alabama's Civil Rights Trail*. Tuscaloosa: University of Alabama Press, 2010.

Grafton, Carl, and Anne Permaloff. *Big Mules and Branchheads: James E. Folsom and Political Power in Alabama*. Athens: University of Georgia Press, 2008.

Green, John Clifford, Mark J. Rozell, and Clyde Wilcox, eds. *Prayers in the Precincts: The Christian Right in the 1998 Elections*. Washington, DC: Georgetown University Press, 2000.

Harvey, Gordon E. *A Question of Justice: New South Governors and Education, 1968–1976*. Tuscaloosa: University of Alabama Press, 2002.

———. "'Wallaceism Is an Insidious and Treacherous Types of Disease': The 1970 Gubernatorial Election and the 'Wallace Freeze' on Alabama Politics." In Harvey, Starnes, and Feldman, *History and Hope in the Heart of Dixie*, chap. 7.

Harvey, Gordon E., Richard D. Starnes, and Glenn Feldman, eds. *History and Hope in the Heart of Dixie: Scholarship, Activism, and Wayne Flynt in the Modern South*. Tuscaloosa: University of Alabama Press, 2006.

Havard, William C., ed. *The Changing Politics of the South*. Baton Rouge: Louisiana State University Press, 1972.

Havard, William C., and Loren P. Beth. *The Politics of Mis-Representation*. Baton Rouge: Louisiana State University Press, 1962.

Holloway, William Vernon, and Charles W. Smith. *Government and Politics in Alabama*. University, AL: University Supply Store, 1941.

Hrebenar, Ronald J., and Clive S. Thomas. *Interest Group Politics*. University Park: Pennsylvania State University Press, 2004.

———, eds. *Interest Group Politics in the Southern States*. Tuscaloosa: University of Alabama Press, 1992.

Ifill, Gwen. *The Breakthrough: Politics and Race in the Age of Obama*. New York: Doubleday, 2009.

Ingle, Bob, and Sandy McClure. *The Soprano State: New Jersey's Culture of Corruption*. New York: Macmillan, 2009.

Jackson, Harvey H. *Inside Alabama: A Personal History of My State*. Tuscaloosa: University of Alabama Press, 2004.

Jacob, Herbert, and Kenneth Vines, eds. *Politics in the American States*. 2nd ed. Boston: Little, Brown, 1971.

Kern, Montague. *30-Second Politics: Political Advertising in the Eighties*. New York: Praeger, 1989.

Key, V. O., Jr., *Politics, Parties, and Pressure Groups*. New York: Thomas Y. Crowell, 1942.

———. *Southern Politics in State and Nation*. New York: Alfred A. Knopf, 1949.

Kousser, J. Morgan, and James W. McPherson, eds. *Region, Race, and Reconstruction: Essays in Honor of C. Vann Woodward*. New York: Oxford University Press, 1982.

Landsberg, Brian K. *Free at Last to Vote: The Alabama Origins of the 1965 Voting Rights Act*. Lawrence: University Press of Kansas, 2007.

Lamis, Alexander, ed. *Southern Politics in the 1990s*. Baton Rouge: Louisiana State University Press, 1999.

Lea, James F., ed. *Contemporary Southern Politics*. Baton Rouge: Louisiana State University Press, 1988.

Lesher, Stephan. *George Wallace: American Populist*. Cambridge, MA: Da Capo Press, 1995.

Lienesch, Michael. *Redeeming America: Piety and Politics in the New Christian Right*. Chapel Hill: University of North Carolina Press, 1993.

Martin, David L. *Alabama's State and Local Governments*. 3rd ed. Tuscaloosa: University of Alabama Press, 1994.

Maxwell, Angie, and Todd G. Shields, eds. *Unlocking V. O. Key, Jr.: Southern Politics for the Twenty-First Century*. Fayetteville: University of Arkansas Press, 2011.

McMillan, Malcolm Cook. *Constitutional Development in Alabama, 1798–1901: A Study in Politics, the Negro, and Sectionalism*. Chapel Hill: University of North Carolina Press, 1955.

Melanson, Philip H. *The Secret Service: The Hidden History of an Enigmatic Agency*. New York: Basic Books, 2005.Nash, Jere, and Andy Taggert. *Mississippi Politics: The Struggle for Power, 1976–2008*. Oxford: University Press of Mississippi, 2009.

Novkov, Julie. *Racial Union: Law, Intimacy, and the White State in Alabama, 1865–1954*. Ann Arbor: University of Michigan Press, 2008.

Permaloff, Anne, and Carl Grafton. *Political Power in Alabama: The More Things Change . . .* Athens: University of Georgia Press, 1995.

Perry, Huey. *Race, Politics, and Governance in the United States*. Gainesville: University Press of Florida, 1996.

Ransone, Coleman B., Jr. *The Office of Governor in the South*. Tuscaloosa: Bureau of Public Administration, University of Alabama, 1951.

Rich, Robert F., and William D. White. *Health Policy, Federalism, and the American States*. Washington, DC: Urban Institute, 1966.

Rogers, William Warren, and others. *Alabama: The History of a Deep South State*. Tuscaloosa: University of Alabama Press, 1994.

Sabato, Larry. *Goodbye to Good-Time Charlie: The American Governor Transformed, 1950–1975*. Lexington, MA: Lexington Books, 1978.

Scher, Richard K. *The Modern Political Campaign: Mudslinging, Bombast, and the Vitality of American Politics*. Armonk, NY: M. E. Sharpe, 1997.

———. *Politics in the New South: Republicanism, Race, and Leadership in the Twentieth Century*. 2nd ed. Armonk, NY: M. E. Sharpe, 1997.

Schlesinger, Joseph A. "The Politics of the Executive." In Jacob and Vines, *Politics in the American States*, 210–37.

Skocpol, Theda. "Strategies of Analysis in Current Research." In Evans, Rueschemeyer, and Skocpol, *Bringing the State Back In*, 3–37.

Stewart, William H. *The Alabama State Constitution: A Reference Guide*. 1st ed. Westport, CT: Greenwood, 1994.

Sullivan, Patricia, ed. *Freedom Writer: Virginia Foster Durr, Letters from the Civil Rights Years*. Athens: University of Georgia Press, 2008.

Tarr, G. Alan. *Understanding State Constitutions*. Princeton, NJ: Princeton University Press, 2000.

Thomas, James D., and William H. Stewart. *Alabama Government and Politics*. Lincoln: University of Nebraska Press, 1988.

Tullos, Allen. *Alabama Getaway: The Political Imaginary and the Heart of Dixie*. Athens: University of Georgia Press, 2011.

Tyler, Pamela. *Silk Stockings and Ballot Boxes: Women and Politics in New Orleans, 1920–1963*. Athens: University of Georgia Press, 2009.

Van Der Slik, Jack R., ed. *Politics in the American States and Communities: A Contemporary Reader*. Boston: Allyn and Bacon, 1986.

Walker, Joe E. "Yes, Virginia, Issues and Images Both Count in Politics." In Van Der Slik, *Politics in the American States and Communities*, 116–19.

Walton, Hanes. *When the Marching Stopped: The Politics of Civil Rights Regulatory Agencies*. Albany: State University of New York Press, 1988.

Warmoth, Henry Clay. *War, Politics, and Reconstruction: Stormy Days in Louisiana*. Columbia: University of South Carolina Press, 1930.

Webb, Samuel L., and Margaret E. Armbrester, eds. *Alabama Governors: A Political History of the State*. Tuscaloosa: University of Alabama Press, 2001.

Webster's Unabridged Dictionary and Thesaurus Online. *www.merriam-webster.com*.

Yackle, Larry W. *Reform and Regret: The Story of Federal Judicial Involvement in the Alabama Prison System*. New York: Oxford University Press, 1989.

Articles

"Alabama Chapter Hosts Lobby Day." *Bulletin of the American College of Surgeons* 96 (2010): 54.

Apergis, Nicholas, Oguzhan S. Dincer, and James E. Payne. "The Relationship between Corruption and Income Inequality in the States: Evidence from a Panel Cointegration and Error Correction Model." *Public Choice* 145 (2010): 125–35.

Arington, Michele. "English-Only Laws and Direct Legislation: The Battle in the States over Language Minority Rights." *Journal of Law and Politics* 7 (1990): 325–52.

Askew, J. Thomas. Review of William Vernon Holloway and Charles W. Smith, *Government and Politics in Alabama*. *Journal of Politics* 3 (1941): 381–82.

Beckwirth, E. H. "Alabama Law and Jurisprudence." *Alabama Lawyers Journal* 14 (1925–1926): 18.

Black, Earl. "Southern Governors and Political Change: Campaign Stances on Racial Segregation and Economic Development, 1950–69." *Journal of Politics* 33 (1971): 703–34.

Boyd, William J. D. "New Study Ranks State Legislatures: Citizens Conference Cites Procedures, Operations." *National Civic Review*, March 1971, 155–58.

Brace, Paul. "The Political Economy of Collective Action: The Case of the American States." *Polity* 20 (1988): 648–64.

Brewer, Albert P. "Constitutional Revision in Alabama: History and Methodology." *Alabama Law Review* 48 (1997): 583–612.

Brown, Robert L. "From Whence Cometh Our State Appellate Judges: Popular Election Versus the Missouri Plan." *University of Arkansas at Little Rock Law Journal* 20 (1997): 313–25. Brown is repeating a view he doesn't share.

Burns, Nancy, Laura Evans, Gerald Gamm, and Corrine McConnaughy. "Urban Politics in the State Arena." *Studies in American Political Development* 23 (2009): 1–22.

Canon, Bradley C. "Reactions of State Supreme Courts to a US Supreme Court Civil Liberties Decision." *Law and Society Review* 8 (1973): 109–34.

"Capital Poll: Public Attitudes toward Alabama Public Schools." *Alabama School Journal*, December 1, 2008, 3.

Clausen, Christopher. "America's Design for Tolerance." *Wilson Quarterly* 31 (2007): 26–32.

Cohen, Harris S. "On Professional Power and Conflict of Interest." *Journal of Health Politics, Policy, and Law* 5 (1980): 291.

Cooper, Melvin G. "The Alabama Ethics Act—Milestone or Millstone." *Cumberland-Samford Law Review* 5 (1974–75): 183–213."Crimson Tide." *Weekly Standard*, November 13, 2010.

Day, Terri R. "Nasty as They Wanna Be Politics: Clean Campaigns and the First Amendment." *Ohio Northern University Law Review* 35 (2009): 647–84.

DeBow, Michael. "The State Tobacco Litigation and the Separation of Powers in State Governments: Repairing the Damage." *Seton Hall Law Review* 31 (2001): 563–97.

"Democratic Input for King." *Inside Alabama Politics*, April 30, 2010, 4.

Fair, Brian K. "Equality for All—The Case for a New Declaration of Rights in the Alabama Constitution." *Cumberland Law Review* 33 (2002–3): 339–85.

Farina, Steven M. Review of Larry W. Yackle, *Reform and Regret: The Story of Federal Judicial Involvement in the Alabama Prison System. Michigan Law Review* 88 (1990): 1883–88.

Feldman, Glenn. "Race, Sex, Class, and the Status Quo Society: Developing Racial, Political, and Religious Attitudes in 1940s Alabama." *History* 91 (2006): 360–85.

Flynt, Wayne. "Alabama's Shame: The Historical Origins of the 1901 Constitution." *Alabama Law Review* 53 (2001): 67–76.

Force, Robert. "State Bills of Rights: A Case of Neglect and the Need for a Renaissance." *Valparaiso University Law Review* 3 (1969), 125–82.

Frank, Mitch. "Alabama's Most Courageous Politician." *Time*, August 15, 2003. http://content.time.com/time/nation/article/0,8599,476249,00.html.

Green, Joshua. "Karl Rove in a Corner." *The Atlantic*, November 2004. http://www.theatlantic.com/magazine/archive/2004/11/karl-rove-in-a-corner/303537/.

Hamilton, Virginia Van der Veer. "Lister Hill, Hugo Black, and the Albatross of Race." *Alabama Law Review* 36 (1984): 845–60.

Hammons, Christopher W. "Was James Madison Wrong? Rethinking the American Preference for Short, Framework-Oriented Constitutions." *American Political Science Review* 93 (1999): 837–49.

Hansen, Wendy L., and Neil J. Mitchell. "Disaggregating and Explaining Corporate Political Activity: Domestic and Foreign Corporations in National Politics." *American Political Science Review* 94 (2000): 891–903.

Harmel, Robert. "Minority Partisanship in One-Party Predominant Legislatures: A Five-State Study." *Journal of Politics* 48 (1986): 729–40.

Hildreth, W. Bartley. "The Politics of a Windfall: Allocating Special Offshore Oil and Gas Receipts in Four Southern States Facing Fiscal Retrenchment." *International Journal of Public Administration* 11 (1988): 581–600.

Hillyer, Quin. "Not Our Cup of Tea." *American Spectator*, February 15, 2010. http://spectator.org/articles/40092/not-our-cup-tea.

Hird, John A. "Policy Analysis for What: The Effectiveness of Nonpartisan Policy Research Organizations." *Policy Studies Journal* 33 (2005): 83–105.

Horton, Scott. "Crazy in Alabama: The Imminent Threat Posed by Teachers." *Harper's Magazine*, March 2008. http://harpers.org/blog/2008/03/crazy-in-alabama/.

Huebner, Timothy J. Review of *The Politics of Rage* by Dan T. Carter. *Florida Historical Quarterly* 75 (1996): 97–99.

Isom, Warren Rex. "The Office of Lieutenant Governor in the States." *American Political Science Review* 32 (1938): 921–26.

Itkin, Matthew D. "Felon Disenfranchisement and the Systemic Racism of the Criminal Justice System." *Journal of Race, Gender, and Ethnicity* 4 (2009): 72–76.

Katsinas, Stephen G. "George C. Wallace and the Founding of Alabama's Public Two-Year Colleges." *Journal of Higher Education* 65 (1994): 447–72.

Knack, Stephen. "Social Capital and the Quality of Government: Evidence from the States." *American Journal of Political Science* 46 (2002): 72–85.

Lamis, Alexander P., and Nathan C. Goldman. "V. O. Key's Southern Politics: The Writing of a Classic." *Georgia Historical Quarterly* 71 (1987): 261–85.

Lancaster, Lane W. "Alabama State Reorganization." *National Municipal Review* 34 (1945): 69–73.

———. Review of *Alabama's Balancing Budget* by Paul E. Alyea. *Journal of Politics* 4 (1942): 416–19.

Latimer, Margaret K. "'No-Party' Politics at the End of the Wallace Era." *Publius* 9 (1979): 215–27.

Lewis, John. "Reflections on Judge Frank M. Johnson, Jr." *Yale Law Journal* 109 (2000): 1253–56.

Lutz, Donald S., and Richard W. Murray. "Coalition Formation in the Texas Legislature: Issues, Payoffs, and Winning Coalition Size." *Western Political Quarterly* 28 (1975): 296–315.

Lutz, James M. "Regional Leadership Patterns in the Diffusion of Public Policies." *American Politics Research* 65 (1987): 387–98.

Martin, Roscoe C. "Alabama's Administrative Reorganization of 1939." *Journal of Politics* 2 (1940): 436–47.

Meier, K. J. "The Political Economy of Consumer Protection: An Examination of State Legislation." *Western Political Quarterly* 40 (1987): 343–59.

Mohr, Clarence L. Review of Gordon E. Harvey, *A Question of Justice: New South Governors and Education, 1968–1976. Journal of American History* 90 (2003): 1090–91.

Morehouse, Sarah M., and Malcolm E. Jewel. "States as Laboratories: A Reprise." *Annual Reviews in Political Science* 7 (2004): 177–203.

Murphy, Paul L. "The Early Social and Political Philosophy of Hugo Black: Liquor as a Test Case." *Alabama Law Review* 36 (1984–85): 861–79.

Murphy, Walter F. "The South Counterattacks: The Anti-NAACP Laws." *Western Political Quarterly* 12 (1959): 371–90.

Norrell, Robert J. "Labor at the Ballot Box: Alabama Politics from the New Deal to the Dixiecrat Movement." *Journal of Southern History* 57 (1991): 201–34.

———. "Law in a White Man's Democracy: A History of the Alabama State Judiciary." *Cumberland Law Review* 32 (2001–2): 135–63.

Opheim, Cynthia. "Explaining the Differences in State Lobby Regulation." *Western Political Quarterly* 44 (1991): 405–21.

Parker, Will. "Still Afraid of Negro Domination: Why County Home Rule Limitations in the Alabama Constitution of 1901 are Unconstitutional." *Alabama Law Review* 57 (2005): 545–63.

Parks, Norman L. "Tennessee Politics since Kefauver and Reece: A Generalist's View." *Journal of Politics* 28 (1966): 144–68.

Pearson, Joyce A. McCray. "The Federal and State Bills of Rights: A Historical Look at the Relationship between America's Documents of Individual Freedom." *Howard Law Journal* 36 (1993): 43–73.

Perry, Stuart H. "Politics and Judicial Administration." *Annals of the American Academy of Political and Social Science* 169 (1933): 75–85.

Persky, Jonathan D. "Ghosts That Slay: A Contemporary Look at State Advisory Opinions." *Connecticut Law Review* 37 (2004): 1155–233.

"Peterson Phenomena." *Inside Alabama Politics*, May 21, 2010, 3.

Reutzel, Todd. "These Stones Will Cry Out: A Critique of Government Displays of the Ten Commandments." *Tennessee Law Review* 72 (2004): 905–48.

Rodriguez, Peter, Klaus Uhlenbruck, and Lorraine Eden. "Government Corruption and the Entry Strategies of Multinationals." *Academy of Management* 30 (2005): 83–96.

Saltzburg, Steven J., and Edward J. Imwinkeiried. "Keeping the Reformist Spirit Alive in Evidence Law." *University of Pennsylvania Law Review* 149 (2000–2001): 1277–93.

Sanders, Randy. Review of Jeff Frederick, *Stand Up for Alabama. Journal of American History* 95 (2008): 273–74.

Sandholtz, Wayne, and William Koetzle. "Accounting for Corruption." *International Studies Quarterly* 44 (2000): 31–50.

Sanger, Carol. "Regulating Teenage Abortion in the United States: Politics and Policy." *International Journal of Law, Policy, and the Family* 18 (2004): 305–18.

Shepard, Kris. "Conservatism and Its Cousins in Twentieth-Century America." Review of Glenn Feldman, *From Demagogue to Dixiecrat* and other books. *Historical Journal* 41 (1998): 901–8.

Shepherd, Joanne M. "The Influence of Retention Politics on Judges' Voting." *Journal of Legal Studies* 38 (2009): 169–206.

Shores, Janie L., William Mike House, and Paul Simon. "Tributes to Senator Howell Heflin." *Alabama Law Review* 48 (1997): 417–40.

Simmons, James R. "Altruistic Corruption: The Downsian Bureaucrats Revisited." *Administrative Theory and Praxis* 21 (1999): 265–79.

Sollars, David L. "Institutional Rules and State Legislator Compensation: Success for the Reform Movement?" *Legislative Studies Quarterly* 19 (1994): 507–20.

Spence, Susan Thompson. "The Usurpation of Legislative Power by the Alabama Judiciary: From Legislative Apportionment to School Reform." *Alabama Law Review* 50 (1998): 929–68.

Sturm, Albert L. "The Development of American State Constitutions." *Publius* 12 (1982): 57–98.

Tabarrok, Alexander, and Eric Helland. "Partisan Judicial Elections and Home Court Advantage." *Corporate Legal Times*, March 2002. http://www.independent.org/newsroom/article.asp?id=225.

Thomas, Martha. "The 'New Woman' in Alabama: 1890–1920." *Alabama Review* 43 (1990): 163–80.

Thompson, Joel A. "State Legislative Reform: Another Look, One More Time, Again." *Polity* 19 (1986): 27–41.

Tobin, Richard J. "Some Observations on the Use of State Constitutions to Protect the Environment." *Boston College Environmental Affairs Law Review* 3 (1974): 473–93.

Toma, Eugenia F., Indrias Berhane, and Corinna Curl. "Political Action Committees at the State Level: Contributions to Education." *Public Choice* 126 (2006): 465–84.

Uelmen, Gerald F. "Crocodiles in the Bathtub: Maintaining the Independence of State Supreme Courts in an Era of Judicial Politicization." *Notre Lame Law Review* 72 (1997): 1134–45.

Viadero, Debra. "Head of Alabama Teachers' Union Tests Power in Governor's Race." *Education Week*, May 21, 1990. http://www.edweek.org/ew/articles/1990/03/21/09310022.h09.html.

Walton, Hanes, Jr., and James E. Taylor. "Blacks and the Southern Prohibition Movement." *Phylon* 32 (1971): 247–59.

Watkins, Zina L. "Lobbyists and Interest Groups: Sources of Information." *CRS Report for Congress*, May 9, 2008.

Webster, Gerald, and Rebecca H. Webster. "Taxing Issues: Geography, Politics, and the 2003 Tax Reform Referendum in Alabama." *Southeastern Geographer* 44 (2004): 190–215.

Wilson, Shaun. "A Little Bit of Alabama: On Australia's Low Tax Consensus." *Australian Review of Public Affairs*, May 30, 2005. ww.australianreview.net/digest/2005/05/wilson.html.

Winders, Jamie. "Bringing Back the (B)order: Post 9/11 Politics of Immigration, Borders, and Belonging in the Contemporary US South." *Antipode* 39 (2007): 920–42.

Court Decisions

Ankrom v. State, So. 3d, 2011 WL 3963006 (Ala. 2011).

Baker v. Carr, 369 U.S. 186 (1962).

Barber v. Cornerstone Community Outreach, Inc., 42 So. 3d 65 (Ala. 2009).

Baze v. Reese, 553 U.S. 35 (2008).

Boles v. Parris, 952 So. 2d 364 (Ala. 2006).

Dobson v. Allied-Bruce Terminix Companies, Inc. This decision was reversed by the US Supreme Court in *Allied-Bruce Terminix Companies, Inc. V. Dobson*, 513 U.S. 265 (1995).

Ex parte Ford Motor Co., 47 So. 3rd 234 (Ala. 2010).

Ex parte King, 50 So. 3rd 1056 (Ala. 2010).

Harris v. Alabama, 513 U.S. 504 (1995).

Loving v. Virginia, 388 U.S. 1 (1967).

Lynch v. Alabama (official citation forthcoming).

Mack v. Carmack, __ So. 3d __, 2011 WL 3963006 (Ala. Crim. App. 2011).

Marsh v. Alabama, 326 U.S. 501 (1946).

Opinion of the Justices, 81 So. 2d 678 (1955).

Reynolds v. Sims, 377 U.S. 533 (1964).

Riley v. Cornerstone Community Outreach, Inc., 57 So. 3d 704 (Ala. 2010).

Smith v. Allwright, 321 U.S. 649 (1944).

Smith v. Board of School Com'rs of Mobile County, 655 F.Supp.939 (S.D.Ala.), rev'd 827 F.2d 684 (11th Cir. 1987).

State v. Cornerstone Community Outreach, Inc., et al., Ex parte State of Alabama et al. (in re: Governor Bob Riley et al. V. Cornerstone Community Outreach, Inc., et al., and State of Alabama v. Chad Dickie et al.). 1090808. May 21, 2010.

State v. Manley, 441 So. 2nd 864 (1983).

Wallace v. Jaffrey, 472 U.S. 38 (1985).

Weissinger v. Boswell, 330 F.Supp. 615 (M.D. Ala. 1971).

Unpublished Sources

Ansolabehere, Stephen, John M. de Figueiredo, and James M. Snyder Jr. "Why Is There So Little Money in US Politics?" NBER Working Paper No. 9409, January 2003. http://www.nber.org/papers/w9409.pdf.

Hammitt, Kenneth. "Southern Realignment: Evolution, Maintenance, and Impact of Political Parties." Unpublished American University honors capstone (thesis). Fall 2007–Spring 2008.

Kelly, Donald L. "Unethical Leadership in Higher Education and the Precarious Journey to Recovery: A Case Study of the Alabama Community College System." Dissertation written at the University of Alabama, 2009.

Lin, Victor L. "The Possible Consequences and Effects of Moderately Restrictive Term Limits on the California State Legislature." Senior honors thesis, Department of Political Science, University of California, San Diego, March 28, 2011.

Miller, Nancy Martorano. "Paths, Events, and Strategic Choices: The Evolution of American State Legislatures." Paper presented at the American Political Science Association 2009 Annual Meeting.

Miscellaneous candidate press releases (2010).

Miscellaneous Comcast and Facebook messages (2008–11).

Tuomala, Jeffrey C. "In Defense of Chief Justice Roy S. Moore" (2003). Liberty University, Faculty Publications and Presentations, Paper 35.

Wängnerud, Lena. "Variation in Corruption between Mexican States: Elaborating the Gender Perspective." Paper presented at the American Political Science Association 2010 Annual Meeting.

Wrzenski, Rhonda Louise. "Is It Really 'All about the Benjamins'? Exploring the Role of Campaign Self-Finance in the State Legislative Electoral Process." Paper prepared for the annual Conference on State Politics and Policy, Houston, February 16–19, 2012.

Miscellaneous Internet Sites

Alabama Judicial System (http://judicial.alabama.gov)

Alabama State Bar (www.alabar.org)

American Scene (http://theamericanscene.com)

Birmingham Blues (www.queervoice.net)

Boston.com (www.boston.com)

Brennan Center for Justice (www.brennancenter.org)

Bureau of the Census (www.census.gov/population)

CNN.com (www.cnn.com)

Colorado Independent (www.coloradoindependent.com)

Congressional Reports Service (www.loc.gov/crsinfo)

Conservative Activist's Home Page (www.conservativeusa.org)

Counter-Terrorism Training and Resources for Law Enforcement (www.counterterrorismtraining.gov)

Crooks and Liars (www.crooksandliars.com)

Daily Kos (www.dailykos.com)

Defenders Online (www.thedefendersonline.com)

Department of Archives and History (http://archives.state.al.us)
Digital History (www.digitalhistory.uh.edu)
Exxpose Exxon (www.exxposeexxon.com)
Fix (www.washingtonpost.com/blogs/the-fix)
Freedom Works (www.freedomworks.org)
Free Ratio (www.freeratio.org)
Free Republic (www.freerepublic.com)
Gallup.Com (www.gallup.com)
Godlike Productions (www.godlikeproductions.com)
Governing (www.governing.com)
Irregular News (www.irregularnews.com)
Left in Alabama (www.leftinalabama.com)
Liberty University Faculty Publications and Presentations (http://digitalcommons.liberty.edu/lusol_fac_pubs)
Locust Fork News-Journal (www.locustfork.net)
Museum of Broadcast Communications (www.museum.tv)
National Abortion and Reproduction Rights Action League (www.naral.org)
National Bureau of Economic Research (www.nber.org)
National Endowment for the Humanities (www.neh.gov)
National Organizers Alliance (www.noacentral.org)
Newser (www.newser.com)
OpenSecrets.org (www.opensecrets.org)
PBS: Public Broadcasting Service(www.pbs.org)
Pipl-People Search (www.pipl.com)
Political Scene (www.tmcnet.com)
Politico.com (www.politico.com)
SaintsReport.com (www.saintsreport.com)
Science Blogs (http://scienceblogs.com)
Social Science Research Network (http://ssrn.com)
Steve Flowers (http://steveflowers.us)
Topix (www.topix.com)
US Chamber of Commerce (www.uschamber.com)
US News: Money (http://money.usnews.com)
Voices for Alabama's Children (www.alavoices.org)
Wire Eagle (http://wireagle.auburn.edu)
Womens News (www.womensnews.org)
For full book publication data on individual essays and reviews, see the book entry by editor(s).

Personal Interviews

Benn, Alvin. Personal interview, May 11, 2010.
Byrne, Bradley. Personal interviews, January 5–July 20, 2010.
Hubbard, Representative Joe. Personal interview, December 5, 2010.
Mabry, Dr. Henry. Personal interview, September 11, 2012.
Merrill, Representative John. Personal interviews, November 4, 2010; December 22, 2011; and August 3, 2012.
Orr, Senator Arthur. Personal interview, June 19, 2012.

Poole, Bill. Personal interview, July 19, 2010.
Riley, Governor Bob. Personal interviews, September 10 and December 13, 2004 and November 16, 2010.
Sims, Cliff. Personal interview, December 6, 2011.
Sparks, Commissioner Ron. Personal interview, July 27, 2010.
Sweet, Virginia. Personal interview, September 9, 2010.
Walker, R. B. Personal interview, August 31, 2010.
Wieder, Ben. Telephone interview, January 13, 2012.

Index